P.J.B. Mahony.
ND(N+)

NAVIGATION AND DIRECTION
THE STORY OF HMS DRYAD

BY THE SAME AUTHOR

The Royal Navy Today
The Russian Convoys
British Sea Power
The Rescue Ships (with L F Martyn)
The Loss of the Bismarck
The Attack on Taranto
Operation Neptune
The Arctic Convoys

ISBN 085937 087 9
© 1977 Vice Admiral B B Schofield CB CBE

*Published by Kenneth Mason Publications Ltd, Homewell,
Havant, Hampshire. Designed by Sadlergraphics and printed by
Coasby Plus Ltd, Emsworth, Hampshire*

NAVIGATION AND DIRECTION

The story of HMS Dryad

BY VICE ADMIRAL B B SCHOFIELD CB, CBE

KENNETH MASON

Acknowledgements

The author would like to thank all those of his brother officers who, by their letters to him, provided much of the material contained in this book. They are too numerous to mention individually but he is especially grateful to Captain C J Wynne-Edwards DSC* RN, Commander J M Porter RN and Lieutenant-Commander J D D Moore DSC RN all of whom read the script and made many valuable contributions and useful suggestions. It must also be stated that without the enthusiastic support of Admiral Sir Geoffrey Miles KCB KCSI, Vice Admiral J S C Salter CB DSO OBE, Captain Eric Brand RN, Captain Sir David Tibbits Kt DSC RN and Commander David Pollock RNVR the project would never have been launched. Thanks are also due to Lieutenant-Commander R Dyer RN for his unique record of the reminiscences of Admiral of the Fleet Sir Henry Oliver GCB KCMC MVO DL.

He wishes to record his appreciation of the facilities placed at his disposal by Rear Admiral G I Pritchard and Captain J F Cadell RN during their periods in command of *HMS Dryad* and to the staff of the establishment for their ready help in dealing with the problems of research and production as well as to the young ladies of the typing pool who produced the final copy.

The author and publisher wish to thank all those who have given permission for quotation and/or reproduction from books, articles and illustrations of which they hold the copyright, in particular The National Maritime and Imperial War Museums, the Photographic Unit of the Public Relations Office of the Commander in Chief, Home Command and the Fleet Air Arm Museum of the Royal Naval Air Station, Yeovilton.

Contents

Illustrations

Prologue

'*Of all the arts and professions which have at any time attracted notice, none has ever appeared to be more astonishing and marvellous than that of navigation, in the state at which it is at present; an art which doubtless affords one of the most certain irrefragable proofs of the amazing powers of human understanding. This cannot be made more evident than when, taking a retrospective view of the tottering inartificial craft to which navigation owes its origin, we compare it to a noble and majestic edifice, containing 1000 men, together with their provisions, drink, furniture, wearing apparel and other necessaries, for many months, besides 100 pieces of heavy ordnance; and as it were on the wings of the wind, across immense seas to the most distant shores.*

'*And yet, if such a ship sailed along the coast only, and never lost sight of the shore, as the navigators of old used to do, we might be tempted to look on navigation as an easy and trifling business. But the finding of the straightest and shortest way over an ocean of more than sixty or eighty degrees in longitude, and thirty or forty in latitude; or across a track of 4000 to 6000 miles in extent, by day and by night, in fair weather or in foul; as well as when the sky is overcast as when it is clear, and often with no other guide than the compass, and the being able to determine the true position of the ship at sea by the height of the sun, though this latter is often enveloped in clouds, or to direct its course by the moon and stars with such exactness and precision, as not to make a mistake of the value of half a degree, or thirty miles; this at least shows the progress and great perfection of an art practised by a class of people, of whose understanding many conceited and supercilious landsmen have but a mean opinion, and whose plain and simple manners they frequently take the liberty of turning into ridicule, forgetting how much they are indebted to their skill and prowess.*'

From *A History of Voyages and Discoveries made in the North*
published in German Circa. 1780
(C H Layman in *ND Bulletin* Vol 30)

The Queen, accompanied by the Duke of Edinburgh, inspects the guard of honour during a visit to HMS Dryad in 1973.

Chapter I

THE EVOLUTION OF
THE NAVIGATING OFFICER

'And after this sort he proceedeth from place to place until he arrive unto his desired porte, which is a conclusion infallible if there be no other impediments (whereof there hath been good consideration had) which may breed errour, for from such negligence may arise many inconveniences.'

The Seaman's Secrets by John Davis, 1607

Introduction

The art and science of navigation is of great antiquity and its practice must have commenced in several different parts of the world, wherever in fact men had need to use the sea for the transport of goods. Amongst the earliest navigators of which we have knowledge are the Phoenicians who are reputed to have circumnavigated the continent of Africa in about the year 60 BC. The Vikings too voyaged to Iceland, Greenland and probably North America in the 8th Century AD, but ocean navigation as opposed to coasting and short sea voyages did not become general until the fifteenth century.

According to Commander W E May, a former Navigating Officer and an acknowledged expert on early navigation, the Polynesians, whose civilization reached its peak before the thirteenth century, are reputed to have sailed their frail craft across the equator from the South Sea Islands to Hawaii. They sailed north with the help of the sun by day and the Pole star by night, having noted that the latter did not orbit like the rest of the constellations. With the help of a half coconut shell, called the Sacred Calabash, in which a hole had been bored 20° below the furthermost rim and which was half filled with water to act as a level, they observed Polaris and when it showed just above this rim they knew it was time to alter course to starboard. They then sailed east keeping the star just above the rim of the shell until they reached Hawaii.

The early Portuguese navigators employed the pig's keen sense of smell to warn them of their approach to land. When the Master estimated that he was about to make a landfall, the pigs would be released from their pen and so keen was their scent for land that they would rush to the ship's side sniffing ecstatically long before those onboard could see the land. As Commander May remarks 'The Pig Navigator suffered from an absence of any form of lane identification, like the early forms of Decca, but in those days the explorer was thankful to reach any land and was not always particular which country he reached first.'

According to Ovid (43 BC) the Master of a ship, whose place was at the stern although he did not actually steer, was expected to understand the course of the winds, the prognostications of the sky, the action of the rudder or steering oar and the sails as well as the suitability or otherwise of the various harbours. It was not however until twelve centuries later that an attempt was made to draw up a comprehensive code of behaviour for ships' crews. This was done by order of Eleanor of Aquitaine and introduced into England in about 1190 by Richard Coeur de Lion on his return from the third Crusade, though the author remains a subject for speculation. The code is known as The Laws of Oleron from the name of the island off the north west coast of France on which they were drawn up and sealed. They contain some interesting rules bearing on the navigation of ships, *eg*

'Everything onboard being under the care of the Master, he is required to understand thoroughly the art of piloting and navigation that he may control the pilot.'

In the fifth article of the Laws, provision was made to enable the Master to discharge any man, and especially the pilot, for incompetency, in which case his wages were forfeit. In the twenty-third article a sterner fate was decreed for a pilot who caused his ship to be lost:

'It is established for a custom of the sea that if a ship is lost by default of the lodesman, the mariners may, if they please, bring the lodesman to the windlass and cut off his head without the mariners being bound to answer before any judge, because the lodesman had committed high treason against the undertaking of the pilotage, and this is the judgement.'

In Plantagenet and even in Tudor times the men employed to sail the ships in which soldiers were embarked, were subordinate to the latter and the Captain at Arms did not necessarily know anything about navigation and so had to rely on the Master to take him where he wanted to go. The formation of fighting fleets led inevitably to the great naval battles which emblazon the pages of history. Amongst the instances in which navigation can be said to have played a part in achieving victory may be cited the surveying of the Traverses in the St Lawrence river by Captain James Cook which enabled Wolfe to land and capture the city of Quebec; Hawke's victory at Quiberon Bay and those of Nelson at Copenhagen and the Nile. In more recent times the relocation of the battleship Bismarck after she had escaped from the shadowing cruisers led to her destruction.

The Navigating Officer and his modern successor, whether at sea or in the air has still an important part to play in the conduct of maritime operations. In the words of a distinguished member of the profession, the late Admiral of the Fleet Sir John Cunningham, a former First Sea Lord 'If I might quote from my own experience, I should say that the position occupied by the Navigating Officer of a ship is one which enables him to obtain a better grasp of all the duties which go to make for the efficient organization of a ship of war than is obtainable in any other specialist branch. He sees and participates in every gunnery and torpedo exercise, every tactical and strategical exercise; he is concerned vitally with problems affecting the main propulsion of the ship, the upkeep of material and the endurance of the ship both from the point of view of fuel and of her stores and provisions, and has ample opportunity for studying personnel questions in all aspects; in addition he acquires specialist knowledge of the handling of ships and fleets, of meteorology and the varying moods of the sea itself.'

The beginning of navigation instruction in the Royal Navy

The earliest record we have of the existence of formal instruction in navigation in the Royal Navy is contained in a letter addressed to the Navy Board by one Thomas Slitter through the Commissioner of the Navy at Chatham and dated 24 February 1677* (*The Mariner's Mirror*, Volume 16 page 422).

It appears by the records of the Clerk of the Cheque's Office in Chatham, that in former times there was a stipend allowed to a mathematician for reading a mathematical lecture to His Majesty's Servants relating to his Navy and instructing them in the art of navigation and other parts of mathematics thereby 'to render them more serviceable to the King and Country.'

After a reference to one Richard Burley who held the position from 1631 until his death shortly after the Restoration in 1660 (except for the years 1641 to 1649) since when it had been vacant, he makes formal application to be considered for the post:

'That if it pleased His Majesty to bear me as an Able Seaman on any of his ships in this harbour and allow me victuals and wages accordingly I would undertake, for the said allowance to read a lecture in navigation and the other parts of the mathematics thereto subservient, once a fortnight, at such a convenient place and time (without prejudice to the King's service) as should be appointed by the Commissioner upon the place for the best advantage of all those desirous to learn.'

The curriculum proposed by Mr Slitter was extensive and included spherical trigonometry and the taking of astronomical observations, subjects which since the beginning of the seventeenth Century, were being increasingly studied in connection with the use of the quadrant, cross-staff and back-staff – forerunners to the sextant, and also the use of logarithms.

The first official steps to provide instruction in the art of navigation were taken during the reign of Queen Anne with the issue of an Order in Council dated 14 March 1702. It stated that it was a matter of very great consequence to the nation that all possible care should be taken to instruct such young gentlemen then serving and those who in the future would be appointed to serve as 'volunteers' in Her Majesty's Fleet, not only in the theory but also in the 'practick part' of navigation because they were the future officers of the Navy. As F B Sullivan has pointed out (*The Mariner's Mirror*, Vol 62, p 311 The Naval Schoolmaster during the eighteenth century and the early nineteenth century by F B Sullivan), this desirable state of affairs was to be brought about by the introduction onboard ships of 'schoolmasters' who would receive a Midshipman's pay plus an allowance of £20 per annum, known as Queen Anne's Bounty. Before he could be entered onboard one of HM Ships, the would-be schoolmaster had to produce a certificate from the Corporation of Trinity House to show that he was qualified and also one from 'Good Substantial People' to certify that he was of a sober life and conversation. In fact the Order seems to have regularised a practice which, according to Trinity House records, was already operating.

As the 18th century progressed, the Admiralty's concern to improve the standard of navigation increased. A forcible reminder of the Navy's shortcomings in this respect had been given by the loss of Admiral Sir Cloudesley Shovell's squadron on the Scillies in 1707. However, little change was made in the schoolmaster's duties until the dawn of the 19th century and the great technical changes which ensued necessitating a restructuring of naval education. Although this led to changes in the status and duties of the schoolmaster there was a marked shortage of volunteers for service in this capacity. This led in 1837 to the introduction of the Naval Instructor and Schoolmaster who, in a short time, obtained a permanent career structure.

The Schoolmasters then serving were allowed to continue to do so under the same conditions as previously until in the course of time there were no more.

The Master

By the Laws of Oleron, the Master was originally in charge of the ship's furniture and tackle as well as being required to have a thorough knowledge of navigation and pilotage, but with the advent of ocean navigation a distinction began to be made between the two and the pilot became a man with local knowledge of what we call pilotage waters. The Regulations and Instructions relating to *His Majesty's Service at Sea* dated 1731, the first to be issued in book form, under the heading 'The Master', Article VII states, 'He is to have care of navigating the ship under the direction of his superior officer and to see the Log and Log Book be duly kept; and to keep a good lookout'. The Captain of course was in overall charge of the ship and told the Master where he wanted to go and it was up to the latter to take him there.

The loss of HMS Impregnable

A classic example of the dichotomy between the Captain's and the Master's responsibilities is provided by the grounding of the 90 gun ship *HMS Impregnable* on the Poles shoal outside Chichester Harbour on 19 October 1799 and her subsequent total loss.

The Court of Inquiry charged with investigating the matter, acquitted the Captain, Jonathan Faulknor, of blame for the loss of his ship and attributed it to the negligence of the Master. A few years later in 1803, we find Admiral the Honourable Sir George Elliot writing, 'As to navigation in those days hardly anybody but the Master knew anything of it. We had no chronometers and knew nothing of lunar observations . . . I remember some of our squadron between three and four hundred miles out of their longitude in going from Gibraltar to the West Indies.'

HMS Dryad III, a single screw sloop, launched at Devonport in 1866.

That there was difficulty in getting volunteers to be trained as Masters is shown by an Order in Council, dated 15 August 1805, which reads:

'The great inconvenience experienced by Your Majesty's Navy for the want of persons properly qualified to execute the duty of Master onboard Your Majesty's ships and vessels, being very considerably increased as we have judged it right to turn our attention to that class of officers with a view to ascertain the means by which an inconvenience of such magnitude to Your Majesty's Naval Service can be obviated, and persons in every respect qualified for such appointment be induced to offer themselves for, and attach themselves to, Your Majesty's Service, and having induced the Commissioners of Your Majesty's Navy to state to us, for our consideration, such causes as in their opinion operated to prevent persons qualified to serve as Masters in the Navy from offering their services; they have . . . represented to us that the encouragement at present held out to that useful class of officers appears to them to be insufficient to induce proper persons to offer themselves for Your Majesty's Service . . .'

Two years later Masters were granted the same (newly instituted) uniform as Surgeons and Pursers under an Order in Council dated 29 June 1807. They were required to pass a scale of examinations for the different rates of ships over which the Masters and Wardens of Trinity House presided. The following year they were accorded the status of Lieutenant and precedence of Surgeons in mitigation of their complaint that when captured or cast away on an enemy's coast they were treated as 'foremastmen.'

13

King's Regulations and Admiralty Instructions

In the 1808 edition of what had now become known as *King's Regulations and Admiralty Instructions,* the duties of the Master were more fully defined and included:

a Responsibility for seeing that the inboard end of the cable was secured.
b To deliver to the Captain everyday at Noon an account of the situation of the ship, the latitude and longitude, the variation (deviation) of the compasses, the bearing and distance of the place sailed from or that to which she was bound and any other particulars that the Captain shall direct.

In 1825 in a revised edition of KR and AI Masters were given the entire charge of the stores heretofore kept by the boatswain and carpenter for which they received an additional allowance of £80 a year in the case of a First Rate and £37 a year in the case of a Sloop. The pay of the Master of a First Rate at that time was £14 a month and his status was defined in the following terms:

'An officer ranking immediately after the Lieutenants, appointed by the Commissioners of the Navy to assist in fitting and to take charge of the navigating and conducting a ship from port to port under the charge of the Captain. The management and disposition of the sails, the working of the ship into her position in the order of battle, and the direction of her movements in the time of action are also particularly under his inspection; and he is moreover charged with the stowage of the hold. He is to be careful that the rigging, sails, and stores are duly preserved. To see that the log and log book be regularly and correctly kept, accurately to observe the appearance of coasts, rocks, and shoals, with their depth of water and bearings, noting them in his journal. To see the hawse clear when the ship is at anchor and to provide himself with proper instruments, books of navigation, and maps. It is likewise his duty to examine the provisions, and accordingly admit none into the ship but such as are sound, sweet, and wholesome.'

He also had to keep the spirit room keys and attend all issues of rum. He was responsible that the correct amount of fresh water was kept onboard; and reported daily to the Captain the amount of beer and water remaining.

Masters of the Fleet

In 1838 a few of the senior Masters known as Masters of the Fleet were granted the rank of Commander and five years later, in 1843, an important step was taken when Masters, who had previously been appointed by warrant, were granted commissioned rank, as were also pursers, doctors, chaplains and naval instructors.

Under an Order in Council dated 24 October 1853, Masters were required to pass in Navigation at the Royal Naval College, the history of which will be found in the following Chapter. Then in 1860, the Hydrographer, Rear Admiral J Washington as Head of the Hydrographic department which, since its establishment in 1795, had been responsible for all matters affecting navigation, put forward a scheme for the training of Masters in Pilotage and he also suggested that they be merged in the Commanders' and Lieutenants' list.

Introduction of the Navigating Officer

Yet another change was made in 1864 when Masters with 15 years service became

Staff Commanders and Masters of the Fleet, Staff Captains. In 1867 the title Master was abolished and under an Order in Council of 26 June of that year Masters became Navigating Lieutenants, Second Masters became Navigating Sub Lieutenants, and Master's Assistants became Navigating Midshipmen. The rank of Navigating Cadet was introduced and those of Staff Commander and Staff Captain retained. Instead of passing for line of battle ships at Trinity House after three years service in the rank of Master, the new Navigating Lieutenants were required to pass for ships of the first class drawing 26 feet of water or more. Promotion to Staff Commander was by selection. However they were still a separate and subordinate class as the Regulations of the period show.

'Navigating Officers, whatever their rank and seniority may be, are, in all matters of command, and in all details relating to the duties of the Fleet, and to the discipline and interior economy of Your Majesty's Ships, to be held subject to the authority of any officer not below the rank of Lieutenant who may be in charge of the executive duties of the ship, or in charge of any other special service or duty, of whatever seniority such officer may be'.

As an award for meritorious service in the presence of the enemy they could be transferred to the executive list with their own seniority.

In 1867, three years after taking office as Hydrographer, Rear Admiral G H Richards proposed to the Board of Admiralty that the examinations for Lieutenant and Navigating Lieutenant should be assimilated with a view to stimulating recruitment for the Surveying service. The Board took six years to reach a decision on the matter and in 1873 announced their intention of employing a number of executive officers in navigating duties subject to their passing an examination in Pilotage at the Hydrographic Office. Two years later it was made compulsory for every executive officer to pass an examination in Pilotage.

Introduction of Lieutenants (N)

Meanwhile it was decided to reduce the number of Navigating Officers on the Active List from 432 to 265, 15 of whom would be Staff Captains. Then in 1879 it was decided to replace the class of Navigating Officers by Lieutenants for Navigating duties to be known as Lieutenants (N). Entries into the former branch, nevertheless, continued until 1893 and the last of the Staff Captains, J D Moulton, did not retire until 1913, so bringing to an end a branch of the Royal Navy with the longest continuous record of service.

However, the system continued by which officers who wished to specialize in navigation merely volunteered to do so and, if accepted, were appointed to a small ship to learn the tricks of the trade. After serving for three years they passed a viva voce examination for First Class ships before a Board of three officers at the Hydrographic Department.

In May 1883, the Hydrographer was invited to comment on a report by four senior officers concerning navigation and pilotage in the Fleet and he remarked favourably on the Portsmouth pilotage classes which he considered preferable to the individual instruction of officers in their ships, but there had been a falling off in the number of officers volunteering to specialize as Lieutenants (N). A conservative Navy resented their taking command by seniority with regular Commanders and

Lieutenants, and their exclusion from ship's duties, a relic of the old days of Masters, welcomed by some but rejected by others, had not enhanced their position. However the Hydrographer attributed the situation to uncertainty regarding their future. Amongst the surveyors only one Lieutenant Commander with eight to nine years seniority in the rank was promoted to Commander each year. In the event, failure to remedy this state of affairs, worked to the great advantage of the (N) branch as will be related later.

Notes bearing on the navigation of HM Ships

In 1889 the Hydrographic Office issued a new publication entitled *Notes bearing on the Navigation of HM Ships* which gives a good picture of the state of the art in the Royal Navy at that time. It dealt with the correction of charts, light lists, and sailing directions, the proper use of charts as aids to navigation, patent logs and sounding machines, making plans of bays and harbours visited, the use of the sextant, the care of chronometers, keeping a remark book and a compass journal, all matters with which future Navigating Officers were to become well acquainted. As in wartime the compass might receive damage, officers were reminded of the value of fixing the ship's position by the use of sextant angles and the newly supplied station pointers. Perhaps the most remarkable innovation listed was a tripod 'to hold the lamp over the standard compass' which 'will be found of great service in fixing the position at night'. The Thomson sounding machine which had been first supplied to HM Ships in 1885 was not to be regarded as an unerring guide if obliged to run in for the land in thick weather. New editions of this informative publication appeared in 1891-2 and 1893. A fifth edition, no copies of which remain, was followed by a sixth in 1909, thereafter the information was included in the different volumes of Sailing Directions.

Lieutenant House's Speed and Distance Table

One of the simplest and yet most useful aids to navigation before the slide rule came into common use, was a Speed and Distance Table compiled by Lieutenant A E House to whose grandson, Lieutenant R E D House RN, the author is indebted for some of the information given below.

At the turn of the century in the days before the advent of radar and all the other modern aids to Navigation available today, a young surveying officer called House joined the surveying ship *Daphne* in the Persian Gulf. One day he had the idea of compiling a Speed and Distance Table which he forwarded to the Admiralty and which was considered so useful that it was issued to all the ships in the Fleet and because it might easily blow overboard it was labelled in black letters TO BE PASTED ON A BOARD. It showed the distance run at various speeds in intervals of time from one to sixty minutes. In 1910 Captain House as he became, was appointed King's Harbourmaster at Wei Hai Wei and he lived until the year 1955. Being a Younger Brother of Trinity House, at the annual dinner in 1956 given by the Elder Brethren to the Younger ones his name was included amongst those who had died during the previous twelve months. He is described as 'a gentle, kindly man who by no great feat of invention and by means of no scientific ingenuity produced a small device to help his fellow navigators' and for this his name will long be remembered.

Enter Lieutenant H F Oliver Royal Navy

Also in 1889 an event which was to prove of even greater moment to the future of the (N) branch occurred. An impecunious Lieutenant Henry Francis Oliver serving in the flagship of the Pacific Fleet, *Triumph,* decided that the most satisfactory way of solving his financial problems was to apply for surveying duties. He spent the next four and a half years on this arduous but most rewarding duty and was recommended for promotion to First Class Assistant Surveyor. He had taken the opportunity during a visit to Malta to pass provisionally as a Navigating Officer for First Class ships and when in March 1894 the Hydrographer refused to approve his advancement in the surveying service, he decided to leave it and return to general service as a Navigating Officer. The impact of this future Admiral of the Fleet on the branch was to prove decisive. He quickly sensed that the great changes taking place in the RN at that time which included an increase in the tonnage, draught and speed of the major units, would demand an even higher standard both of navigation and of ship handling, well beyond the competence of officers like the elderly Navigating Officer of the ship in which he had taken passage back to England from Australia in 1897. Although a former instructor in the cadet training ship *Britannia,* Oliver noticed that he had not bothered to adjust his compasses since leaving England, nor when the ship entered the southern hemisphere had he reversed the heeling error magnets in the binnacle, so when the ship rolled the compass card would swing 30° to 40°.

After an eventful six years as Navigating Officer in various ships, during which he showed marked ability and made good use of the knowledge he had gained as a surveyor, on 1 January 1900 Oliver was promoted to Commander and on 9 September of that year was appointed Commander (N) of *Majestic* (14,900 tons) flagship of the Commander in Chief Channel Fleet, at that time Vice Admiral Sir Harry Rawson. In March 1901, Rawson was relieved by that gallant officer Vice Admiral Sir Arthur Wilson VC and it was shortly after the change in command that Oliver performed a feat of navigation which was to become legendary. Let him tell the story in his own words, which he does with becoming modesty:

'The annual manoevures in the same year (1901) commenced at midnight; we were off the west coast of Islay in foggy weather with the (eight) battleships in single line ahead steaming 13 knots, making for the Scilly Islands. We never saw Rathlin Island or a scrap of Ireland and the fog continued all that day and the next night. When we were south of the Tuscar (a rock off the south easterly point of Ireland) we reduced speed to 6 knots and sounded continuously. About 4 am, Sir Arthur Wilson was in the charthouse on the fore bridge where I got him some ship's cocoa and we talked about the chance of getting into St Mary's which was our main base. I said that if I saw the Bishop Lighthouse (off the south west corner of the Scillies) for long enough to get a good fix, I could get the Fleet in. We passed westward of the islands and when at a safe distance south of them by dead reckoning and soundings, altered course for the Bishop Rock, picking up its fog signal and keeping on. When it was pretty loud, the fog lifted for a few minutes. I got a good fix, a bearing and sextant angle, and then the weather shut down again. There were buoys at the bends of the channel and no large alterations of course and I had been in that way once before. We anchored in thick fog in single line ahead. Later the sun came out and I got some sleep that afternoon, the first for three nights.'

To have steamed 470 miles by dead reckoning in tidal waters and thick weather and then to make a successful landfall and subsequently anchor eight battleships safely in a narrow rockbound anchorage was indeed a remarkable achievement, considering the navigational equipment available in those days.

Vice Admiral B C Watson who qualified in 1910, joined the *Majestic* as a Midshipman in March 1903 and he recalls how on arrival onboard he was informed that the Navigating Officer wished to see him on the quarter deck. 'There I was introduced to a rather gruff-looking elderly man with a black beard' who informed him 'I have had a letter from your mother and you can count on me as your sea Daddy, so come to me if you get into any trouble'. Two days later Watson was keeping the forenoon watch. 'It was a fine Sunday morning and Church which was being held on the messdeck was just ending when loud shouting was heard forward. I looked over the side and saw a man's head bobbing up and down in the water between the picket boat lying at the boom and the ship's side'. It was the picket boat's stoker who had slipped off the boom whilst making his way inboard. Everyone inboard was giving him advice but no one did anything. Suddenly a figure in blue dived from the boat deck 30 feet up and seized the dazed rating and pulled

HMS Mercury, built in 1878 and allocated in 1903 as floating Navigation School.

him into the ship's side when both were hauled to safety. Returning to the quaterdeck Watson was astonished to encounter 'Oliver not only in his frock coat dripping with water but also his cap and looking for all the world just like a walrus'. With typical modesty Oliver disappeared down below to change his clothes and without saying anything to anybody. The story of the gallant rescue, however, leaked out and appeared next morning in the local paper much to his disgust.

During his time in the *Majestic* Oliver became increasingly convinced that the (N) branch was badly in need of reform. 'Some young officers became Ns to have an easy time in harbour' he has recorded, 'and they usually had no better instruments than their old Britannia sextants; they never took a star sight or a sight in an artificial horizon if they could help it. I once saw an old Commander (N) go onboard a Cardiff collier in uniform, with his deck watch to get a comparison. When the noon positions were signalled at sea he was usually many miles out in his longitude'.

Princes Among men

In an entertaining book entitled *'Fabulous Admirals'* by Commander C L Lowis AFC RN (Retired) p 237-8 the author relates a story which gives a popular view in the Service of certain Navigating Officers of that time. 'In harbour they led a detached life in some quiet nook, carefully correcting charts with the Admiralty Notices to Mariners . . . they even escaped the daily Divisions or Church Parade by arranging to wind their chronometers at that time . . . Tankie, the Midshipman attached as Assistant Navigator, having collected the key from the keyboard sentry, used to report to the Pilot, generally in the middle of his breakfast, and the two would descend to the gloomy depths where the chronometers lay in state.

'Most Pilots wound their clocks in profound silence, but one of the old school made quite a ritual of the daily occasion . . . every day he would turn to his Tankie and say "Who are the salt of the earth?" and the Tankie was obliged to respond "the Navigating Branch, sir" the short ceremony being brought to a close by the Pilot's response "And the princes amongst men". In fact the Sergeant Major of Marines being the least concerned with the ritual surrounding the chronometers, was made responsible for checking with the Navigating Officer at 0900 each day that this officer had done his duty and of subsequently reporting to the Captain "Chronometers wound, Sir".'

It was to change this image that Oliver devoted his efforts during the next few years. That all was not well with the branch is suggested by a remark of Lord Brassey's in a lecture given at the Royal United Services Institute on 6 March 1891 and which he attributed to Captain Kiddle. 'The modern Navigating Lieutenant is drifting into the position of the officer he displaced and, if reports are true, the majority wish to avoid the duty.' The Hydrographer and titular head of the (N) branch at this time was the famous surveyor, Rear Admiral Sir William J L Wharton KCB FRS who had been in office since 1884. During the 18 years which had elapsed since he assumed the post, the Navy had completed the change from sail to steam and now comprised 55 battleships and more than 100 cruisers. As has been mentioned, larger faster and deeper draught ships were being commissioned, new and better navigational equipment was becoming available such as a patent log that did not wear out at speeds above 12 knots and a mechancial sounding machine to supplement the old hand lead and line.

In 1902 the Channel and Mediterranean Fleets met and anchored off Lagos, in southern Portugal, when Admiral Sir John (Jackie) Fisher, then Commander in Chief Mediterranean, invited his brother Flag Officers and Captains to dine. Included in the invitation was Commander H F Oliver and after dinner Fisher took him on one side and gave him the opportunity to air his views about the future of the (N) branch. At that time Fisher's mind was full of plans for improving the entry and training of naval officers generally, so the moment could not have been more propitious. Oliver has recorded how he used 'to talk things over with some of the keen Navigators in the Channel Fleet and with Herbert Richmond, my old shipmate in the *Stork*, who was now First and Torpedo Lieutenant in the *Majestic'*. Subsequently he and Richmond wrote a paper in which they suggested the creation of a Navigation School and which they circulated to the other Navigating Officers in the Fleet. However, they were advised not to show it to Admiral Sir Arthur Wilson as 'he was very strict and might try me by court martial.'

The old Royal Naval Academy at Portsmouth in 1754. (By courtesy of Portsmouth Naval Museum).

Chapter II

THE FOUNDING OF THE

NAVIGATION SCHOOL

'The pilots or lodesmen shall be examined of the knowledge and experience they ought to have of the fabric and working of ships, and of the course of the tide, of the sandbanks, currents, shells, rocks, and other impediments that may render difficult the entry of the rivers, ports and harbours in which they are established. A pilot undertaking to conduct a vessel while he is drunk, shall be fined five livres and shall not exert the function of pilot for one month.'

From an Ordinance of Louis XIV of France dated 1681

'More depends on the conduct and ability of the Master than on any other in the ship. If the First Lieutenant be called the Captain's right hand man, the Master may be said to be his right arm, aye, and right leg too for he can scarcely move without him.'

Captain Glascock's *Manual for the Naval Officer* 1848

Fisher, Richmond and Oliver

In 1903, Fisher was appointed Second Sea Lord and took with him to the Admiralty as his assistant, Richmond, who had been promoted to Commander at the end of 1902. After some hesitation, he and Oliver decided to show the paper on the (N) Branch which together they had written, to Fisher who, after reading it sent for Oliver and told him 'he was appointing a Court of Inquiry at Portsmouth into (N) officers' (Much of the information in this chapter has been compiled from the personal recollections of Admiral of the Fleet Sir Henry Oliver as related to Lieutenant Commander R Dyer). Richmond remarks in his diary on 26 March 1903, 'Oliver is delighted, naturally . . . It really is wonderful to have a man at the Head of Affairs who can take the matter up as Fisher has, who is so absolutely approachable and ready to listen to suggestions and act on them.' Oliver had already hinted to Fisher that Captain H D Barry, formerly in command of the *Duke of Wellington,* would make a good chairman and it was left to him and Richmond to select the other members. The final list as approved by Fisher was as follows:

Captain H D Barry, Director of Naval Ordnance and Torpedoes
Commander F S Miller, formerly Navigating Officer *HMS Revenge*
Commander H F Oliver, formerly Navigating Officer *HMS Majestic*
Commander A Hayes-Sadler, formerly Navigating Officer *HMS Emperor of India*

Commander H W Richmond, Naval Assistant to Second Sea Lord
P Dale-Russell Esq., Secretary to the Committee and Private Secretary
to Rear Admiral J Durnford

As all the members of the Committee, except Oliver and Richmond, were married, most of the work of drafting the findings fell on these two as an entry in Richmond's diary for 3 May 1903 confirms. As was to be expected the Committee gave overwhelming support to the proposals in the Oliver-Richmond paper. 'A lot of witnesses were called' Oliver has recorded, 'who knew my plans. A few other (N) officers were called who knew nothing about it, but Richmond was outside in the waiting room and "instructed" them accordingly'. The report proposed the setting up of a Navigation School for officers desiring to qualify in navigation and the institution of a First Class Ship course for qualified (N) officers with three or more years experience. After Fisher had read the report, he expressed the intention of appointing Oliver in command of the new Navigation School and of promoting him to Captain in the next half-yearly promotions on 30 June. In Richmond's words 'Jack said we want this school to be a success and Oliver is the man to start it well' (Richmond's Diary 27 May 1903). The Circular Letter dated 15 June 1903 giving effect to the proposals in the Report is reproduced in full in Appendix I.

HMS Mercury

Oliver had hoped for a shore establishment with sea-going tenders for the new school, but Fisher told him there was no provision in the Naval Estimates for it and that he would have to make do with a 25-years-old cruiser, *HMS Mercury* of 3370 tons disarmed and lying on the Motherbank at Spithead awaiting disposal. He was also given a flat-iron gunboat, *Plucky,* for pilotage and compass instruction in the Solent. Nothing shows better the remarkable character of this future Admiral of the Fleet than the way in which he set to work to convert this dirty, dilapidated, old vessel into a floating Navigation School. He used the heavy gun metal racers which had been left in the ship as cash to pay for the work done by the Dockyard. The ship's complement amounted only to 36 seamen and about 45 stokers, so he obtained RNR seamen and stokers on loan from the depot. Although provided with two small dynamos, she was not wired for electric light, 'We therefore cadged wire fittings and lamps from the Channel Fleet ships at Portsmouth and the Gunner and Chief Engineer did the work.' When it was completed, Oliver reported officially that the *Mercury* was electrically lit, but gave no details as to how this had been achieved. A few months later, her complement was increased by four torpedo ratings, who in those days maintained the electrical equipment on which Oliver commented 'the mills of God grind slowly!' The *Mercury* was fitted with a hand çapstan and after carrying out her commissioning steam trial, it was decided to test the anchor gear by mooring ship. When it came to unmooring, it took all hands including the stokers on watch to break each anchor out and the whole operation occupied an entire day. This was clearly a situation not to be tolerated, and was overcome by the use of a small steam driven boat-hoist and a steel wire deck tackle which could be secured to the cable.

There was no enclosed space in the ship large enough for instructional purposes, so a large deckhouse was constructed on the quarter-deck with an instructional compass on top, alongside which a sheltered chart table was fitted. To escape from port duties which would interfere with instruction, Oliver took the ship up Southampton water, on the principle of 'out of sight out of mind.' With only himself, a Commander and two Lieutenants (N) to take the First Class Ship, Qualifiers, and Warrant Officers courses, the last named of which took place onboard the *Plucky*, Oliver was hard pressed to manage, but he succeeded in obtaining the assistance of a Captain F S Miller who was on half pay while writing a book on handling ships and who brought his work onboard and helped Oliver to arrange the instructional programme.

From time to time the distinguished scientist, Lord Kelvin, would go to sea with Oliver in the *Plucky* to test new types of compasses on which he was working; three versions of his patent sounding machine were tested in the *Mercury* before the Hand Machine Mark IV was accepted for use in the Royal Navy.

The first qualifiers

The first class of Qualifiers to be trained in *Mercury* numbered nine of whom four reached the rank of Commander. One of them, G N Henson, has left us his impressions of it. 'On 2 August 1903, I joined *Mercury* with a class of about 10 Sub Lieutenants for a course in practical navigation which was completed on 27 November 1903. The then Captain H F Oliver was the Commanding Officer and there were three senior Navigating Officers to instruct us in the different subjects'.

'I can still recall the appalling state of the ship as, when we joined, dockyard workmen were still working onboard from about 7.00 am until 5.00 pm doing what was known as a dockyard refit. We lived with all our belongings in our Brittania sea chests and slept in hammocks. There was a very cold and rough bathroom with round tin baths and a great shortage of hot water. We messed in the wardroom with all the other officers and this was a higher standard than the average gun-room.

'Shortly after joining, when the dockyard workmen left, we were taken to sea, and I well remember a very uncomfortable time in bad weather. We remained at sea for a few days and after we got clear of the Isle of Wight, the boilers were put out to economise the use of coal and we cruised about in the English Channel and were exercised in practical navigation including the taking of star sights when possible.

'The course was the first to be held and Captain Oliver was very keen that all Navigating Officers should have a knowledge of surveying and he personally took us to do a complete survey and make a chart of Haslar Creek. He provided all the necessary gear for doing this including instruments, and I found this very useful in later years. He was also very keen that we should be able to fix the ship's position by taking star observations.

'After leaving *Mercury*, I was appointed to a battleship as an Assistant Navigator for a period of six months and at the end of this time, May 1904, I was appointed as Sub Lieutenant (N) to *Speedwell*, a more or less modern gunboat employed on fishery protection duties and taking RNR seamen to sea. We took about 40 at a time and they were allowed one round of ammunition per man. We would drop a flag-buoy and steam past it a few hundred yards away whilst they fired at it. The chief object of the exercise was to get back into harbour as soon as possible.

'In September 1905, I was appointed as Lieutenant (N) of *HMS Dryad'*. (A twin screw gunboat of 1670 tons, 3500 HP, with a maximum speed of 18½ knots. Length 250 feet, beam 30 feet, draught 10 feet). 'In January 1906 she was ordered to be paid off on becoming a tender of the newly formed Navigation School ashore and about the middle of February I left her and handed over to Lieutenant Commander E R G R Evans who had recently returned from his South Polar Expedition.'

As Oliver has recorded, *Mercury* did not really prosper until Admiral Sir John Fisher became Commander in Chief Portsmouth at the end of 1903. (He took up his appointment on 31 August 1903). Certainly the following year, 1904, much more was achieved. Two classes of Qualifiers totalling 17 Lieutenants passed through the School and 32 Lieutenants (N) already qualified under the previous scheme introduced in 1873, underwent a course for First Class ships. Amongst the former were four future Flag Officers R H Lane-Poole, J A G Troup, K D McPherson, and J S G Fraser, whilst the latter included H O Reinold (a future Captain of *HMS Dryad*) and the Hon A C Strutt (later Squadron (N) of the Battle-Cruiser Force) both of whom became Flag Officers.

Amongst Oliver's achievements during the next two years was the temporary conversion of the *Mercury* into a yacht for the visit of Prince George and Princess Mary (later HM King George V and Queen Mary) who visited Portsmouth as guests of the Commander in Chief. Oliver relates an amusing story about the visit:

'On the day it was blowing rather hard and so the Princess and Lady Fisher did not come out but the Prince and Commander in Chief and the Misses Fisher braved it. I knew that there would be a lot of signalling, so I took the Commander in Chief's Signal Staff from *Victory* out with spare flags and other gear. At one time when a lot of signalling was going on, Fisher said to me that he didn't think much of my signal staff and I was able to say they were his own. The Prince said "He rather had you there Fisher!" ' (Dyer ibid)

The Anglo-French Review 1905

Shortly afterwards Oliver was given the task of organizing a Royal Review of the combined British and French Fleets by King Edward VII in celebration of the recently achieved *entente cordiale*. The Review was to be followed by an official ball at the Royal Naval Barracks for which it had been decided the 10 French battleships would be berthed inside Portsmouth Harbour. To get them all in on one tide meant that they must enter harbour at five minutes intervals and this allowed no time for anything going wrong. Oliver tackled the task with his customary efficiency and with the co-operation of the dockyard pilots backed by a number of Navigating Officers from the fleet, the task was accomplished without a hitch. For this excellent organization Oliver was made a Member of the Royal Victorian Order and the Senior Pilot received a gift from the King. The French Government gave Oliver a silver medal two and a half inches in diameter, in a carved box. An indirect result of the Review, during which the *Mercury* was assigned to the Lord Mayor of London and his party, was the subsequent presentation by the City of London of two handsome silver centre-pieces to replace a number of silver salt cellars and spoons which had mysteriously disappeared during the Review! These silver cups now form part of *HMS Dryad's* prized mess silver.

The staff of the Navigation School in 1906. (L to R) Lieut (N) A H Smyth RN, Lieut (N) W R C Moorson RN, Lieut (N) A F Dixie RN, Lieut (N) G P Ross RN, Lieut (N) H A Le F Hurt RN, Lieut (N) J E T Harper RN, Captain H F Oliver RN, Commander H W Grant RN.

Despite these interruptions, 23 officers took the Qualifying (N) Course in 1905 and 31 the First Class Ship course. Of the former W T R Ford, G F B Edward-Collins and A J Robertson reached flag rank, three became Captains and three Commanders.

The need for a shore establishment

Because of the increasing number of examinations which became necessary and which, in fairness to those undergoing them, had to be held in harbour, it was becoming more and more obvious that a shore establishment with sea-going tenders was essential. The Navigation School had fully justified itself and the fleet was crying out for trained Navigating Officers. Fortunately Oliver's friend and patron, Fisher, was now First Sea Lord so his representations on that score did not go unheeded.

It was becoming apparent that the Royal Naval College, Greenwich was not proving entirely suitable as a location for the War Course School and the Admiralty had decided to establish local War Course Schools at the Home Ports. Oliver managed to get his proposals for a shore establishment linked to that of the Portsmouth War Course School as the following letter dated 31 May 1905 from the Admiralty to the Commander in Chief Portsmouth shows:

'I am commanded by My Lords Commissioners of the Admiralty to request that you will direct Captain Frederick T Hamilton MVO, *HMS Excellent,* Captain H F Oliver, *HMS Mercury* and Major S Davidson RE, Superintendent Civil Engineer, to confer with Captain Edmund J W Slade MVO, RN College Greenwich, as to the provision of accommodation for the Navigation School and War Course in the RN College, Portsmouth.'

The Old Naval College

The conference took place on 29 August and proposed that the War Course should be accommodated in the library building opposite the Commander in Chief's residence and that the Navigation School should be allocated the Old Naval College. However before the latter could be put to its new use, considerable repairs and alterations were necessary, the cost of which was estimated at £11,750. The Board accepted the Committee's recommendations without demur.

The Naval College

The building to which Captain Oliver now turned his attention was already 173 years old and well steeped in navigational history. It had been built as the result of a letter from the Lords of the Admiralty to the Navy Board dated 3 March 1729 which ran:

'Gentlemen,
His Majesty having been pleased to direct by Order in Council dated the 21st of last month, upon an humble memorial from this Board that an Academy shall be erected in the Dockyard at Portsmouth for the better education and training of 40 young gentlemen for His Majesty's Service at Sea, instead of the Establishment now in force for Volunteers on board His Majesty's Ships. We do hereby desire and direct you to consider and lay before us, as soon as conveniently may be, a draught or plan of such a building as you may judge to be proper for the reception not only of the aforesaid young gentlemen, but also a Mathematical Master, Three Ushers, and a French Master, by whom they are to be instructed, together with an estimate of the charge thereof; and you are also to give us your opinion at what place in the Yard the said building may be most conveniently erected.'

Nine days later, in what must have been a record for a speedy reply in those days, the Navy Board forwarded 'a plan of the south part of His Majesty's Dockyard at Portsmouth, wherein is described a place in the south-east angle of the said yard, where, in our opinion, the said building may be most conveniently erected; which estimate amounts to £5772. 4s.' Unfortunately no drawings of the original design remain, but an engraving of the completed building dated 1754 can be seen in the Naval Museum in Portsmouth Dockyard. It shows the existing west front and the cupola which was used as an observatory for at least a century after it was built. It also appears that the north and south wings enclosing the courtyard were separated from the main building and the latter, originally intended to be shorter was extended during building to include a large study subsequently used as a billiard room and later, a squash racquets court. The first and second floors were a honeycomb of small cabins and offices but the ground floor provided a good example of eighteenth century architecture, especially the large L-shaped mess room with its cornice of tudor rose design. The Naval Academy took four years to build and was opened in the early summer of 1733. The curriculum included navigation, gunnery, writing, arithmetic, french, drawing, fencing, and dancing. The course lasted three years but many of the scholars completed it in less. On leaving the Academy, the scholar received a certificate from the Headmaster which read:

'Mr . . . . has (in so many years, months, and days) finished the Plan of Mathematical Learning, and made a manuscript copy thereof; in consequence, he is judged qualified to serve in HM Navy.'

The manuscripts were bulky volumes recording in copper plate handwriting the students' progress from simple addition to the calculations necessary for obtaining the longitude by chronometer, and they are embellished with sketches and paintings. Details of various sailings are given as well as methods of marine surveying. Under gunnery and fortifications the student was taught how to pile cannon balls in geometrical figures. The manuscript compiled by Captain George Tyrrell who joined the Academy in 1803 was presented to the Navigation School by Lord Teignmouth in 1922.

That it was not all that might be expected of a naval establishment is indicated

The old Navigation School in Portsmouth dockyard.

by a report on it in July 1774 which states, 'kitchen utensils are amazingly dirty. The scholars' heads abound in vermin.'

In 1776 one of the few scholars of whom any detailed information survives, James Trevenen, and two other of his class of 1773, joined *Resolution* under the command of Captain James Cook for that famous navigator's third and last voyage which ended with his death. In December of that year three scholars were expelled and eight confined for insolent and riotous behaviour. The records of that period do not reveal many famous names amongst those who entered the Royal Navy through the Academy, an exception being Captain Sir Philip Broke of *Shannon* fame who entered the College as a volunteer in 1792 and whose manuscript was for some years lodged in the training ship *Britannia.* However opposition to the College continued strong and in 1801 we find Lord St Vincent writing, 'The Royal (the prefix was granted following the visit of King George III in 1773) Academy at Portsmouth, which is a sink of iniquity, should be abolished.' Nevertheless in 1807 the building was enlarged to take seventy scholars and the Reverend James Inman, a Senior Wrangler, joined the staff as Professor.

Inman's term of office

Whilst at the Academy Inman compiled his famous *Navigation and Astronomy for the use of British Seamen* known to many generations of Navigating Officers as *Inman's tables.*

A new constitution had been drawn up and published in an Order in Council dated 1 February 1806. It provided for the following staff:

Governor	First Lord of the Admiralty (ex officio)
Lieutenant Governor	A Post Captain. Pay £500 increased to £700 in 1813
Professor (Headmaster)	An able mathematician from Cambridge. Pay £8 per scholar per annum
Preceptor	For disciplinary duties. Pay £300 per annum, increased in 1813 to £350
Housekeeper	A disabled and meritorious Lieutenant
Writing Master	Salary £100 per annum
Drawing Master*	Salary £100 per annum
Fencing and Dancing Master	One guinea per head per annum
Surgeon	

Note From 1811 to 1836 this post was held by John Christian Schetky a ship portraitist of outstanding talent who became marine painter to Kings George IV, and William IV and to Queen Victoria.

During Inman's 30 years in office the standard of training greatly improved. The scholars turned out at 4.45 am and discipline seems to have been taut. One of the students, George Mundy, later an Admiral of the Fleet and Commander in Chief Portsmouth wrote to his mother on 10 February 1818:

'I sleep in a very nice little cabin all by myself and always keep the door locked and the key in my pocket. We have coffee and milk for breakfast, very good dinners also suppers. Most of the boys keep what they call a 'mess' or drink tea every night, but that is on condition that their fathers pay 3s a week and it is sent in the bill every half year so that it would come to £3 in a half-year. So I suppose that Papa would not let me keep one . . . One of the boys invited me to drink chocolate with him one night and I must say it was excellent. The masters here are very strict indeed, but they never flog, only lock them up in a dungeon and have a soldier to guard it. PS I am now in my little cabin with the door locked.'

Inman who for 18 years combined his instructional duties with that of President of the School of Naval Architecture, introduced a system of marks and merit tickets to encourage his scholars and in 1833 we find Cooper Key (later Admiral Sir Astley) writing, 'this last month I have a second merit ticket, instead of the first which I got last time . . . I am going on in drawing very well, I am now doing sepia and I will soon begin painting. I like drawing very much indeed.' A tribute to Schetky.

The College is closed

However, the opponents of College education for young officers had never given up the struggle and finally they had their way. In 1836 it was decided to close the school and during the debate on the Navy Estimates the following year Sir George Graham said, 'We thought the decision to which the Admiralty had come respecting the suppression of the Naval College was, on the whole, a wise one.' He was of the opinion that any scheme of naval education should blend both the theory and practice of shipbuilding; he also thought that the cockpit of a man of war to be the best school for carrying this scheme into execution. Thus on 30 March 1837 the College closed and Dr Inman was granted a pension of £460 a year which he enjoyed until his death in 1859 at the age of 83.

The building did not lie idle for long. An Order in Council dated 8 July 1838 proposed:

'Whereas we had had under consideration the subject of affording additional means of scientific education to the young gentlemen and officers of your Majesty's Fleet; and whereas we are of opinion that this desirable object may be obtained at a very moderate expense by taking advantage of the buildings of the late Royal Naval College at Portsmouth, and by an addition to the present establishment of Your Majesty's Ship *Excellent* we beg leave most humbly to submit the proposal to Your Majesty's sanction.'

The College re-opens

Thus on 1 January 1839 the College reopened as part of the command of Captain Thomas Hastings of *HMS Excellent* and remained part of that establishment for 35 years. The uses to which the College was put during the next three and a half decades were many and various: courses in mathematics, the study of steam engines, courses for unemployed officers, and as a venue for examinations for Naval Cadets. Admiral Sir Percy Scott records in his autobiography 'the existing day for us all at length arrived, and about 100 little boys presented themselves at the Royal Naval College for examination. A week afterwards I was gazetted a naval cadet in HM Navy' (1866). However the main purpose of the College was the scientific education of officers in general. In 1870 a committee appointed to enquire into the whole question of the higher education of naval officers proposed that the vacant buildings of Greenwich Hospital be taken over as an RN College in place of the one at Portsmouth and this was put into effect by an Order in Council dated 16 January 1873 and another chapter in the life of the old building closed.

During the next 33 years the College, deprived of its role, became little more than a hotel for Sub Lieutenants and other miscellaneous officers undergoing courses in the port. Sub Lieutenants passing out in gunnery, torpedo and pilotage lived there. The Captain of *Excellent,* was still in command of the establishment and lived in the Governor's House; a Lieutenant of the College acted as Executive Officer and occupied what were to become the Commander's quarters. Only the Pilotage Course still held there maintained its long link with navigation and in 1900 even this tie was broken when the courses were transferred to the Royal Naval College Greenwich.

When the building was allocated to Oliver in 1905, it was in a pretty dilapidated state. The end of one wing had sunk and the outer walls had cracked from top to bottom necessitating shoring up whilst new foundations were laid. Electric lighting, a new hot water system and extra bathrooms were needed. The hall floor required to be relaid and a lodge constructed for the hall porter, but most important of all was the erection of fire-proof partitions for in Oliver's words, 'it has become a dangerous fire trap.' Approval was given for the work to proceed, as has been mentioned. On 1 January 1906 the School was formally opened, and in accordance with custom given a ship's name — *Dryad* — being that of one of the sea-going tenders now allocated to the establishment.

The Navigation School opens ashore

With the opening of the Navigation School ashore and in order to meet the new responsibilities with which it was charged, Oliver had managed to obtain an increase in the staff which now comprised one Commander (N) who was also in command of the tender *Harrier* and eight Lieutenants (N) one of whom was in command of the other tender *Plucky.* The old *Mercury* was paid off and besides the *Harrier* and *Plucky* a third tender was allocated, the gunboat *Dryad* which gave its name to the school. The gunboat tenders made a great difference to the work of the School and enabled longer cruises to be made as, unlike the *Mercury,* they had sufficient sleeping accommodation for all the pupils at once. The *Plucky* was used for Warrant Officer pilotage classes doing day trips in the Solent.

The first Qualifying class after the opening of the School comprised 11 Lieutenants who included amongst their number a future Admiral of the Fleet, John H D Cunningham. (See Appendix II.) They completed the five months course at the end of May 1906 and were followed by another class of 10, two of whom failed. The Qualifying course included a surveying cruise and Oliver relates a story about one of these cruises in the tender *HMS Dryad* of which he was in command. The First Lieutenant of the tender was Lieutenant E R G Evans (later Admiral Lord Mountevans) (See Appendix II) who was to become famous not only for his work with Scott in the Antarctic but also for his exploits in command of *HMS Broke* during World War I. One forenoon after a frustrating attempt at teaching 'two very dull Lieutenants' how to run lines of soundings, Oliver returned to the ship for lunch and ordered Evans to take them away during the afternoon, remarking that if he (Oliver) did 'either they would be put overboard or else I should be.' When later that day the boat returned, on being asked how he got on Evans replied 'not so badly, but they have both been overboard.' Evens was a very strong man!

A total of 20 qualified (N) officers attended the First Class Ship course during the year, one of whom A H Norman reached flag rank. 'The Subs were a problem at first,' Oliver remarks, 'as they arrived in batches of 50 or 60 most of them stone broke after the expensive messing at Greenwich and many actually in debt'. He took the matter up with the Commander in Chief, and subsequently the Captain of the RN College, Greenwich visited *Dryad* to see how young officers could be fed adequately with good plain food at a cost of 1s 6d per day.

The Sub Lieutenants' Pilotage course

The syllabus of the Sub Lieutenants' Pilotage course was contained in a handbook called *The Pilotage Handbook* which was drawn up by the staff of the Navigation School under Oliver's supervision and published for the first time in 1906. It was reissued by the Admiralty in 1908 and 1912 and the contents were subsequently incorporated in the Admiralty *Manual of Navigation*. The course included a six day cruise in one of the tenders during which they took turns as Navigating Officer, Officer of the Watch, Helmsman, heaving the lead or operating the new patent sounding machines. Oliver commented 'Many could not heave the lead and had never steered a ship and got awfully sick on these cruises.' As there was no ground for recreational facilities surrounding the School, Oliver, who was a bachelor and lived on the first floor of the east wing which eventually became the Captain's House, sacrificed part of his garden in the rear of the building to allow the construction of a gymnasium where the young officers could exercise. As he says, 'they had no money and were otherwise hanging about doing nothing or getting into mischief'. He also teamed up with the new Submarine School which had just started under Captain (later Admiral Sir) Reginald Bacon by which mixed teams could be formed. These 'innovations' were apparently regarded with some mistrust by the old established Schools *Excellent* (gunnery) and *Vernon* (torpedo).

Soon after the School was transferred ashore. Oliver introduced a short course for Senior Officers in fleetwork, cruiser searching, and handling ships and these courses continued until November 1913.

The Commander in Chief inspects the School

The Navigation School was situated right alongside the residence of the Commander in Chief Portsmouth and throughout its 35 years of existence in those premises this was a factor to be borne very much in mind by successive Captains and Commanders of the establishment. Oliver has recalled that Admiral Sir Charles Douglas who succeeded Fisher as Commander in Chief 'was very friendly to us, and he used to wander over in the forenoon smoking his cigar, yarning, and looking at things.' One day he decided to carry out an official inspection of the School and whilst the 'elderly Marine servants' who had been engaged as mess waiters and to look after the officers undergoing courses, 'were well polished up to form a guard' there were

The handsome L-shaped mess in the old Navigation School.

no Marine buglers to sound the salute. The Commander, H W Grant, not to be defeated, borrowed two blue-jacket buglers from the *Dryad* and *Harrier* and stationed them out of sight in the basement area below the front door, whilst two of the Marine guard were furnished with bugles. On the Commander in Chief's arrival the pseudo Marine buglers went through the motions of sounding off, whilst the hidden buglers, alerted by a prearranged signal, did the blowing; the deception it seems was not discovered!

Some years later it was suggested that the School should fly a white ensign on a flagstaff over the entrance so as to distinguish it from the surrounding dockyard stores which were built of the same brick. 'No fear,' said the then Executive Officer, 'the hall porter would be sure to forget the time of sunset and we should be certain to get a rude signal from the Commander in Chief next door.'

Captain Oliver relieved by Captain Power

Early in 1907 Captain L E Power MVO was appointed in command of the Navigation School vice Oliver. He had been Master of the Fleet during the Coronation Review on 16 August 1902 and had formerly commanded the cruiser *Edgar*. He was a holder of the Shadwell Testimonial.

In his turn over to his successor, Oliver revealed the delicate situation which existed between the Hydrographer, the Director of Naval Education, and the Navigation School. About the DNE, Oliver remarked bluntly, 'the Navigation School is the only training establishment that the DNE has not got his nose into.' By firmness and tact he navigated successfully between the scylla and charybdis of the two departments while maintaining good relations with both.

The Hydrographic Department and the (N) Branch

The Hydrographer of the Navy, by virtue of his responsibility for advising the Board of Admiralty on all navigational matters as laid down in paragraph 16 of his Instructions dated January 1889, was *ipso facto* Head of the Navigation Branch which was a section of his department. However, from the start, Oliver was determined that the Hydrographer's authority should not extend to the Navigation School and he had persuaded Fisher, when the School was established, to agree that this should be so. One day, however, he received an official telegram from the then Hydrographer, Admiral Sir William Wharton, announcing that he intended to inspect the school. The close proximity of Admiralty House, enabled Oliver to walk over with the telegram and show it to the Chief of Staff, (the Commander in Chief being away at the time) and the following day he received another telegram cancelling the visit. He thereupon wrote to the Hydrographer and informed him that if he wished to visit the School unofficially at any time he would be delighted to show him around. There is no record that the invitation was accepted, but Wharton's successor, Admiral Sir A M Field, who took office in August 1904, visited the School and was shown round 'in the capacity of an ordinary visitor.'

Although over the years amicable relations were preserved between the Hydrographer and the School, which was responsible for trying out new navigational equipment on the former's behalf, the marriage between the two sections of the Hydrographic Department was never entirely happy. In 1905 a committee, of which Oliver was a member, was formed to consider the appointment of (N) officers to certain branches and recommended the appointment of an Assistant Hydrographer (N) to replace the Superintendent of Sailing Directions and the creation of two separate departments. Four years later in 1909, when the Board had considered the report, the First Sea Lord, Sir John Fisher, and the Hydrographer both gave it their approval but it fell into the clutches of the Treasury which opposed it. The resulting argument has been fully described elsewhere (*The Admiralty Hydrographic Service 1785-1919* by Vice Admiral Sir Archibald Day pages 251-252) and although the Hydrographer again returned to the charge on the grounds that two separate departments would ease the burden of work falling on his own department and, which included *inter alia* – the Navigation School, defence navigation, compasses, chronometers, meteorology, pilotage, groundings and collisions, jurisdiction over moorings in Admiralty harbours, navigational equipment, fleet programmes, and fisheries damage claims, after two years of deliberation, in July 1911 the Board decided against the creation of a separate (N) department whilst approving certain additions to the Hydrographer's staff. These included a Naval Assistant (N) to the Assistant Hydrographer (N). Once again the Treasury intervened and a further two years elapsed, but in April 1913 the Hydrographer succeeded in obtaining approval for the creation of a separate Navigational department under a Director of Navigation responsible to a Superintending Sea Lord. His duties included all the matters listed above. The first holder of the emancipated post was Captain Philip Nelson-Ward MVO who had recently relinquished command of the battleship *Formidable* in the Atlantic Fleet; he remained in office for just over three years and retired with the rank of Rear Admiral in July 1916, on his relief by Captain John A Webster MVO.

The Navigation School's progress

The School was now well established but the number of officers applying to qualify in Navigation dropped to 13 in 1907, one of whom K E Creighton reached flag rank. Eleven officers took the First Class Ship course, amongst them A F B Carpenter who gained a VC for his gallant exploit in command of *Vindictive* during the assault on Zeebrugee in April 1918 and who retired with the rank of Vice Admiral. Another of the class was J D Campbell who after serving as Director of Navigation was Captain of the School from December 1926 to December 1928 and retired with the rank of Rear Admiral.

To compensate for the small number of Qualifiers in 1907, the following year a total of 33 took the Qualifying course of whom three failed and two later reverted to General Service. Four of them reached flag rank namely H R Moore (see Appendix II), E R Corson, E J Pope, and M L Clarke. Eleven officers took the First Class Ship course in 1908 amongst them O H Dawson who was Captain of the School from June 1932 to July 1934 and who after retiring with the rank of Rear Admiral served as Commodore of Convoys during World War II and was awarded a KBE.

The first Qualifying course in 1909 numbered 14, one of whom J G P Vivian reached flag rank, the second numbered 18 and included J H Godfrey, Director of Naval Intelligence during World War II, R J R Scott and J Powell, all of whom reached flag rank. For the first time a foreign officer, Lieutenant C C Eang of the Chinese Navy was included amongst the Qualifiers. During the year 12 officers returned for a First Class Ship course.

Changes in command

In January 1910 Captain Power was relieved in command of the school by Captain H W Grant who, as Commander, had so ably assisted Oliver with the founding of the school, first afloat and then ashore. He had been promoted to Captain on 31 December 1907 and had subsequently served as Flag Captain to Rear Admiral W B Fisher in the battleship, *Albemarle,* in the Atlantic Fleet.

There were two Qualifying courses in 1910 numbering 16 and 14 and out of the total, four namely J W Clayton, E J Spooner, B C Watson, and P K Kekewich reached flag rank. During the year, 11 officers returned for the First Class Ship course and amongst them were several who had qualified from the first course held in the school.

In 1911, a special class of six Turkish officers took the Qualifying course in addition to two classes of RN officers numbering 15 and nine, whilst 13 officers

The fourth HMS Dryad, a twin screw gunboat launched in 1893 and allocated as tender to the Navigation School, when it opened ashore in 1906, to which it gave its name.

took the First Class Ship course. Of the first batch of RN Qualifiers W S Chalmers was appointed Assistant (N) in the battle-cruiser *HMS Lion,* flagship of Rear Admiral David Beatty commanding the battle-cruiser squadron. The former, after his retirement in the rank of Rear Admiral, wrote a widely acclaimed life of Admiral of the Fleet Earl Beatty. Two others of the class who attained flag rank were K H L McKenzie and W G Benn, the last named surviving the sinking of the battleship, *Royal Oak* of which he was in command, by U47 in Scapa Flow on 14 October 1939; he subsequently became Director of Navigation and played a notable part in the amalgamation of the (N) and (D) branches.

Relief of Captain Grant

On 15 January 1912, Captain Grant was relieved in command of the School by Captain E L Booty MVO who had commanded the cruiser *Ariadne* in the Home Fleet and who, before promotion to Captain on 31 December 1908, had been Commander (N) of the battleship *Caesar,* flagship of Vice Admiral Lord Charles Beresford in the Channel Fleet. After being relieved, Captain Grant commanded the cruiser, *Hampshire* on the China Station and in the Grand Fleet, but in 1915, at Oliver's request, he joined the Admiralty as Assistant Director of Operations where he remained until the end of the war. He retired in 1919 to become Director of Cable and Wireless (Holdings) Limited, a post which enabled him to visit the numerous cable stations which the company had established throughout the world and in so doing to improve greatly their amenities and recreational facilities. He also founded a club in London for personnel home on leave and with no homes of their own to go to.

The events of 1912

In 1912 a total of 27 officers qualified in two classes of 14 and 13 respectively. Two Turkish, two Greek and one Egyptian officer also took the Qualifying course and 15 officers the one for First Class ships. Despite the steady increase in the size of the fleet as the naval armaments race with Germany reached full spate, only one course of 12 Qualifiers was held in 1913, but a record number of 27 officers underwent the First Class Ship course, amongst whom was W G Tennant, who was destined to reach the rank of Admiral after a distinguished career (see Appendix II). The following year, 1914, two Qualifying classes were held numbering nine and 11, and 15 officers completed the First Class Ship course. Commander G B Rudyard-Helpman DSC of the second batch of Qualifiers and who was still a Sub Lieutenant when he did the course, writes that before joining *Dryad* he and his 11 classmates did a month's mathematical course at the Royal Naval College Greenwich. Their cruise in the tender took them as far as the Isle of Man and they surveyed a portion of Falmouth harbour. After qualifying he and S J L Bennett were appointed (N) of the new M class destroyers *Meteor* and *Miranda* in the Harwich Force, L M Bridge went as (N) of the old seaplane tender *Ark Royal* which did such good work during operations off the Dardanelles, whilst J M H Fisher went as Assistant (N) in the cruiser *Good Hope,* flagship of Rear Admiral Sir Christopher Craddock which was lost with all hands at the Battle of Coronel on 1 November 1914.

Another event in this memorable year was the publication of the first *Admiralty Manual of Navigation and Nautical Astronomy.* It was compiled by Commander W E F Aylmer, who had qualified in 1906, and a well known Naval Instructor John White MA.

The outbreak of World War I

On 1 September 1914, soon after the outbreak of World War I, the Navigation School closed down and for the next four and a half years the buildings were used to accommodate officers on temporary duty in the port. Captain Booty departed to take up his appointment as Commodore in command of the 10th Cruiser Squadron and the staff dispersed to take up their war appointments.

During the four years of war the foundations so well and truly laid by Captain Oliver were tested in the hardest of all schools — active service. The great Anglo-German naval armaments race had reached its climax and the British Home Fleet, about to be renamed the Grand Fleet comprising 28 battleships, four battle-cruisers, eight armoured cruisers, eight light cruisers, four flotilla cruisers, and 58 destroyers assembled in Scapa Flow in the Orkneys to await events. Each ship down to and including cruisers carried a qualified Navigating Officer. Very few ships were fitted with gyro compasses. *Indomitable,* in which the author was serving as a snotty, had a German Anschultz but it was rarely serviceable, and the accuracy of the standard magnetic compass depended on careful adjustment which was liable to alter whenever the main armament was fired. The Fleet was manoeuvred by flag signals and both its order and disposition had to be changed to suit the prevailing circumstances. The Navigating Officer's duty was to advise his Captain on the action to be taken and those who had learned to recognize signals as soon as they were hoisted reaped the benefit of their knowledge since Signalmen were trained not to rely on memory when reporting the meaning of a signal. Lieutenant (later Admiral Sir Bertram) Ramsay, Signal Officer and Flag Lieutenant to Admiral Sir Douglas Gamble in the battleship *Dreadnought* describes a hair-raising passage of the Pentland Firth by the Grand Fleet at night during a full gale during which the battleships *Conqueror* and *Monarch* collided, but remarks, 'the standard of navigation and ship handling, however, was high and accidents were rare.' (*Full Cycle* by Rear Admiral Peter Chalmers, page 22)

The battle of Jutland

Students of the battle of Jutland will recall that there was a serious discrepancy between the estimated geographical positions of Admiral Jellicoe's flagship, *Iron Duke,* and that of Admiral Beatty's flagship, *Lion,* which led the Commander in Chief to think that he was further away from the German High Seas Fleet than he in fact was. When the error was discovered, rapid deployment was necessary and the faultless way in which this was achieved was proof of the high standard of fleetwork which had been attained. Commander (later Vice Admiral) Oliver Leggett, Master of the Fleet in the *Iron Duke* and Commander the Hon A C Strutt in the *Lion* were both very experienced Navigating Officers, but the latter's ship had been in close action with the enemy with unfortunate repercussions on the navigation of the flagship of the battle-cruiser force as Lieutenant (later Rear Admiral) W S Chalmers RN Assistant (N) to Strutt has described. 'The action continued on a northerly course with renewed violence, the *Lion* being hit twice without serious damage. One of these hits, however, caused a temporary interruption in the navigation of the flagship . . . I was working on the chart in the Admiral's plotting room . . . when I felt the deck under my feet give a sudden heave. At the same moment the chart table over which I was leaning, split in the centre and the windows fell in exposing the chart and myself to the full blast of a head wind. I placed both hands on the chart, but the wind was too quick for me and before I could realise what had happened, the chart was torn in two and the business half of it flew through the window. I last saw it fluttering over the sea like a frightened seagull . . . I climbed on to the compass platform and reported the incident to the Navigating Officer (Arthur Strutt) who was keeping the reckoning in his notebook. He handed me the book and told me to get another chart and plot it all over again. D(avid) B(eatty) who was standing beside him having heard the order, turned to me and said 'mind you get a check from the *Princess Royal'* (our next astern). This was typical of Beatty's coolness and clarity of mind in the height of action'.

(*The Life and Letters of David Beatty* by W S Chalmers, pages 241-2)

As Beatty drew the German Fleet, all unsuspecting, towards the British battlefleet, Jellicoe was waiting impatiently for information which would give him the relative position of the enemy to his own fleet, but 'it so happened that the *Iron Duke* by her own reckoning was four miles north-west of her true geographical position and the *Lion,* by hers, put herself seven miles east of her actual position. The accumulated error of the two flagships was therefore about 11 miles in an ESE direction' (ibid). Fortunately as already mentioned, Jellicoe's masterly handling of the situation overcame this handicap and the Grand Fleet deployed across the line of advance of the German Fleet.

Despite the closing down of the Navigation School, during the war some 18 officers were allowed to qualify provisionally at sea, one in 1916, three in 1917 and 12 in 1918. In 1916 at the Hydrographer's suggestion, the Navigation department at the Admiralty once again became a branch of the Hydrographic department, but the Director was given increased responsibilities. Soon after the end of the war, in February 1919 a list of the subjects for which he was responsible to the Board was drawn up and in March of that year seamanship was added. As will be seen this arrangement continued unaltered for 26 years. Whilst it can be said that it worked reasonably well, there was always a feeling in the branch of a certain loss of prestige compared with gunnery and torpedo branches, both of which were represented by a divison of the Naval Staff.

A signed photograph of Sir Henry Oliver when he was a Vice-Admiral in 1920.

Chapter III

THE INTER-WAR YEARS

'The Arte of Navigation demonstrateth how by the shortest good way, by the aptest direction and in the shortest time, a sufficient ship be conducted.'   John Dee 1570

The Navigation School reopened on 3 January 1919 under the command of Captain A C S Hughes-D'Aeth who, despite his lugubrious surname, lived to the good age of 81. He had commanded the cruiser *Minotaur,* flagship of Rear Admiral H L Heath in the Second Cruiser Squadron at the battle of Jutland and been awarded a CB for his services on that occasion. When Heath transferred his flag to the battleship *Dreadnought* after promotion to Vice Admiral, D'Aeth went with him as his Flag Captain and stayed with him until the end of the war.

Resumption of Senior Officers courses

Soon after the School reopened the Senior Officers course at the Navigation School was resumed as part of an enlarged technical course and it provided some of its most interesting work. In addition to the subjects previously mentioned, lectures were given by Staff Officers on the wider aspects of navigation and fleetwork, radio direction finding, meteorology, aerial navigation and action plotting, as well as demonstrations of new navigational instruments.

There were no startling changes or inventions during World War I to affect the Navigation branch comparable with those which took place 25 years later during World War II. The Qualifiers' curriculum differed little from that laid down in Admiralty Circular Letter of 15 June 1903 though adjusted and updated to cover the advent of improved aids to navigation such as the gyro compass and changes in the shape and composition of the Fleet. The staff of the School, comprising a Commander (N) as Executive Officer and up to a total of 10 Lieutenant Commanders (N) or Lieutenants (N) remained fairly steady throughout the inter-war years.

The first students to return to the School were the 18 officers who, as already mentioned, had qualified provisionally at sea during the War. They were given a short refresher and/or First Class Ship course. Amongst them was A R M Bridge who was Captain of the School from May 1937 to June 1939 and subsequently reached flag rank.

Post war Qualifying classes

The first post war class of Qualifiers numbering 12 completed their course in October 1919. They were followed by a class of five in April of the following year and included H J Egerton who retired as a Vice Admiral in 1948. Despite the arrangements which Oliver had made when the School originally opened to prevent any interference by the Director of Naval Education, the Admiralty decided that, after four years of war, once the backlog of wartime aspirants for (N) had been dealt with, future Qualifiers should spend two months at the RN College Greenwich in order to brush up their knowledge of spherical trigonometry, astronomical navigation and meteorology. (This largely theoretical instruction was, later and in a shortened form, incorporated in the Navigation School syllabus).

At the RN College Greenwich

At that time the RNC Greenwich was the nirvana of the old pre-war naval instructors who had entered the service direct from the universities. Some of them had been to the RN Colleges at Osborne and Dartmouth and served in the training cruisers or been appointed to ships carrying Midshipmen. These last were mulcted of 3d a day out of their princely salary of 1s 9d a day to contribute toward their instructors' pay! There were some very fine men amongst these instructors but, except for those who combined their duty with that of Chaplain, it is not surprising that they were usually the leading candidates for the first boat ashore in harbour and for an arm chair in the wardroom at sea. Later on when they were made responsible for all naval education, action plotting, and meteorology, their leisure time was considerably restricted.

The senior member of the directing staff at Greenwich when the author joined that establishment as a member of the 1920 Qualifying class, was Instructor Captain S F Card who was known as the Dean, a title which the Admiralty is said to have approved on condition that it did not carry with it an increase in emoluments. He had a sallow complexion with a black beard tinged with grey and even in plain clothes always wore a high stiff collar. In the manner of professors he had written a book on *Navigation and Nautical Astronomy* which all of us were encouraged to buy at a local bookseller at the cost of 12s 6d (62½p). Strange to relate there were never any secondhand copies available. In charge of the Qualifying classes was Instructor Commander Maurice Ainslie who had joined the training ship *Britannia* as an Instructor Lieutenant in 1901 and, in his younger days, had earned fame as a rugger player. He was an enormous man with a large black beard and was known throughout the service as 'The Wombat'. When not in uniform, he usually wore an old norfolk jacket and trousers adorned by a large patch in the seat of his pants. He was certainly a great character and he delighted in covering the blackboard with vast mathematical proofs which the class were seldom able to follow. He would claim that his method was more 'elegant' than that of Captain Card which he regarded as somewhat 'rigorous'. At some point he would introduce the magic formula — sine one minute — at the same time rubbing out most of what he had previously written. This was regarded by the class as distinctly underhand and usually produced boos and protests, but the Wombat reminded us that university

The Navigation School crest and motto.

professors are not accustomed to being interrupted during the course of their lectures. We of the 1920 class meekly accepted our fate and the only event of note during our stay at the University was the engagement (and subsequent marriage) of one of our number, C P Christie, to the Astronomer Royal's daughter, Stella Dyson. However the 1921 class which included Eric Brand and a very amusing and remarkable officer, Geoffrey Cross, was more rumbustious and determined to get one up on this wizard of the blackboard. They invited him to a contest in the small bar of the College but, despite the odds, the Wombat saw them all off and as one of them has recorded, 'he wobbled away into the darkness on his bike, with our monthly exam papers fluttering off his carrier like leaves in autumn.' (See *Britannia at Dartmouth* by S W Pack page 125)

Although we made such fun of the Wombat, it was never meant unkindly and those whose lot it was to be instructed by him will support the verdict 'one felt rather humble and proud to have known such a famous eccentric' (ibid, **p** 166).

In June 1920, on the successful completion of our stint at Greenwich, our class, numbering 14 reported to the Navigation School. Included in the total were two officers from the Royal Canadian Navy, one of whom L W Murray, as a Rear Admiral was Commander in Chief of the Canadian Eastern Sea Frontier during World War II and on retirement studied law and became a barrister. We also had two Greek officers who showed their appreciation on Qualifying by presenting the School with an ivory statuette of the Venus de Milo, complete with plinth.

Other members of our class were Gerald Curteis who, after promotion to Captain, retired to become Deputy Master of Trinity House, a post which he held for 13 years; O L Gordon who commanded the cruiser *Exeter* during her last gallant fight against a superior Japanese force off Sumatra and subsequently spent three and a half years as a prisoner of war in Japan; H A Rowley who was Captain of the School from January to June 1939 and subsequently lost his life when commanding the cruiser *Gloucester* when she was sunk off Crete by German aircraft.

The Navigation School in the 1920s

On 1 August 1919, Captain J E T Harper relieved Captain J A Webster MVO as Director of Navigation after completing his exhaustive report on the battle of Jutland. A very experienced Navigating Officer, he knew that he would have great difficulty in reconciling the reckoning of the various ships involved so he arranged for the wreck of the battle cruiser, *Invincible,* to be located in order to provide a geographical position from which to work. The vicissitudes of the Harper Report before it was eventually published are well known. After retiring in the rank of Vice Admiral he wrote two books. *The Truth About Jutland* (1927) and *The Riddle of Jutland* (1934).

On 30 November 1920, Captain Hughes-D'Aeth was relieved in command of the School by Captain Oliver Leggett CB who, as already mentioned, had been Master of the Fleet to Admiral Jellicoe and who had just relinquished command of the battle cruiser *New Zealand* in which the Admiral had made a tour of the Dominions in order to establish a pattern of post war Imperial Defence. For a picture of the Navigation School at the time when Leggett assumed command, we are indebted to Captain Eric Brand, a member of the 1921 Qualifying Course. The Commander of the School at the time was Commander (later Admiral of the Fleet Sir) John H D Cunningham, noted for the caustic remarks which flowed freely from his tongue. Brand writes:

'In those days practically all the staff were married — the School being about the only shore job available for (N) officers — and the whole place could be described — and invariably was — as mouldy. Except for the lovely mess room itself and its beautifully sprung dance floor, there was nothing to recommend it. The ante room for Qualifiers and Sub Lieutenants was an uninviting place and there was a door to the Captain's office in the middle of it. The cabins were bare and poorly furnished, whilst those in the north wing, due to lack of heat, were known as Siberia. For us Qualifiers, we at least had a job to get on with, but it was little wonder that the Subs, who were accommodated there, when undergoing their pilotage and torpedo courses, loathed the place. It was in fact a thoroughly depressing establishment.
'At that time there were three tenders attached to the School, the three recently completed and adapted war-time twin screw minesweepers, *Alresford, Caterham* and *Carstairs* with a maximum draught of eight feet . . . There was one Lieutenant in our class who really had little aptitude for specialisation, in fact it was a mystery to the rest of us how he had obtained a watchkeeping certificate. When we sailed on our cruise, it fell to him to be the first to do duty as (N) of the ship, which meant that he would have to take her out of Portsmouth Harbour. He was naturally worried about this, so during the preceding weekend he hired a rowing boat and got his wife to row him out along the various leading marks in the channel. Unfortunately he did not rehearse the Swashway, so when Cunningham told him to go over it, he was at a loss what to do and, revolving round the compass in an agonised fashion, said to me (I was doing duty as Officer of the Watch) "I can't see the bloody numbers!" to which

I was able to whisper helpfully — "Try putting the arrow down". Needless to say he failed to qualify.'

In 1922 a special class of 17 RNR officers were appointed to the School to undergo a shortened (N) course and the following year four more, but there is no record of any further courses at that time.

Not all those who attended the Qualifying course at the old School during the inter-war years found the experience congenial. One such records 'having chosen to specialise, I imagined a civilised approach from the Course Instructor. Utterly devoid of humour, this was not to be. There were some strong characters amongst our dozen. Two were sacked halfway through and the rest of us protested to the Captain to say that we had volunteered for this Long Course and were prepared to work hard, but not to be treated like children. We made our point and survived to qualify but not before two of us had been called to account. One hot July night we were given the task of establishing the latitude of Portsdown Hill by circum-meridian star sights in an artificial horizon. When we reached the site of our observations, we found we were not alone on that wide stretch of grass, a well known venue for courting couples. In fact what was going on around us was considerably more interesting than our assignment. Moreover the activities of our neighbours seriously interfered with the execution of our appointed task. So, confident that the the latitude of that particular portion of the South Downs had already been established by other means, we adjourned to the neartest pub and sent in a blank return, which was not at all well received.' (Letter to the author from Vice Admiral Sir John Hayes).

Experience of young Navigating Officers

Those who successfully passed the Qualifying examination went to the Admiralty Compass Observatory at Ditton Park near Slough for a two week gyro compass course prior to being appointed to one of the smaller ships on outlying stations, the flotilla leaders of destroyers attached to the main fleets, preceded in some cases, by a period as Assistant (N) in a battleship or battle cruiser flagship. The whole idea was to gain practical experience in the art of navigation of which they had just learned the theory and in ships in which a mistake might not prove too costly! Captain A J Baker-Creswell DSO who qualified in 1927 found himself appointed to the sloop *Veronica,* on the New Zealand station, writes:

'One could imagine no finer training for a young Navigating Officer than two and half years in the South Pacific with every hazard one could think of. One night on passage between the Fiji Islands and Tonga, I was lying on my bunk in the charthouse during the middle watch, when I was suddenly woken by a white faced Gunner, whose watch it was, saying "We're aground! We're aground!" I believed that we were in at least 1500 fathoms at the time, but I rushed out on deck and saw to my horror, in the gleam of a searchlight, that we were indeed surrounded by rocks, some of which were as high as the bridge. I sent for a rope and was lowered over the side on to the nearest rock which slowly began to sink under my weight. I then realised that we had happened on a large field of pumice stone thrown up by some volcanic erruption. We nudged our way through the floating mass and resumed our passage but, soon after, the Chief reported to the bridge that the condensers were red hot and we would have to stop to clear the inlets which were completely blocked with pumice. The next day on looking at the chart I noticed that the course I had laid off passed over a dotted circle marked "Site of Falcon Island – last seen 1898". On reaching the position, I ran a line of soundings and the least depth I obtained was 20 fathoms. A month later we were returning to Fiji by the same route when, to my astonishment, on reaching the same position, there was Falcon Island about three miles long and a mile and half wide, rising to a height of 400 feet. It was a bit of luck that we happened on it in daylight.'

On another occasion the *Veronica* was instructed to fix the position of Ninafou Island which was to be used by an international expedition from which to observe a total eclipse of the sun. 'It was difficult to fit this visit into our programme,' he writes, 'only a few hours could be spared in the middle of one day. I therefore decided to fix it by equal altitudes and a meridian altitude of the sun. Having no encircling reef, it was a difficult place on which to land and being only 50 miles south of the Equator, the heat was considerable. In order to observe the sun in an artificial horizon, I had to remove my helmet and after the first observation, I passed out with heat stroke. My Chief Quartermaster managed to revive me just in time for the noon observation then I passed out again. Frantic efforts had to be made to revive me for the vital second half of the equal altitude which I managed to take and my calculations showed that the island was eight miles from its charted position.'

Another episode which he recalls was locating a coral head, 'rising like Cleopatra's needle to within six feet of the surface' using a home made sweep comprising two large cannon balls connected by a length of sounding wire. The pinnacle lay right in the route used by large freighters picking up sugar at Fiji.

Commander J N N Synnot who qualified in 1932 was appointed to the sloop *Dundee* on the West Indies Station for his first job. He recalls that, 'a very early task was to convey the Governor of the Leeward Islands from St Johns Antigua to Barbuda, 50 miles to the north, for his annual visit. On leaving St Johns I picked up what I thought was the recommended stern transit of "Two conspic. white houses" which led clear of the numerous and dangerous coral reefs and all went well for a time with the Governor and the Captain chatting together on the sunlit bridge about pilotage through coral reefs. Suddenly I saw a patch of discoloured water ahead. To impress the Governor and to save time we were doing our maximum speed of about 17 knots and, as the patch came closer, I noticed the colour change from dark blue to an ominous brown, indicating a depth of not more than six feet. Our pride had to go by the board. I ordered "hard a starboard" followed by "hard a port" and we skirted round some 10 feet from the coral outcrop. Later I discovered I had used the wrong pair of "conspic white houses!" Thus does one learn in the hard school of experience.'

Lieutenant (later Vice Admiral Sir) John Hayes recalls a hair-raising experience on the first occasion on which he acted as a Qualified (N). 'Those who know Bahrein Lagoon and the 90° turn into a tiny coral cut to gain the outer channel, the ultramarine race falling off the ramparts to form a river current, can picture the scene with only a crude beacon to tell the moment of helm over, which was starboard 25. When the rudder action first listed the ship in its own direction, before opposing momentum took over, there was a nasty crunch and a tell tale thickening in the wake. No doubt but that the bilge keel had touched and no moment to stop for divers to examine. So in the first five cables of my navigating career, I fulfilled what all who have never felt that feeling in the stomach say you should do in order to become a fully fledged navigator "take ground" but preferably without damage!' He reminds us that 'in those days the Navigator of a sloop was also the Paymaster which meant that, in my case, in addition to a basic pay of 13s 6d a day and 2s 6d (N) allowance, I was given another 2s 6d for the privilege of being court martialled should my accounts be in error. It was said at the time that more Navigators suffered in this respect than for the grounding of their ships and certainly having been given just a week's course after the long course, in accounting and vitualling, it cost one more anxiety. It was a cheap bargain for Their Lordships; and although when errors in the cash account or rum return became apparent, the letter from the Admiralty was probably more polite than had you been wearing white between your stripes — The Accountant Officer of *Nonsuch* is requested to explain how he arrived at the following conclusions — nevertheless the mailed fist was there. Morning star sights were mathematics one understood; the victualling account in favour of Mr Sorabji Prestonji of Bombay was something only Supply Petty Officer Venables understood and in whose hands of loyalty or otherwise one sank or swam. You quickly learned the technique of pouring out the baskets of so-called chickens on to the quarterdeck to reveal a residue of plucked sparrows; but the ledger and the victualling account shared my dawn chart table with Polaris, Capella, and Betelguese. The latter were reliable and familiar; the former were neither.'

The Shadwell Testimonial Prize

This prize was founded in 1880 in memory of the late Admiral Sir Charles F A Shadwell KCB FRS and is bestowed annually on an officer of a rank not higher than Lieutenant Commander who has never been classed as an Assistant Surveyor, for the most creditable plan of an anchorage or other marine survey, accompanied with sailing directions recently executed by the officer himself.

In the year 1937 the prize was shared by Lieutenant (later Vice Admiral Sir) Ian Hogg and Lieutenant (later Captain) Maurice Butler-Bowdon both of whom have searched their memories to produce accounts of how they achieved this distinction.

'I qualified in the summer of 1936,' writes Admiral Hogg, 'and not being one of the brightest or most industrious of students, I was appointed to a sloop in the Persian Gulf — regarded in those days as something of an oubliette for the more wayward types — and reputedly the hottest place in the world, while the humidity often approaches 100%.

'The task of the sloops was to combat slaving and gun running — a popular sport much practised between the Trucial coast of Arabia and Persia. There was a thriving oil industry at Bahrein, Kuwait, and Abadan but elsewhere in the Gulf its enormous resources were as yet untapped. Indeed whenever the sloops went to Bombay to refit, they towed an oil barge back to stock up the Naval Base at Jufair.

'Life for me was agreeably uneventful until one day early in 1937 a signal was received from the Admiralty stating that Lieutenant Hogg was required to make a survey of a lagoon at Um al Qaiwain — a small insignificant village on the south east coast of the Gulf. The survey was required urgently because Imperial Airways were looking for bases for their planned flying boat service to India and the Far

East. Although a period of three weeks during our long (N) course had been devoted to surveying and included practical work in the River Dart, most of the class of which I was one, regarded the subject as one best left to the professionals, so the prospect of embarking on what could be a vitally important one was daunting to say the least of it.

'Fortuitously, my ship *Bideford,* was on passage to Bombay when the signal was received and on arrival there, I was able to throw myself on the mercy of the Royal Indian Navy which supplied me with theodolites, steel tapes and all the other paraphernalia and — most important of all — a copy of the *Admiralty Manual of Surveying* which became my only reading on our return journey to the Persian Gulf.

'We made straight for Um al Qaiwain. Today the Trucial coast is well surveyed, but in 1937 the Sailing Directions contained an ominous warning to the effect that care must be taken in approaching the coast as, owing to tribal disputes, the villagers frequently moved their dwellings further along the coast. However Um al Qaiwain was in its right place and we anchored off the Sheik's palace. The Captain and I at once went ashore to call on the Sheik and seek his agreement to a survey of his lagoon. The proposal was quite incomprehensible to him and he viewed our stay with the deepest suspicion, but was somewhat mollified when I pointed out that the only visible sign of our work would be some poles with red and white flags on them (happily the national colours of his Sheikdom). Less happily for us, as discovered later during the triangulation, the flags proved an irresistible attraction to the villagers who made off with them at frequent intervals.

'The lagoon was quite extensive, covering several square miles behind the town with access from the sea by a narrow channel, navigable only by ship's boats. Here and there sandy islets could be seen and beyond, the desert with patches of coarse scrub. I reckoned the survey would take perhaps three weeks and require the services of eight ratings and the Sub Lieutenant (conscripted). It was obviously impracticable to live onboard, so I hired an Arab dhow — not the most salubrious of accommodation, but spacious enough for us all to bed down on deck under an awning borrowed from the ship. The ship's skiff was also appropriated for our stay in the lagoon and was in constant use for getting ashore and for running lines of soundings.

'In the early stages, getting ashore was nearly to prove our undoing. Daily temperatures were well into three figures in the sun and there was no shade. It was endurable but we soon found that wading ashore from the skiff, drying off and then getting wet again, produced the most appalling blisters on one's legs and thighs. An SOS was sent to the ship and soon afterwards we embarked the Doc who, I think, found our circumstances somewhat distasteful, but after a day or two, he got us fit for further effort and returned to the ship — thankfully! In the evening the ship's company enjoyed the enterprise of the duly appointed cook of the mess while I wrestled with balancing the triangulation under the flickering light of a hurricane lamp and later recorded the lines of soundings taken during the day.

'Bit, by bit, the survey developed. Coastlining, fixing a tide pole, tidal observations and even a geographical fix of Um al Qaiwain by star sights and an artificial horizon (of which the mercury was regularly covered with sand) were completed.

'At last it was finished. The dhow was returned to its rightful owner and such flags as had not been purloined were recovered and the survey party re-embarked. The fair chart, however, remained to be drawn and I soon found that the heat and the humidity were such that in poring over the chart more sweat than indian ink was splashed over it. There was only one time of the day when it was cool enough to do reasonable work, between 2 am and 5 am daily, and that was when the fair chart was drawn.

'It had proved a great challenge and a new interest for all of us who lived in the dhow for three weeks. Sad to relate, our labours had revealed numerous shallows and drying banks, and it was quite apparent that no flying boat would ever land there. Perhaps someone has found a use for our labours.'

It was in a different part of the world that Butler-Bowdon was called upon to make the survey which shared the honours with Admiral Hogg.

He was serving as (N) officer of the sloop *Wellington* (Now a prominent feature on the Thames embankment and headquarters of the Honourable Company of Master Mariners) during her first commission on the New Zealand station and much time was spent visiting the numerous islands in the Pacific under British jurisdiction. Many of them were inaccurately charted and 'I was able to do quite a bit of surveying and also correct the position (usually longitudinal) of many reefs and islands,' he writes, and with becoming modesty, states that, 'it may have been the quantity rather than the quality of my work which earned me a half share in the 1937 Shadwell award.' In fact it was a running survey of Gardner Island, one of the Phoenix group (eight small islands lying between 2½° and 4½°S and 171° and 174½°W) which won him the award. 'Landing looked a bit hazardous especially with valuable instruments,' he records, 'and did not seem warranted as there was a convenient wreck on the SW shore which still had a useful mast.' With the help of a rangefinder and bearings from the magnetic compass he produced a plan which was subsequently published as a correction in *Notices to Mariners*. He received a barograph for his share of the prize which still faithfully records the vagaries of British weather.

First Class Ship courses

After a period varying between three and four years, Qualified (N) Officers returned to the Navigation School for what was then called a First Class Ship course, but which was later more appropriately named an advanced course. It lasted seven weeks and included a comprehensive study of strategical and tactical plotting, enemy reporting, deployment, search and interception, weather forecasting and an introduction to air navigation. It was generally preceded or followed by a refresher course at the Admiralty Compass Observatory. From then on (N) officers could expect a continuous succession of sea appointments graduating up through cruisers to battleships and carriers. Captain F B Lloyd OBE who succeeded Captain J L Storey CBE DSO as Master of the Fleet recalls that after qualifying in 1925 he was at sea, with two short exceptions, from then until February 1943, having been promoted to Captain the previous December.

The instructional staff

A few officers, after completing their First Class Ship course were re-appointed to the School for instructional duties. They usually began by instructing the comparatively easy Sub Lieutenants Pilotage courses before being assigned to the more difficult Qualifiers and First Class Ship courses. Captain Brand recalls, 'In January and February I took through a regular Sub's course and then I was told off with K M L Robinson as my mate to take the 1926 Qualifiers course starting in April, so we really had to get down to it and learn our stuff. We decided that we would begin with Section VIII (Pilotage) which I would take and which we felt certain we could manage, but instead of the usual practice whereby the Instructor not performing sat in front of the class, we agreed that he would sit at the back from where he could make inconspicuous signals to assist the Lecturer should he find himself in trouble.

'The course, numbering eight, duly assembled and I spent the first hour outlining the programme including the cruise etc and in the course of my remarks I emphasized that I and my colleague did not profess to know everything and, that if this caused them some surprise, they should bear in mind that a few years hence some of them might well find themselves in a similar position. About 10 am I started on Section VIII with some 30 minutes to go before the stand-easy bell. At 1020 Tom Brownrigg (Master of the Fleet in the Mediterranean in World War II) asked a question about some page in Lecky's *Offshore Distance Tables*. I turned to it and to my horror realised that I had never seen it before and so had no idea what it was about. I shot an agonised glance to Robinson only to receive a wave of the hand which clearly indicated, "count me out" so I played for time and was saved by the aforesaid bell! The next day Robinson was lecturing on astronomics and an argument broke out whether a sign should be plus or minus. I tried to work it out and found myself on the side of the class, however Robinson clinched the argument by saying, "well, anyhow that's what the Manual says and you must accept it." When we put our heads together after the class was over, we found an uncorrected Errata in the front of the book!' A similar fate overtook the author when lecturing on tides to a Subs course which included HRH the late Duke of Kent. When I upbraided the royal pupil for making a mistake in a simple tidal problem I had set the class, he protested that he had followed the example shown in the back of the Tide Tables. When I checked this I found there was a mistake in the example which may well have been there unnoticed for years!

Qualifier's surveys

The Qualifying Course included a fortnight's cruise during which a survey was carried out of some small area, selected after consultation with the Hydrographer. As a Qualifier we surveyed the entrance to the Hamble River and later as Commander I took the 1932 class to do a stretch of the Orwell River. These surveys were hard work and nearly always a race against time. Brand who surveyed Loch Crinan with the 1926 class recalls, 'I can see one group now, late on a Saturday evening, standing up to their waists in cold water, for the tide had risen, remaking a station which hadn't worked properly'. Subsequently, whilst coaling in the Clyde, he took the class to visit the well known makers of magnetic compasses, Messrs Kelvin, Bottomley and Baird, in Glasgow. 'There in a room full of beautiful new binnacles, my young officers began twiddling the shining brass covers round and round, much to the annoyance of the Manager. When we all assured him that it was a unique opportunity to do this because, after a few months at sea, they would never do so, he was astonished. He said they had been making these binnacle covers with their sliding doors, to enable bearings to be taken in bad weather, for years and no one had ever told them that they were never used at sea.'

Enter the Boatswain

The title of Boatswain dates from Saxon times and is therefore one of the oldest among seafarers. In the reign of Edward the Confessor (1042-1066) he is mentioned as being in charge of the rowers, and in the days of sail he was not only responsible for the masts, yards and cordage, generally referred to as the standing and running rigging as well as the hawsers, but he was also responsible for discipline. He was, in fact, the Master's right hand man. Later he became one of that worthy band of Warrant Officers who formed the backbone of the old Navy. It was, therefore, most appropriate when, in 1925, Their Lordships decided that the Navigation School should take on the training of prospective Boatswains, especially as has been mentioned, the Director of Navigation was the Adviser to the Board on matters of seamanship.

The first class of nine selected Petty Officers started their course in *Dryad* in August 1925 with Lieutenant Eric Brand as their instructor, and comprised 10 weeks of advanced seamanship followed by an eight week Pilotage course. 'I really knew nothing which could be called "advanced seamanship" ' Brand writes, 'However I was given a free hand to get on with it and I soon found out that Portsmouth held a number of interesting places from which I could get help and to which I could take the class. The most useful of these was the Royal Marines Barracks at Eastney where something was known of Repository, a term devised by the Garrison Gunners for the art of handling heavy weights on shore such as guns and their mountings. A few far-seeing Royal Marine Officers, with very little support, were trying to evolve the idea of a Mobile Naval Base and beach work generally, such as building piers with tubular scaffolding and making hardways.' He goes on to relate how 'the members of the class were taken aback by my immediate confession (as they told me afterwards) that I knew nothing of Advanced Seamanship, but that we were going to work it out together' and this they successfully did.

To assist the would-be Boatswains in their Pilotage course, Brand devised what he calls The Astronomical Spotting Table. 'The only practicable astronomics in the Bosuns Pilotage course was the use of the sextant to take a meridian altitude and Mr Bush, the Schoolmaster, and I were trying to explain how the sextant arm should be moved to ensure that the sun touched the horizon tangentially. I sent Mr Bush to fetch a tobacco tin, a piece of string and the large brass gong which stood in the Hall. Having tied the gong on to the string, he was to take it up to one of the cabins on the top floor of the centre block, open the window and slowly haul the gong up and down as ordered by me. To give more light to the basement rooms surrounding the courtyard, the walls were whitewashed for about four feet up and the line between the top of the whitewash and the brick formed a very good simulated horizon. I lined up the Bosuns with their sextants on the far side of the courtyard facing the wall against which Bush was controlling the movements of the artificial sun, and took up position in the middle of them. Then in my best gunnery voice I shouted "start the run", the object of the practice being to observe the height of the "sun" at maximum elevation ... At the end of each run I compared my meridian altitude with those of the class and it was surprising to see how their results improved.' Surprising too was the effect of this innovation on the rest of the staff. 'One by one the windows round the courtyard went up and astonished staff officers looked out to see what this noisy gunnery racket was all about,' and even the Captain was moved to ask for an explanation of this unusual performance.

The course was most successful and the future Boatswain's all passed their exams and in due course were promoted to Warrant rank. The following spring a meeting was held at the Admiralty to consider a suggestion emanating from Whale Island that Boatswains should be abolished as they were not qualified to act as Officers of Quarters and therefore mere passengers in a ship of war. Brand was deputed to represent the Navigation School and supported by the Director of Naval Education, A P McMullen, shot down the opposition, the latter replying to a salvo from the gunnery experts that teaching seamanship on a blackboard was nonsense, with the remark, 'of course I have been saying for a long while that modern seamanship is nothing more than applied mechanics.'

Sometime later when Brand was Navigating Officer of the battleship *Barham*, flagship of Rear Admiral Ernle Erle Drax, the Admiral ordered the ship's Boatswain, Mr Bonney, to rig sheers and lift a whaler. This he did successfully, but the Admiral queried the strength of the topping lift which he thought looked too weak. A dismayed Mr Bonney sought out Brand and showed him his calculations, which the latter checked and found to be correct, so he undertook to tell the Admiral. 'Whoever heard of Bosuns calculating?' Drax remarked. Brand then explained that Mr Bonney was one of the New Pattern Boatswains, as they came to be called, whereupon the Admiral sent for Mr Bonney and tendered him an apology.

The second class of Boatswains was taken by Lieutenant Commander (later Captain) Godfrey French in 1926 and comprised 12 Petty Officers of whom one was a PT instructor. For Lieutenant-Commander (later Commander) C R Burgess OBE the third class which he was detailed to take ended in romance for he married the sister-in-law of the Major in charge of the Eastney part of the course. The courses continued at intervals until the outbreak of world war 2.

Meteorology

Meteorology has always been very much part of the stock in trade of the Navigating Officer, but it took a long time for senior officers to appreciate its operational importance. As however the art of forecasting improved under the stimulus provided by the development of aircraft, it came to be recognised as a factor to be considered in planning operations, of which the Normandy invasion will surely be regarded as the supreme example. It should be mentioned that as the science developed the instructor officers were made responsible for the meteorological work in the ships in which they were borne and that it was Instructor Commander (later Rear Admiral Sir) John Fleming (KBE DSC) who was the Met Officer on Admiral Ramsay's staff for Operation Overlord.

The Naval division of the Meteorological Office of the Air Ministry was formed in 1921, the first Superintendent being Captain L C Garbett CBE. He was subsequently joined by Lieutenant Commander (later Captain) T R Beatty a member of the author's Qualifying course and by Lieutenant Commander C R Burgess who wrote a textbook *Meteorology for Seamen*. In 1937 a Naval Meteorological branch of the Admiralty was formed with the staff of the former division in the Air Ministry and in 1939 this became the Naval Meteorological Service.

The Sub Lieutenant's courses

Compared with the young gentlemen of the old Naval Academy, about whom something has been related in Chapter II, the Sub Lieutenants undergoing courses at the Navigation School in the inter war years were paragons of virtue! Certainly, taking it full and bye, they gave very little trouble. The more general availability of the motor car, however, presented problems and on one occasion when I was executive officer of the establishment we received a rude signal from our close neighbour, the Commander in Chief, ordering the immediate removal of the wreck parked outside the entrance. Wreck, it certainly was being a very ancient car, apparently held together by wire and bits of string! I sent for the owner and enquired how he came by such a monstrosity. 'Sir,' he replied in a tone betraying the injured innocence of youth, 'I swopped it for an old Burberry.' However testimony to the value of the Sub Lieutenant's pilotage course comes from Vice Admiral Sir John Hayes when he was appointed Sub Lieutenant of the cruiser *Danae* on the North America and West Indies station. 'A turning point in my naval life,' he writes, 'occurred one night in 1935 when anchored off Grand Cayman Island, then nothing but a beach, some turtles, and a casuarina tree but now a world casino resort. The usual party of wardroom officers had to go ashore in a whaler across the beach to a reception given by the Commissioner. I was duty aboard and the Navigating Officer had gone ashore. It blew up from force 3 to 8 in half an hour from a direction which placed the *Danae* on a lee shore: a cable or two if she dragged before going aground. So off he went to sea with Sub Lieutenant Hayes as Navigator. We roamed around safely during the night and at daylight, the wind having dropped, went in to anchor and retrieve the stranded wardroom. There was nothing more to this than what one had been taught as a Sub. Get your leading mark to run in on, find a cross bearing, which in this case was lacking and so fall back on soundings — Five cables, sir, four — three — two — one — standby — let go — the Captain dropped the anchor flag, apparently astonished by such ju-ju from the Sub. Happily we were in the right place, so I put in to qualify in (N). In those days one had to sit an examination in signals (which aspiring Signal Officers did not) but which in any case interested me and, that hurdle jumped, I found myself as the junior and youngest member of the 12 Lieutenants selected for the 1936 long course.'

Another instance in which the first principles taught in the Sub Lieutenant's

An open bridge as fitted in a Southampton class cruiser of the 1936 era.

courses proved of unexpected use, is given in the following letter to DND which appeared in the *ND Bulletin* for December 1948:

'We had no idea where we were, but I was worried subconsciously for days because the sun rose and set so late. I made the best estimate I could of sunrise and sunset (as far as surrounding hills allowed) took half the day period thus obtained, added it to sunrise and made it 1300 within a minute or two. As our watches were keeping +6 time, I said that, ignoring the difference between sun time and apparent time, our longitude must be about 105° West. Actually this turned out right within 1°, but was far from our estimated position.'

Improving the image of the branch

All of us who served on the staff of the Navigation School during the inter war years were concerned to improve its image and that of the branch generally. Lieutenant (later Captain) Godfrey French who qualified in 1922, in a paper written five years later, suggested that the Navigating Officer should be regarded by his Captain as his Staff Officer (Operations). 'For instance,' he wrote, 'in every ship there are questions on the conduct of the ship in battle and during the approach, on the anticipation of the Admiral's intentions in battle, on the capabilities and probable manoeuvres of other types of vessels and aircraft, whilst more particularly in a cruiser, there are problems on searching, sweeping, spreading and reconnaissance and on attack and defence of trade, on all or any of which the Captain may require expert advice and assistance.'

Combining (N) and SOO

At one time the experiment was tried of combining the duties of Squadron (N) Officer with that of Staff Officer Operations (SOO) in the flagships of the Admiral, Second in Command, Mediterranean Fleet, the Battle Cruiser and First and Second Cruiser Squadrons. Commander (later Admiral Sir Geoffrey) Miles who was appointed to the dual post in the Battle Cruiser Squadron under Admiral Sir Frederick Dreyer with his flag in *Hood* describes it as 'the hardest two years of my life.' 'I shall always remember,' he writes, 'one spring cruise when we had had filthy weather in the Bay and no sights. When negative PZ was made we had to proceed to Vigo. Visibility was about three and a half miles and as we were about to make our landfall, the voice of Fred Dreyer came up the voice-pipe "Commander Miles, don't forget you are navigating 10 million pounds worth of the country's money" this was the value at that time of the three battle cruisers.'

The author who held the dual appointment in the Second Cruiser Squadron from 1934 to 1936 was fortunate in having a very understanding Admiral because whilst it was easy enough to wear both hats during normal peacetime exercises, during combined fleet manoeuvres or in times of crisis such as arose when Mussolini invaded Abyssinia, serving two masters, the Admiral and the Captain, was apt to become difficult. The impracticability of such dual appointments was later recognised by the Admiralty as is shown in the minutes in a docket raised by the Director of Navigation in 1937 on the subject of the unfavourable prospects for promotion of Commanders (N) vis-a-vis those who reverted to General Service. In a final minute Admiral of the Fleet Lord Chatfield, the First Sea Lord, wrote:

'If the Navigating Officers have, in fact, a less favourable chance of promotion it can only be due to the fact that when they are in the zone they are less strongly recommended than their confreres; in other words they are considered to have less chance of success in the higher rank.

'When one remembers that the Navigating Officer has a unique experience in handling a ship and may be considered to be an expert in one of the most important responsibilities of the Captain of a ship, it is unfortunate that there should be something lacking in him otherwise which fails to quality him so well for promotion.

'I consider that the fault lies in the general life of the Navigating Officer, as of course, has been frequently realised before . . . I therefore feel very much in favour of D of N's recommendation that the Navigating Officer should be given a better chance by such means as not employing him as Navigating Officer after four years seniority . . .

'Finally I concur in DCNS's remarks regarding the employment of the Fleet Navigating Officer as Principal Staff Officer to the Admiral. I do not consider this is practicable.'

The Navigation School crest

Among the ideas put forward to improve the standing of the School was a suggestion that it should have an officially recognised crest and motto. Bob (later Admiral Sir Maurice) Mansergh, prompted by Eric Brand then serving on the Directing Staff, applied his extensive knowledge of heraldry to the task and produced a design based on the origin of the name *Dryad* which is derived from the Greek 'Drus' meaning 'tree', a dryad being a wood nymph believed to inhabit a tree. It depicted a sprig of oak proper, the acorns gold, surmounted by a pair of dividers and overall the name *Dryad* and a naval crown. However the heraldic experts at the Admiralty had other ideas and proposed a globe proper surrounding by a ship's wheel white with the points of the compass between the spokes red, surmounted by the name *Dryad* and a naval crown; beneath the crest a motto 'Nobis Tutissimus Ibis' (With Us Thou Wilt go most safely). While accepting the Admiralty's alternate design, the then Captain of the School demurred over the motto and suggested that the superlative 'tutissimus' was going a bit far as alas HM Ships have been known to be wrecked, and he proposed the less boastful 'tutus' which was finally adopted. So it remained, as far as the author has been able to ascertain, until 1961 when Portsmouth Dockyard was requested by the School to construct a replica of the badge and scroll for mounting on the east wall of the newly constructed guardhouse. When delivered in October of that year, it was noticed that it bore the motto first proposed by the Admiralty. Subsequent correspondence with the Admiralty revealed that when in 1949 the Ships Badges Committee carried out a post war review, the badge of *HMS Dryad* had been officially registered with the word 'tutissimus' and reference to Chatham Dockyard where the sealed patterns of all ship's badges are kept, confirmed this. The matter was finally clinched by a letter from the Chairman of the Ship's Badges Committee dated 14 October 1974.

The Annual Dinner

Borrowing the idea from *HMS Vernon*, it was decided to start an annual dinner for all Navigating officers, past and present. A Committee was formed to comb the old Navy Lists and draw up a list of all (N) officers living which included a few of the old Staff Commanders. These were circularised and asked if they would support the idea. The majority of the replies were favourable and in April 1926 the first dinner took place with, appropriately, Admiral of the Fleet Sir Henry Oliver as the guest of honour. It proved a great success and, with the exception of the war years, has become an annual event.

In 1936, shortly after Admiral Sir William Fisher had hoisted his flag as Commander in Chief Portsmouth, the Sub Lieutenants at the School ran riot one night and called the Portsmouth Fire Brigade to a non-existent fire in the School. The racket which ensured when the fire engines drew up brought 'Tall Aggrippa' as Fisher was nicknamed, from a dinner party over which he was presiding to see what all the noise was about. The Captain of the School at the time, W H Gell DSO, was sent for the following afternoon and spent a *mauvais quart d'heure* with the great man who insisted that all those responsible be severely dealt with. Relations between the two establishments remained somewhat strained and it was with a view to healing the breach that Gell invited the Commander in Chief to be guest of honour at the next Navigating Officer's dinner.

The day arrived and also present was the School's founder, Admiral of the Fleet Sir Henry Oliver, to whom the unfortunate incident was related. When 'Dummy' rose to speak, which he always did in sepulchral tones with a deadpan expression and a dry sense of humour which never failed to send his audience into fits of laughter, he reminisced in his usual manner and ended with a story about the time when he was Captain of the School. It appears that one night some of the Sub Lieutenants returned to the School in an old growler. When the cabby demanded an excessive fare, the spirited young officers carried out Field Gun drill on the cab and smartly exchanged the larger back wheels for the two smaller front ones and vice versa. 'Youth will out' said Dummy as he sat down amid loud applause. The Commaner in Chief who, though a strict disciplinarian, was at heart a kindly man, took the hint and made a speech which completely buried the hatchet and in which he affirmed that such demonstrations of youthful horseplay betokened the very spirit which made the Royal Navy invincible in war. Perhaps it was as well that there were no Subs present to hear his remarks.

The building of the squash court

The east wing contained a large billiard room with three tables and during the author's time as executive officer of the School (1931-33) a full sized squash court was built in the northern half for the loss of only one billiard table, an exchange that was voted well worthwhile.

Nelson and Rodney

Another noteworthy event occurred in 1926 with the commissioning of *Nelson* who, with her sister ship *Rodney,* became known as the unhandiest pair of battleships ever built for the RN. Their design was a compromise to meet the limitations agreed under the Washington Naval Treaty of 1922 and as a result the whole of the main armament of nine 16 inch guns was mounted amidships and forward of the bridge structure, which, in consequence was much further aft than usual. However the fact that the jackstaff was 400 feet away and cut the horizon as seen from the bridge enabled the slightest yaw to be instantly detected and corrected. The effect of this distribution of weight and the very high bridge structure, nicknamed Queen Anne's Mansions, was to make these ships very difficult to handle at slow speed and especially with the wind and sea on the beam.

Their unhandiness was given prominence when the *Nelson* flying the flag of the Commander in Chief Home Fleet, ran ashore on the Hamilton Bank as she was leaving Portsmouth Harbour at the start of the spring cruise in 1935. Very soon after this mishap, which was attributed in part to the inadequate speed of the tug secured to the bows, Captain Baker-Cresswell, who in 1933 has taken up the appointment of Navigating Officer of *Rodney,* was faced with the same manoeuvre, his ship, though Devonport manned, having to dock at Portsmouth. 'Although I knew Portsmouth intimately,' he writes, 'I practised what I preached at the Navigation School (he was previously on the staff). I planned exactly how the ship was to proceed, noting times and distances in my note book. Visibility was poor as we left the dry dock and when the ship was pointed down harbour and all tugs xcept the one at the bow had cast off, it was down to half a mile. When we were breast of South Railyway Jetty, a blanket of fog enveloped us bringing the isibility down to 50 yards. It was not possible to anchor or to turn round, but I old the Captain that I was prepared to take her out on dead reackoning and he greed. Note book and watch in hand, we proceeded seeing neither the Round Tower to port nor Blockhouse to starboard. There was a crucial 20 degree alteration of course to port to avoid the Hamilton Bank which is marked by a buoy. Having made the alteration according to my note book, I looked over the starboard side and there ten yards away was the buoy, so I knew we were all right. What I did not know was that the tug had gone the wrong side of the buoy and, but for the presence of mind of the Forecastle Officer who saw what had happened and immediately slipped the tow, we might well have ended up like the *Nelson*. Moreover I was not aware of what had happened until we anchored safely at Spithead; at the crucial moment the phone between the Forecastle and the bridge had gone dead!'

Entering and leaving the Hamoaze in a heavy ship could be equally daunting as there is a 110 degree alteration of course off Millbay for which slack water was essential. If for any reason the ship was delayed and the ebb had started it could be very tricky. Another port where skill in ship handling was required was Gibraltar where, just as at Malta, the arrival of the fleet generally attracted a large crowd of onlookers and any poor performance quickly became the talk of the town as well as that of the fleet. Baker-Cresswell's skill in handling and berthing the *Rodney* in difficult circumstances, twice earned him Their Lordship's appreciation.

Quartermaster courses

The Chief Quartermaster in a ship had come to be regarded as the Navigating Officer's Yeoman. One of his duties was to extract the charts requiring correction as indicated in the *Weekly Notices to Mariners* from their folios and put them ready for the Navigating Officer to deal with. He also looked after the sounding machines, the patent log and log line, and the hand lead lines. In harbour the four Quartermasters kept watch at the gangway all round the clock and entered up in the deck log the reading of the barometer and hygrometer at the end of each watch as well as recording the time by striking the ship's bell every half hour. He piped away boats and broadcast any announcements required by the routine. At sea the Quartermasters manned the wheel assisted by helmsmen. For none of these duties were the Quartermasters specially trained. In 1923 consequent on the introduction of the new pay code linking substantive with non-substantive rates the Admiralty approved a number of selected Leading Seamen and Able Seamen being drafted to Portsmouth Barracks to undergo a course of instruction at the Navigation School on completion of which they would be awarded the non-substantive rate of Quartermaster which would entitle them to the appropriate additional pay. In the event only one such course took place and it was not until 1946 that the idea was revived.

Chief Petty Officer Glover DSM

The position of Chief Quartermaster of the School is a very important one. In the early days in addition to his responsibilities in charge of all the instructional charts and navigational instruments and the general tidiness of the classrooms, when there were no Qualifiers in residence he had also to wind and compare the chronometers. This meant attendance on seven days in the week. History does not relate who was the first holder of the position when the school opened in 1906 but it became vacant in 1912 just when Chief Petty Officer George David Glover took his pension after 20 years' service in the Royal Yacht Victoria and Albert. He was the only son of Petty Officer William Glover who after serving 12 years in the RN, in 1898 joined the London Fire Brigade from which he retired as Station Officer at Battersea 25 years later. As a small boy George used to assist with the polishing of the brass on the fire tenders at his father's station and he also helped to secure the barrel of beer to the back axle of the tender, which was the invariable custom in those days before proceeding to a fire. At the age of 10, George was sent to the Royal Hospital School at Greenwich where he was taught to dance the hornpipe, and the skill he achieved in this accomplishment stood him in good stead when later he was drafted to the Royal Yacht. During his time there he performed before most of the crowned heads in Europe and amongst his treasured possessions were a signed portrait of Admiral Prince Henry of Battenberg counter-signed by Queen Victoria, and a cigar case presented to him by Kaiser Wilhelm II, Emperor of Germany. He was invited by Czar Nicholas II of Russia to visit St Petersburg (now Leningrad) to teach his children to dance the hornpipe and for his services the Czar presented him with a silver chronometer watch embossed with the Imperial Coat of Arms. He became Chief Quartermaster of the Yacht and was awarded the Silver Medal of the Royal Victorian Order. Three of his four sons joined the RN and his proudest moment was when his third son, Sydney, became a Gunner. He would have been prouder still had he lived to see him obtain commissioned rank as a Lieutenant and gain a DSC and MBE for his services during World War II and ultimately on his retirement as a Lieutenant Commander give 21 years service as Staff Superintendent of the House of Lords for which he received Their Lordship's thanks and the award of an OBE (Civil). The eldest son, George also reached commissioned rank first as a Boatswain and finally as a Lieutenant.

On leaving the Royal Yacht Glover senior was offered service in the Royal Household but for family reasons wanted to live in Portsmouth, so Buckingham Palace's loss was the Navigation School's gain. Glover was one of those rare characters whose sense of duty and loyalty was the guiding passion of his life. During World War I, he was recalled to active duty and for service in minesweepers was awarded a DSM. He rejoined the School when it reopened after the war and died in harness at the age of 60 on 6 September 1932. It was the author's melancholy duty to accompany Captain O H Dawson, then in command of the School and other staff officers to his funeral in Milton Cemetry. Among the many floral tributes was one representing a steering wheel from the Navigating Officers of the Royal Navy whom he had served so faithfully.

Glover was assisted by two other ex-servicemen Hopkins and Porter known to most of us as Mutt and Jeff. The first named had been a member of Admiral Lord Jellicoe's barge's crew in his flagship, *Iron Duke* in the Grand Fleet. Like many a three badge Able Seaman he had taken up barbering as a side line and his skill at this earned him the position of barber to the Commander in Chief. When Beatty relieved Jellicoe, he took over the same barge's crew and they transferred with him to the *Queen Elizabeth* where Hopkins continued to minister to the new Commander in Chief's more luxuriant growth of hair. One day soon after the end of the war, Hopkins received a letter from no less a person than Lord Jellicoe himself in which he asked him whether he would like to be a member of his barge's crew for the round the world trip he was about to undertake in *HMS New Zealand*. The little man jumped at the chance of rejoining his former Chief and replied accordingly. Thereupon Jellicoe wrote to Beatty asking for him to be released. The next thing Hopkins knew was a summons to lay aft to the Admiral's cabin, where an irate Beatty accused him of having the temerity to correspond with the former First Sea Lord behind his Commander in Chief's back. He was made to feel that such a heinous offence could only be punishable by death or such other punishment as hereinafter mentioned. In vain he protested the innocence of his motives. 'Remanded,' said Beatty severely and Hopkins left the cabin utterly dejected. 'I didn't think much of me prospects,' he would relate, 'I saw me three badges all gorn and threepence a day off me pension. In a proper rage 'e was.' But in the end all was well and with his three badges intact he accompanied Jellicoe on his tour before taking his pension and joining the Navigation School as a Chartroom Assistant. There he continued to ply his trade as a barber to the wardroom mess. Commander Gerald Cobb remembers him as a little figure in a white apron, his bright blue eyes smiling over the top of a pair of wire-framed spectacles and on a board placed across the top of the bath in the bathroom in which he used to operate, the beautifully maintained scissors and clippers with which he had trimmed the hair of two of Britain's most famous Admirals. When asked which of the two he preferred, with consumate tact he would reply, 'Well, sir, Admiral Beatty, 'e did 'ave the better 'ead of 'air, sir' and there pause, leaving no doubt as to where his loyalty lay.

On the eve of World War II

As the clouds of war once again began to appear over the horizon, it is an appropriate moment to review the situation of the Navigation branch at the end of the 20 years span between world wars I and 2. Without question the standing of Navigating Officers throughout the fleet had greatly improved and the image of a specialist officer who took little part in the running of his ship had been largely dispelled. The Navigation School itself was far more comfortable and only lack of space prevented any further addition to the amenities.

There was still a feeling throughout the branch that the Director of Navigation at the Admiralty ought to be head of a separate division of the naval staff as he had been during the three years 1913-16, but it was difficult to make a really good case for a change other than that of prestige. Subordination to the Hydrographer did not present any insuperable problems. Liaison between the School and the Director remained good and the former now had a say in the layout of ship's bridges, in which the experience gained by Navigating officers at sea could be taken into consideration.

During the period between the re-opening of the School in 1919 and the outbreak of war in 1939, a total of 287 officers of the RN, 14 from the Royal Australian Navy, six from the Royal Canadian Navy and four from the Indian Navy completed the Qualifiers' course. Of these 28 reached flag rank viz. three Admirals, 15 Vice Admirals and 10 Rear Admirals (see Appendix III), 69 retired with the rank of Captain and 94 with the rank of Commander. Of the total 29 were to lose their lives during the war.

Chapter IV

WORLD WAR II AND THE ADVENT OF RADAR AND

ACTION INFORMATION

'It may therefore be said with complete confidence that every radar equipped combat aircraft, ship, gun and light was — after every off-setting factor has been allowed for — much more than doubled its effectiveness by its radar aids.'

Sir Robert Watson-Watt

The outbreak of World War II

On the outbreak of world war 2, the Navy List showed 26 Commanders who had specialized in (N) but only about one third of these were employed in (N) appointments. In the two main fleets, Mediterranean and Home, the Master of the Fleet in the former was Commander (later Captain) T M Brownrigg who had qualified in 1926 and the Fleet Navigating Officer in the latter was Commander (later Captain) J L Storey who had qualified in 1922. The difference in titles was due to the fact that the Mediterranean Fleet was regarded as the Senior Command, but soon after the war began, it was denuded of most of its ships, the Home Fleet became the main fleet, and the title of Master was granted to the Fleet Navigating Officer of that fleet. There were 83 Lieutenant Commanders (N) and 38 Lieutenants (N) all of whom were employed on navigating duties.

In September 1939 the Navigation School was commanded by Captain H A Rowley who had relieved Captain (later Admiral Sir) Robin Bridge on 16 June 1939. The Qualifying course, 17 strong, was brought to a premature end in August when the likelihood of war seemed increasingly certain and the officers concerned took up the sea appointments for which they had been nominated in such an eventuality. Rear Admiral F B P Brayne Nicholls recalls that he went as Assistant to the Fleet Navigating Officer in *Nelson,* flagship of the Commander in Chief Home Fleet and that after about a year in that appointment, he was considered qualified for First Class ships. He was the only one of the class to reach flag rank, three were promoted to Captain and two to Commander and three lost their lives during the war.

Relief of Captain H A Rowley By Captain J C Armstrong DSC

In December 1939, Captain Rowley was relieved in command of the School by Captain J C Armstrong DSC, who had qualified in 1905 and had been recalled to active duty from the retired list. On him were to fall the problems involved in the transfer of the School to its new quarters in Southwick House from its bombed-out residence in the Dockyard.

Navigation during the war

During the first winter of the war, there was little beyond the blackout to disturb the established routine of the Navigation School and, contrary to what had occurre during world war I, training continued. At sea, needless to say, things were very different. Conditions for the navigation and conduct of ships at sea in the early par of the war were fraught with difficulties. The Navigating Officer was faced with those arising from the deliberate restriction of shore lighting and other navigational aids and, in the shallow waters surrounding the UK, by having to keep his ship within the narrow confines of swept channels in order to avoid the minefields whic the enemy at once started to lay. It became a matter of vital importance for the Navigating Officer to keep his charts up to date with the mass of information emanating form the Hydrographic department giving the positions of wrecks, minefields, boom defences and other obstacles. At night ships had to steam, often at high speed, completely darkened and without the aid of radar which was not to be generally fitted for another 18 months. Station keeping at night was a matter of keeping the faint silhouette of your next ahead in your binoculars. For example the first convoys carrying the British Army to France in 1939 consisted of cross channel ferries employed as troop ships. These sped across the channel at 20 knots while their destroyer escorts did their best to keep station by what was largely inspired guesswork.

Navigators Yeomen

In 1940, in order to provide the Navigating Officer with assistance in his formidable task, the Admiralty instructed each ship to select an Able Seaman to act as full time assistant to him and to be known as the Navigator's Yeoman. The selected rating had to be taught his duties onboard but when trained he became the Navigating Officer's right hand man and was able to help with the correction of charts and the work of the navigation department generally, thus proving himself invaluable. The custom survives to the present day.

Small Ship Navigators

Except in flotilla leaders, destroyers and convoy escorts were not supplied with qualified (N) officers. In many of the smaller ships the duties of Navigating officer were entrusted to Reserve officers of the RNR and RNVR and in many cases their training, especially the latter, of necessity had been brief. It was therefore of paramount importance that qualified RN officers (N) should set the standard and assist these officers in every possible way. Although the quality of the teaching given in *Dryad* proved itself during the war, the continual changes in tactics and weapons in such operations as the defence of convoys, minesweeping and minelayin hore-bombardment and assault meant that Navigating Officers had quickly to adapt to the changing circumstances and rapidly devise new techniques in pilotage, navigation and station-keeping. A lot of this information was passed around the fleet by word of mouth since there was no time to institute shore courses to disseminate it.

War experience of (N) Officers

The intake of Qualifiers in 1940 was below average. amounting to two classes of four and seven respectively. A member of the second batch, Captain A P Culmer recalls that on completing the course, 'I sailed away to my first appointment from Liverpool in *SS Eumaeus* on 27 December 1940. With me was J L West also of the same course. About 12 days later, *Eumaeus* was sunk about 150 miles from Freetown and we lost all our Qualifying notes, sextants, etc. We had done a much shortened long course in the introduction to which we were told, 'even if you do not understand everything, get it down in your notes and when you get to your first appointment your notebook can be your real reference book' but the fates decreed otherwise!

Another member of the class, R H Milward, managed to reach Alexandria safely after a long trip round the Cape in a troop ship, where he joined the sloop, *Grimsby*, commanded by Commander K J D'Arcy who qualified (N) in 1927. After a hectic time escorting convoys to and from Greece and Crete, the ship was told off as escort of a merchant ship to Tobruk where 12 German Ju 88s found her and sent her to the bottom. Warning of the attack was given by shore based radar, but the absence of protective fighters sealed her fate. Milward was subsequently appointed to the cruiser, *Durban* and in 1944 returned to *Dryad* on the staff of the Action Information Training Centre (AITC).

Handling the Queen Mary

Commander (later Rear Admiral) Geoffrey Brittain of the 1928 Qualifiers, found himself in command of the Australian built seaplane tender *Albatross,* lying in Freetown harbour in June 1940. 'The Chief of Staff to the Commander in Chief South Atlantic, sent for me one day,' he writes 'and told me the Admiral wished me to pilot the *RMS Queen Mary* (80,774 tons) from sea to the anchorage off Kissey in two days time. Not having any data for the ship, I used "distances to new course" which I remembered for *HMS Hood* plus 20%. The harbour was pretty full, there being over 100 merchant ships assembled for a slow convoy. Having made my plan, I got permission to move two or three merchant ships, as I was not prepared to try and dodge between them.

'The *Queen Mary* was drawing 40 feet and had to cross a 38 foot patch, so near high water was indicated and I chose the first of the ebb. The turning circle data worked out very well and we got through the boom all right, though there was very little to spare on either side in the gate. As we were approaching our anchor berth, some six miles up river from the boom, the Captain informed me that it would be necessary to lose all headway before letting go. This was a new complication, but we managed to finish up within 17 yards of the planned berth, though I didn't like the idea of a mass of four inch cable lying on the anchor.

'The ship was to sail again next morning and I planned she should sail at the end of the flood so as to cross the 38 foot patch at high water. Steam was ordered for 0730, but when I arrived onboard about 0700 and the Captain and I went up to the bridge and he rang down "stand by" he received an indignant reply from the engine-room, "what's going on? — we ain't got no steam down 'ere." It transpired that the Chief Engineer had interpreted the order for steam as 7.30 *pm* instead of *am.* He was ordered to raise steam as quickly as possible and reported that he could be ready in an hour and a half. This gave me the opportunity of enjoying a Cunard breakfast, rather marred, however, by the thought of the flood having turned to ebb.

'At 0830 we began to weigh just as the ship started to swing to the ebb. The next set back was a report from the foc'sle — foul anchor. We let go again and next time it came up clear, but we had now lost so much time, the ship was swinging to the ebb. I managed to get her pointed and asked the Captain for a bit more speed, so he ordered half ahead and I soon found we were going down Freetown harbour at 20 knots! I stopped engines well before the boom and we shot through with them stopped. As there was shoal water for the *Queen Mary* beyond the boom, I had to alter sharply to port as soon as we were through. The extra Third officer was posted right aft to report when the stern was clear of the boom vessel, but long after the bridge had passed, I made a tenative enquiry to which the reply was, "can't see it yet!" After what seemed an age, he reported "stern clear" and I thankfully ordered, "port 25" and started the engines again. We reached the open sea without further trouble.'

A moment of suspense

Command Gerald Cobb OBE was Navigating Officer of the battleship *Malaya* when she was torpedoed in mid-Atlantic early in 1941. After the mishap she was ordered to steam westward at her best speed and subsequently to enter the port of New York. As the US was not yet in the war, the greatest secrecy was enjoined regarding the fact that she was to be repaired there. However as she limped up the Hudson River, she was met by a fleet of private yachts and that evening the New York papers carried double headlines, 'BATTERED BRITISH BATTLE-WAGON ARRIVES'. So much for security.

After de-ammunitioning and de-fuelling she was ordered to proceed to Brooklyn Navy Yard. This necessitated passing under the famous Brooklyn Suspension Bridge and called for accurate calculation of the amount of clearance between the ship's masthead (after the topmast had been housed) and the bridge. It was found to be minimal and moreover the bridge was known to sag in hot weather, so it was with considerable trepidation that she approached this hazard.

The banks on either side were crowded with sightseers and Cobb who was conning the ship felt his heart in his mouth as he was subjected to the usual optical illusion that they could not possibly clear. The tension on the ship's bridge was acute when suddenly a voice behind him boomed out, 'the next headline will be, BRITISH BATTLEWAGON BATTERS BROOKLYN BRIDGE'. Fortunately the ship passed safely under the bridge and everyone had a good laugh.

They also serve

Commander A E Sutcliff who qualified in 1935 joined the cruiser *Newcastle* as her Navigating Officer on 2 June 1940 as a Lieutenant of six years seniority; he left her five years and one month later with the rank of Commander. During his time as (N) of the ship she steamed 264,751 miles on war service. Typical of the unspectacular, dull, but nonetheless necessary service on which the ship was engaged was a patrol which began on leaving Freetown on 10 December 1940 and ended 133 days later at Simonstown on 21 April 1941 by which time the wardroom wine stock was reduced to half a bottle of Cointreau. Between departure and arrival land was sighted only 13 times usually when refuelling from tankers off the coasts of Brazil, Uruguay, and Argentina. He believes that the above figures establish several records.

The first air raids

The first air attack on Portsmouth dockyard took place on 11 July 1940 and caused no damage to naval establishments. It was followed by another one on 24 July which resulted in serious damage to the dockyard, though the School escaped. Thereafter there were sporadic raids until the night of 5 December when what the Commander in Chief, Admiral Sir William James, describes as 'a nasty attack' took place causing serious damage to Clarence Yard and the Torpedo School, *Vernon.* The Navigation School with its lead-covered cupola and flat roof was particularly vulnerable to attack by incendiaries, so Captain Armstrong organized a fire-watching system from amongst the pupils and staff. The resulting loss of sleep proved detrimental to instruction, especially during the afternoon periods when many pupils found it impossible to keep their eyes open. It so happened that Admiral James was a very keen shot and had been invited to shoot over the estate of a Colonel Thistlethwayte who lived in solitary victorian splendour in a large house in Southwick Park, which lay on the outskirts of Portsmouth to the north of Portsdown Hill. In Admiral Sir William James' book *The Portsmouth Papers* there are several references to his taking a couple of hours off from his demanding duties to shoot 'old T's pheasants.' When informed by Captain Armstrong of the effect which fire-watching and constant alerts were having on instruction in the school, the Commander in Chief arranged with Colonel Thistlethwayte for the officers under instruction to spend the night at Southwick House. Exactly when these nightly moves began it has not been possible to establish, but Captain R H Graham MVO DSC, one of the 1941 Qualifiers, recalls two incidents which took place whilst spending the night at Southwick.

'One night when the sirens had gone and we had dutifully descended to the cellars for shelter, after the lapse of half an hour during which nothing had happened to disturb our peace, there was a sudden clatter in the cellar. We looked up to see Colonel Thistlethwayte appear clad in a heavy woollen dressing gown and seated in a wheel chair, being propelled by two man servants. He was protesting loudly at being dragged down to the basement at that hour of the night.'

'On another occasion, we awoke early one morning and looking out of our bedroom window across the park, we saw the white tresses of a parachute entangled in a magnificent oak tree on the edge of the lawn to the south of the house. Ah, we thought, a filthy hun who had been justly shot down by our wonderful fight fighters and the dark shape at the end of the harness must be his body hanging still and lifeless. Ought we to go and cut him down, and report our action to the Commander in Chief's office? On closer inspection the dangling shape appeared too regular to be that of a body. Then the awful truth dawned on us: it was a land mine which had failed to explode — as yet! We washed and dressed and returned to the Navigation School for breakfast and we heard, subsequently, that the bomb disposal experts came later and removed the offending object.'

However on 10 March 1941, a raid took place during which the Old School received a direct hit. Admiral James records '. . . a real blitz yesterday. The raid lasted seven hours and it was estimated that about 300 planes came over. They did a lot of damage in the yard . . . One bomb knocked out the centre of the Navigation School but another arrived in one of their shelters and rolled down to the wall where I saw

Southwick House as it appeared when requisitioned in 1944.

it in the early morning. I was told that the Wrens in the shelter lifted their feet to let it pass.' (ibid, p 105) The only casualty was a Sub Lieutenant on fire-watch who descended with the roof, but was only shaken.

The move to Southwick House

Despite the considerable damage received, the School continued to function and during raids which took place on 17 April and 3 May Admiralty House, alongside was completely demolished by direct hits. In consequence the Commander in Chief was obliged to move to his war headquarters at Fort Wallington on Portsdown Hill. Although an entry in his diary dated 22 May 1941 reads 'I am glad to say the Navigation School will move shortly to Southwick,' but according to AFO 4109/41 it was not until 27 September that the move in fact was completed. The requisitioning of his property had been stoutly resisted by its gallant owner who ultimately retired to Purbrook House, one of the smaller houses on his large estate where, sad to relate, on 16 November 1943, he died. Four days previously, Admiral James had confided to his diary '. . . alas no more of those wonderful two-hour sessions at Southwick. The House was taken for the Navigation School and old T looks on me now as a double-dyed villain and not a fit person to shoot his birds.'

The Navigation School's new home was an imposing but completely unmodernized victorian mansion standing in a park of some 300 acres which, in the 12th century, was the site of a priory of the Augustine Canon founded by Henry II to house the monks from the ransacked Portchester Castle nearby. It saw the marriage of Henry VI to Margaret of Anjou and later provided shelter for Charles I. In course of time the priory fell into ruins and, at the end of the 18th century, a mansion was built on a site to the north east of where the present building stands. In 1838 this mansion was damaged by fire and the present one was erected in its place. The stables and outbuildings, however, survived the fire and therefore belong to the earlier period.

Considerable alterations were needed in order to adapt Southwick House to its new use. Electric light had to be installed and the first, second and third floor bedrooms had to be converted into classrooms, while the drawing room, dining room, breakfast room and library became the wardroom mess. Living accommodation was provided in nissen huts, hastily erected among the trees in a copse opposite the stables but the park itself, which was leased to tenant farmers, so remained. When the requisition was made, it was generally assumed that the Navigation School would return to its original home in the dockyard when the war was over. No one at that time could foresee the events which were to make *Dryad* the RN's foremost training centre. Before, however, continuing with this theme, we must retrace our steps to the years immediately preceeding the outbreak of world war II which witnessed the birth of what at first was called radio direction finding (RDF) and which today we call radar.

The advent of radar

Like many great inventions, radar had a long period of gestation and after it was born, it took quite a time for its parents to realise what a truly remarkable child they had produced. According to its putative father, Sir Robert Watson-Watt, the reflection of radio waves was discovered in 1923 but 'the history of effective location of ships and the effective detection of aircraft by the utilization of radio echoes begins, not with these important observations but only in 1930 or later.' (*Three Steps to Victory* by Sir Robert Watson-Watt, p 101.) In 1934 a committee under the chairmanship of Professor (later Sir Henry) Tizard was set up for the scientific study of air defence. At its first meeting on 28 January 1935, the idea of producing a damaging effect on aircraft by a ray of radio waves was considered but rejected as impracticable. However, Watson-Watt suggested that the problem of the location of aircraft by radio though difficult, might be worth pursuing, and he was invited to develop his ideas. This led to the construction of a special laboratory at Orfordness on the coast of Suffolk and by mid-September the height of an aircraft flying at 7000 feet and distant 15 miles was successfully measured. The first air exercise in connection with radio location, as it was first called, took place in September 1936, in which two 240 feet towers which had been erected at Bawdsey Manor, near Felixstowe, were used to watch aircraft operating over the North Sea. Bawdsey became the prototype for 20 such stations stretching from Portsmouth to Scapa Flow, the last of which came into operation in July 1939.

While the system of radio location was being developed at Bawdsey, the RAF at Biggin Hill was busy working out new methods of organizing fighter interception on the assumption that the necessary apparatus would soon be available to assit with this. It was only natural that the RAF with its responsibility for the air defence of Great Britain should have had the first claim on the use of the new equipment not only for warning purposes but also as a basis for the direction of fighter aircraft, but the Admiralty too became interested and in 1938 two sets were fitted, one in the battleship *Rodney* and the other in the cruiser *Sheffield* both of which formed part of the Home Fleet. Within the limits of the design which did not permit the aerial to rotate, it proved its claim to detect aircraft and surface craft approaching outside visual range.

Had radar been fitted in all ships when the war began, the loss of the Armed Merchant Cruiser *Rawalpindi* on 23 November 1939 might have had different consequences. Lieutenant Commander (later Commander) Charles Cree DSC who was (N) officer of the cruiser *Delhi* on the northern patrol at the time, recalls, 'we were the next ship in the line and to the southward of the *Rawalpindi*, but we had been pursuing a large unidentified tanker to the westward or we might have made contact with the *Scharnhorst* and *Gneisenau* which sank her. The Captain of the *Delhi* (later Admiral Sir Louis 'Turtle' Hamilton) altered course to the reported position and increased to full speed and turning to me said, 'If I meet the sod I am going to ram her.' I don't think he realised there were two enemy ships. However we did not make contact — we were working on DR not having had any sights for several days — but things might have been different if both the *Newcastle* which made temporary contact and ourselves had been fitted with radar.'

When radar was introduced into the fleet it was received with enthusiasm but it took some time for its capabilities and limitations to be appreciated. As an aid

The old stables at Southwick House which were converted for use as the Action Information Training Centre.

to pilotage, navigation and station-keeping it was readily accepted as the following story by Lieut-Commander J D D Moore DSC who was one of the 1940 Qualifiers shows:

'Some fleet minesweepers of the *Halcyon* class (900 tons) accompanied the first convoy to North Russia in August 1941. My ship was the flotilla leader, *Harrier,* (whose name was bestowed on the post war Aircraft Direction Training Centre at Kete). We were refitting at Southampton and a few days before we were due to sail some boffins arrived onboard unexpectedly to fit our first radar set, then referred to as RDF, which they explained should enable us to detect U-boats on the surface at night. In fact the set was one of the first batch of experimental 10cm wave length radars, the introduction of which had been made possible by the discovery of the magnetron by Randall and Boote. The Chief Telegraphist and I goggled at the cathode ray tube with its line of green light, appropriately called "grass" and noticed that as we rotated the aerial (by hand, of course) blips sprouted up from the grass as the beam passed over nearby ships. Somehow it never occurred to us that the set could equally well detect land.

'The voyage to north Russia proved uneventful, the Germans not having yet appreciated how important these convoys were to become. From time to time we switched on our radar set, the only one in the convoy, for the benefit of the Telegraphists detailed to work it, since there were as yet no trained operators. On approaching the White Sea entrance from the north at the end of our journey, I had the Chief Telegraphist keep watch on the RDF in case we encountered U-boats

69

or even Russian ships. We caught a fleeting glimpse of a barren and featureless coast in making our landfall but suddenly we were enveloped in thick fog just as we were approaching the narrow passage known as the Gourlo which leads into the White Sea and which abounds with shoals. The whole convoy stopped, not knowing what to do next. At this moment up came Chief Telegraphist's cheerful voice through a voice-pipe "Bridge, I think we are picking up land on the RDF." I hastened to the radar office, a little hut at the back of the bridge, and studied a forest of strange looking blips now appearing on the scan. It seemed obvious that these were caused by land and that the three nearest points that could be picked out, correspon ded exactly with three conspicuous headlands on the coast in that vicinity. Laying off a range and bearing of each one on the chart, I found that they all coincided exactly in a point, whereupon I confidently reported to my Captain that we had an accurate fix.

'The result was that we were ordered to lead the convoy through the Gourlo to which end we showed every available bright light that would bear astern. Fixing by radar continuously, we crept forward and the entire convoy duly arrived safely at Archangel, much to the surprise of our Russian allies. Later we were informed by our Russian liaison officer that the Captain of the Russian destroyers sent to escort us in and who naturally knew nothing of radar, had been "liquidated" for failing to find us in the fog!'

The need for fighter protection

However very soon after the outbreak of war it was obvious that the Admiralty's views on the defence of ships against air attack, by which reliance was to be placed mainly on the ship's AA armament, were unrealistic. Although an excellent liaison had been established with Coastal Command of the RAF, it was primarily concerned with reconnaissance and not with fighter protection. The need for the latter soon became evident along the east coast of Britain where the coastal convoys carrying among other goods, vital coal supplies for the London power stations, attracted the attention of the Luftwaffe. To meet this threat the responsibilities of Fighter Command of the RAF were gradually extended until they covered the coast from the Thames to the Moray Firth up to a distance of 40 miles to seaward. All that was possible at this stage was for the convoy of ships being attacked to send out a call for help, but too often by the time the fighters had arrived the enemy had completed his mission and departed.

The first efforts to direct fighters for the protection of ships and shore installations were made during the Norwegian campaign in May and June 1940, and the crude methods that were improvised could be improved only slightly during the first Malta convoys later that year because it was not possible to provide either the competent directors or the material needed.

The development of aircraft direction

The arrival in the Mediterranean in August 1940 of the carrier *Illustrious,* the battle-ship *Valiant,* and the cruiser *Sheffield* all of which were fitted with air warning radar sets, improved the situation in those waters. Captain Charles Coke DSO who was serving as Signal Officer in *Ark Royal* which formed part of the famous force H in the western Mediterranean writes; 'in the first days the system was simple and rarely effective. Sightings of enemy aircraft from ships of the fleet were supplemented by radar reports from *Sheffield*. These reports of the positions of enemy aircraft were transmitted in morse to *Ark Royal* and retransmitted in morse to airborne fighters.

The first improvement was to obtain reports of the position of our own fighters as well as of enemy aircraft, so that the plotting and the calculation could be done in the ship instead of in the air, thus the pilots need be concerned only with the course to steer. The time elapsed between the observation of the radar blip and the receipt by the pilot of his instructions was of the order of four minutes. The radar could give only the approximate position and rarely an indication of height. The plotting equipment I used was an observer's Bigsworth Board and I had no assistance other than the telegraphist who sat alongside me and operated the morse key. Nevertheless some interceptions were achieved and some protection given to the early Malta convoys.'

In the eastern basin of the Mediterranean where Admiral Cunningham's fleet was operating and which had been joined by the *Illustrious* and the *Valiant*, attempts were also being made to grapple with the problem of fighter direction.

THE GENERAL PROCESS OF ACTION INFORMATION

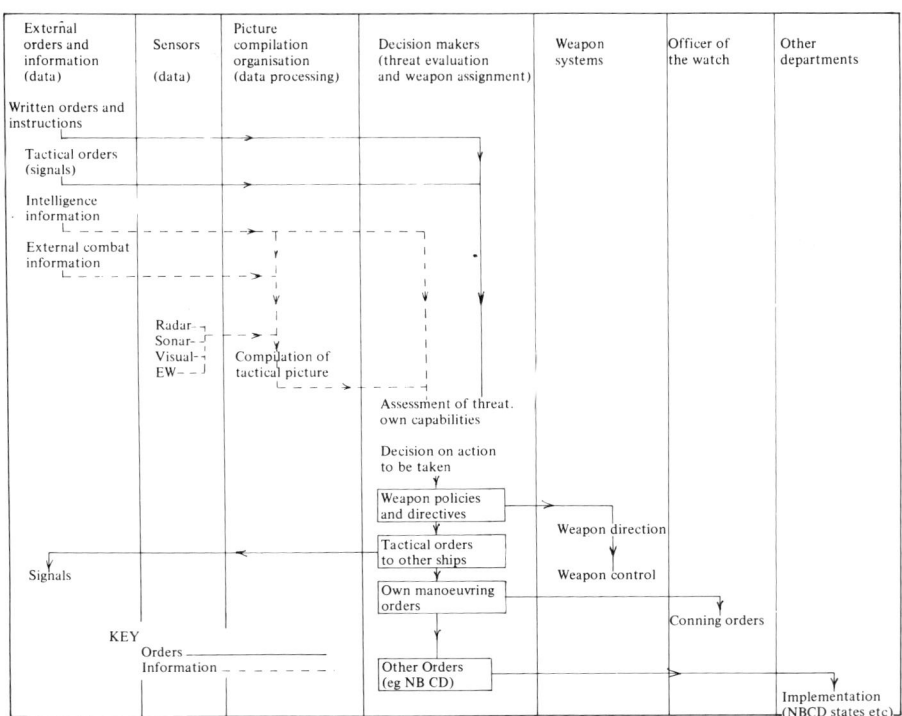

71

Commander G R M Going DSO, one of the heroes of Taranto who subsequently lost a leg when the *Illustrious* was bombed by the Luftwaffe, writes, 'my first contact with aircraft direction was during the golden first commission of the *Illustrious*. This was memorable, not only for Taranto, but also and possibly significantly for the birth of naval aircraft direction. Admittedly the *Ark Royal* working with *Sheffield's* radar had pioneered this, but we were the first carrier to be fitted with Type 79 radar and to use it for the direct control of fighters. This was done using the notoriously inefficient HF/RT backed by W/T and using a perspex covered mooring board for the shipboard plotting and interception. The results achieved by these primitive means were startlingly successful and, despite the inadequacy of our Fulmar fighters, the Mediterranean Fleet, which hitherto had been bombed whenever it put to sea, enjoyed six months of immunity from air attack.'

In command of the *Illustrious* at that time was Captain (later Admiral Sir) Denis Boyd who was later to hold the posts of Rear Admiral (Air) Mediterranean, and Fifth Sea Lord and he, together with Admiral Sir Lumley Lister who preceded him in both these appointments, played a most important part in the development of aircraft direction in the fleet and the establishment of the Fighter Direction Centre at Yeovilton. Here for a while we must leave the story of aircraft direction which is told in Chapter V in order to recount the developments taking place in the field of action information.

The birth of the Action Information Organization

There is a story that 'action information' as it came to be called, was first discussed between two comparatively junior (N) officers in a cafe at Harwich in 1939 during which the table cloth was used to depict a diagram which later became all too familiar to (N/D) officers; be that as it may.

Between the wars the surface tactical plot had received scant attention and had undergone comparatively little development. There were a number of (N) officers who were not at all happy with the equipment at their disposal for this purpose. The improved reliability of the gyro compass and the bottom log had encouraged the development of an automatic plotter known as the Brewerton after its inventor. It comprised a crawler, operated by impulses from the gyro compass and the patent log, which adhered to the chart or plotting sheet by magnetic attraction to a steel plate plate underneath, but whenever the guns fired it was liable to jump and tear the plot. It was superseded eventually by a much more satisfactory type designed by the Admiralty Research Laboratory (ARL).

The normal location of the automatic plotting table in ships other than flagships was in the chart house which, in many ships, was situated on the deck below the compass platform where it was not readily accessible to the Captain and who, after dark, would not want to spoil his night vision by entering a lighted compartment. Lieutenant Commander (later Captain) M E Butler-Bowdon OBE who in the spring of 1939 was appointed Flotilla (N) of the Fifth Destroyer Flotilla being formed from the new J and K class destroyers, realised that it would be advantageous if the ARL plotting table could be viewed from the compass platform. He interested

An aerial view of Southwick House which was used as the Headquarters for the Normandy invasion. The picture shows the excellent natural cover provided by the surrounding trees.

his future Captain (D), Lord Louis Mountbatten in the idea and 'we soon found a mutually convenient position' he writes, 'for the ARL table below the compass platform and for what later became known as the view plot. This took the form of a pyramid shaped trunk with the thin end uppermost and a flat top on which I intended a sheet of glass or two eye-pieces should be placed, but Lord Louis suggested **a** the fitting of magnifying binoculars to the eye-pieces and **b** that each eye-piece should incorporate sheets of polaroid glass which would prevent the light from showing skywards and also interference with the viewer's night vision. It proved a great success.' As will be seen it was not until the fourth year of the war that this fitting was adopted officially.

Commander J N N Synnott, another officer who was to become intimately concerned with the development of the action plotting arrangements, was at sea as Navigating Officer of the cruiser *Birmingham* when war as declared. His ship was employed searching for German shipping in the vicinity of Sumatra and by the end of her third patrol both he and his Captain 'were quite convinced that even in a new cruiser, only completed less than two years earlier, the plotting arrangements were quite inadequate and needed large and drastic alterations and expansion.' In

December 1940 he was appointed to the battleship *Queen Elizabeth* which was within six months of completing a major refit. 'Most surprisingly,' he writes, 'it was found that the ship's plotting facilities were no more advanced than those in *Birmingham* . . . However this ship was designed as a fleet flagship so there was a large Admiral's bridge below the Captain's bridge, still quite bare, but the plans showed only a large chart table, bookshelves, a telephone and a voicepipe or two.' With the willing co-operation of his Captain, he managed to redesign the whole compartment and fill it with equipment, instruments, and communications which he had learned from experience were necessary. This foresight bore fruit when later on the Commander in Chief Home Fleet hoisted his flag in the ship for a short while and was gratified to find that these illicit plotting arrangements compared very favourably with those which had been installed in his former flagship *Nelson* through the acumen of the Master of the Fleet, Commander (later Captain) F B Lloyd.

The formation of an AIO committee

As the war progressed and more and more ships were equipped with increasingly effective radar sets and some with high frequency direction finding (HF/DF) sets as well, the need for a more sophisticated plotting organization grew rapidly. Reports had been received in the Admiralty from Commander (later Vice Admiral Sir) Guy Sayer, commanding the sloop *Cleveland* of the east coast convoy escort force, from Captains D16 and D21 at the Nore, and from the Commander in Chief, Eastern Fleet all of which foreshadowed the need for some form of action information organization and on 12 May 1943, the ACNS (Weapons), Rear Admiral Wilfred Patterson called a meeting of all interested departments at the Admiralty to consider the general policy for handling action information in HM Ships. At this meeting it was decided to form an AIO committee with Captain Sayer, who had taken up the post of Deputy Director, Training And Staff Duties on 1 April, as chairman. The constitution of the committee was promulgated in Office Acquaint Number 260 dated 24 June 1943 and was as follows:

Deputy Director Training and Staff Duties (chairman)
Representatives of the:
>Director of Navigation
>Director of the Signal Division
>Director of Naval Ordnance
>Director of Air Weapon Training
>Director of Torpedoes and Mining
>Director of Naval Construction
>Director of the Gunnery Division
>Director of Electrical Engineering
>Director of Naval Equipment

The Committee's terms of reference were, 'to draw up staff requirements for an Action Information Organization for each class of new construction ship and investigate the best means of altering existing ships.' It was further charged with giving guidance to technical departments on the requirements for developing equipment. The first meeting was held on 8 June 1943 and dealt with destroyers and escort vessels. At its next meeting on 24 June it considered AIO in carriers, and a sub-committee was formed to deal with the complex question of communications. On 9 July the committee met to consider the staff requirements for AIO in capital ships and cruisers and the attachment of an experimental unit to the Navigation School, *Dryad,* was approved. An Admiralty Fleet Order 1454/43 issued on 14 July outlined the policy for AIO in HM Ships. Thereafter the committee met at frequent intervals throughout the summer and autumn.

The construction of an Action Information Training Centre in HMS Dryad

As has been mentioned, the need to develop fighter direction had been made evident soon after the war began and in 1941 an Aircraft Direction School had been opened at Speckington Manor, close alongside the Royal Naval Air Station at Yeovilton, Somerset, where demonstration of the art and the training of RNVR officers and Radar Plot ratings was proceeding apace. With the decision to set up a similar training centre for action plotting in *Dryad* came the appointment of Lieutenant Commander (later Captain Sir) David Tibbits DSC who joined *Dryad* on 14 June 1943 on his return from the far east, where he had held the appointment of (N) officer of *Devonshire.* With no office, no telephone and no terms of reference, he began work. The only available space at Southwick House was the stables, once a lovely old building of coach houses, loose boxes and harness rooms but now blacked out and empty except for an old retainer quartered in what was to become the headquarters of the new development. After a visit to the Fighter Direction Centre at Yeovilton, Tibbits was able to report that the buildings allocated appeared suitable for conversion and he enclosed details of proposed layouts of demonstration models and of the staff needed to operate them. He also suggested that the new organization should take over the instruction in plotting now given in the School. His suggestions were approved and complete plans to implement his proposals were immediately put in hand and forwarded to the Admiralty through the Commander in Chief, Portsmouth on 5 July. While awaiting Board approval, Tibbits visited the Commander in Chief Home Fleet; he also gave a lecture to the current class of (N) Qualifiers on action information.

Board approval was given on 3 August, but did not reach *Dryad* until 6 August and six days later a conference with representatives of the dockyard took place at which final plans for the work were drawn up and forwarded to the Commander in Chief on 20 August together with proposals for the adjustment of the accommodation at Southwick House. In order to hasten the granting of board approval, a copy of the report was delivered personally to the Director of Training and Staff Duties at the Admiralty and three days later approval to build without delay was given; work began the next day.

The first mock-up

On 21 August, another meeting of the AIO committee took place, this time at Bath, where the technical departments of the Admiralty had taken up residence, at which Tibbits undertook to construct the mock-up of the action information centre in a Battle class destroyer within 14 days. A great deal of woodwork was involved and a joiner had been asked for as a matter of urgency, but none was forthcoming and Tibbits found himself assisting the contractors' carpenter and a couple of joiners which he had managed to borrow from the dockyard and Whale Island. The mock-up was completed in 13 days and as the last screw was turned the joiner who had been requested, joined.

The work of conversion of the old stables into a demonstration and training centre for AIO involved a number of different bodies like the Admiralty Signal Establishment, Haslemere, the Superintending Civil Engineer, the Manager of the Constructive Department and the Electrical Engineer Manager in the dockyard as well as the Surveyor of Lands of the Southwick Estate and it says a great deal for Tibbit's tact and ability that the work ran so smoothly. The Director of Navigation, Rear Admiral W G Benn, paid his first visit to the site on 15 September, and the following day, Commander (later Captain) C J Wynne-Edwards, DSC*, who had been appointed to his staff in order to take over the work in connection with the new development, also paid a visit to the embryo AIO. The latter had been in sea-going appointments continuously for the past 10 years, two and half of which during the war as Squadron (N) of the 1st Minelaying Squadron; he was to prove a tower of strength in the Admiralty end of the new development.

The Director of Navigation and the AIO

Meanwhile in anticipation of the new responsibilities with which he was soon to be faced, on 16 July 1943, the Director of Navigation had initiated a docket in which he suggested that the time had come to consider anew the formation of an (N) division of the naval staff, separate from the Hydrographic department to which, it will be remembered, it had reverted in 1916. He gave as his reasons for the change:

a To improve the status of the (N) branch
b To bring precept into line with practice and remove the anomalous position in which this office finds itself by being part of the Hydrographic Department.
c To make clear to everyone its functions both inside and outside the Admiralty.
d To satisfy a long standing wish that this branch should stand on its own feet and be independent of the Hydrographic department.

As however the pressure to develop an Action Information Organization increased as the result of the events narrated above, the Director initiated a second docket (CE4076) dated 29 November 1943 (without waiting to hear the decision of the board on his previous one) in which he proposed the formation of a new section of the (N) department to be known as the AIO section and thereby regularize Commander Wynne-Edwards' appointment. The last named who had taken up his appointment on 12 October lost no time in making contact with Captain Sayer (DDTSD) and the experience and enthusiasm of these two officers with the backing of their respective Directors, gave the whole project the momentum needed to overcome all obstacles (and there were many) leading to the rapid development of AIO in the fleet and to the metamorphosis of the Navigation branch. In a letter to the author Wynne-Edwards writes, 'from the first we were very much concerned to improve the layout of the bridge in all types of ship, with particular emphasis on escorts and fleet destroyers, and to introduce a tactical plot immediately below some part of the bridge which could be seen at any time by the Command through a 'view plot' without leaving the bridge. In most cases this entailed much structural alteration, preceded by the building of wooden mock-ups in which the optimum arrangements of displays and equipment could be devised. Some of these were constructed in the dockyards and building yards, and others in *Dryad* at Southwick.'

Development of the view plot

On 15 November 1943, an important meeting of the AIO committee took place to decide on a policy for fitting plan position indicators (PPIs) on ships bridges and also the requirement for a viewing device to enable the PPI and the plot in the bridge plotting room to be viewed simultaneously from the compass platform, a problem which Butler-Bowdon with the help of Lord Louis Mountbatten had tackled when commissioning *Kelly* in 1939. The problem was considered both by the Admiralty Research Laboratory and the AITC in *Dryad* and at the last named after a difference of opinion between Tibbits and Wynne-Edwards as to the design, the latter personally made a mock-up of the proposed bridge hood late one night in the joiner's shop which met the requirements and was accepted by the AIO committee when shown to them on 20 January 1944, as a result of which an order for six was placed with ARL.

Increase of staff for D of N

On 16 December 1943, a third docket (CE 59850/43) was launched by the Director of Navigation in which he applied for an additional officer on his staff, whose appointment had been approved in principle but not implemented. He cited the growth of the work in connection with the AIO and as a result Lieutenant Commander J N N Synnott joined his staff with the acting rank of Commander in which he was confirmed at the end of the year. His experience in the field of action plotting has already been mentioned and this was yet another most fortuitous appointment for which the Appointments Officer at the Navigation School, Lieutenant Commander Ivan B Farrant was responsible.

To return to the D of N's second docket (CE 4076) as it began its routine journey round the various interested divisions of the naval staff. As might be expected, the Director of Training and Staff Duties strongly supported the proposal. The Director of Naval Equipment, on the other hand, thought the new organization ought to come under the Director of Naval Ordnance, a suggestion with which the Director of the Gunnery Division and the Director of Radio Equipment agreed. The Directors of Naval Construction and Torpedo and Mining, each staked out a claim to be the co-ordinating authority. After the docket had been circulating for five months, the Head of the Civil Branch called it in and in a masterly minute dated 2 May 1944 summarized the conflicting interests and recommended that the Director of Navigation should be the co-ordinating authority of the new organization and that he be given a material section to deal with it. This proposal received board approval on 7 June 1944, but the battle was not yet won.

In a docket dated 27 August 1944, the Director of Navigation returned to the charge and again requested the separation of his department from that of the

Hydrographer in view of the greatly increased work in connection with AIO with which he now had to deal. Although minutes by members of the Board were sympathetic, the First Lord, Mr (later Viscount) Alexander (of Hilsborough) turned it down.

Disbandment of the AIO Committee

In September 1944, a confidential pamphlet on the Action Information Organization (CB 04357) compiled by D of N's staff, was issued to the fleet. On the 11th of the same month a meeting of the naval staff to consider all outstanding matters concerning AIO was held and as a result, five days later, on 16 September, the Director of Training and Staff Duties raised a docket in support of proposals put forward by both the Director of Navigation and *HMS Dryad* to the effect that the first named should now take over full responsibility for the Action Information Organization and also for the training and employment of RP ratings. While the docket was circulating, the Director of Navigation, the Director of Air Weapons Training, and the Deputy Director of Training and Staff Duties visited the Home Fleet and between 26 and 28 October gave a series of lectures onboard the fleet flagship. Board approval to DTSD's docket was given in November and the decision was published in AFO 5971 dated 16 November 1944. Meanwhile the AIO committee, having fulfilled the function for which it had been created was disbanded as from 11 November 1944.

Director of Navigation becomes independent of the Hydrographer

The Director of Navigation was now in a much stronger position than he had ever been and in another docket (HO 212/44/2/5) dated 29 November 1944 he sought to regularize his position vis-a-vis the Hydrographer having regard to the greatly enhanced status of his department. It had the desired effect. Six months later, the First Lord reversed his previous decision and Board approval was given to the revised responsibilities of the Director of Navigation which were promulgated in OM 359 dated 6 September 1945. (See Appendix IV).

Progress with the AITC

To return to the Navigation School where by the new year (1944), the lower floor of the stables had been converted into an instructional plotting room and all plotting training was now being done in the AITC. The first battleship/cruiser model was nearing completion, including the control room, and the staff and the WRNS plotters were materializing. The former included Electrical Lieutenant G Fitzgerald RNVR, Instructor Lieutenant Commander R Moss and Lieutenant Seaton RNVR. The contractors had demolished the old wall and gates of the courtyard and begun the construction of the workshop block, the loft floor had been reinforced with additional joists, planking and concrete and Admiralty approval for the construction of accommodation buildings had been received. Other events of note were participation by the staff of the AITC in the design of the plotting rooms in a new cruiser

Swiftsure and the aircraft carrier, *Minotaur* and the appointment of Lieutenant Millard RNVR as liaison officer with the Fighter Direction Centre at Yeovilton. This last cemented the close link up which had been established between the two establishments not only by choice but also by necessity, as Wynne-Edwards explains, 'in parallel with all this activity on the surface side, the development of fighter direction equipment in the carriers was being carried out with even greater priority. Aircraft Direction Rooms were rapidly becoming more sophisticated. The large, vertical, illuminated perspex plot had been produced, on the back of which radar and other information was plotted by Radar Plot Ratings in looking-glass writing with chinagraph pencils. Radar sets of greatly increased power and discrimination were coming into use; plan position indicator (PPI) displays were being developed on which air interception courses could be deduced and transmitted to fighter aircraft. At sea aircraft direction was carried out by Fighter Direction Officers (FDOs) who were a new specialist branch composed almost entirely of RNVR officers. Within the Admiralty the whole of this activity came under the jurisdiction of the Director of Air Warfare and Training (DAWT).

Here was something of a quandary. In the short term there was nothing anomalous in the separation of the Fighter Direction Officer training from that of the Operations Room Officer (ORO), but both were served by the Radar Plot Rating and there was therefore an immediate need to concentrate the training of these ratings to cover all aspects of both air direction and surface plotting. In order to achieve this it seemed most desirable that one branch should assume responsibility for co-ordinating this training. The Air Warfare and Flying Training divisions were adamant that the plotting and direction of naval aircraft must remain wholly under the umbrella of control by airmen. To me it seemed of vital importance that, in the long term, control of all action plotting whether air or surface, must be co-ordinated within one specialist branch, and that realistically this could only be done by the Navigation branch. To achieve this the (N) branch must be given control of the RP rating. Throughout the spring and summer of 1944, the arguments on either side were marshalled and rehearsed in many an Admiralty docket and at many a meeting.'

Selection of Southwick House as headquarters for 'Overlord'

On 19 January 1944, the author relieved Captain Armstrong in command of the Navigation School, *Dryad* and he had barely had time to familiarize himself with what was taking place there when he was informed by the Commander in Chief Portsmouth, Admiral Sir Charles Little GBE KCB, that he would receive a visit within the next day or two from a Major General (later Sir Frederick) De Guingand who would acquaint him with the purpose of his visit which was one of great secrecy. The General duly arrived and announced that as Chief of Staff to General (later Field Marshal Viscount) Sir Bernard Mountgomery, Commanding 21 Army Group, he had been entrusted with the task of selecting a suitable headquarters near the south coast for the launching of the Normandy invasion. After being shown round Southwick Park which, in its winter setting, looked somewhat bleak, he stated that it seemed to him an ideal situation as by the spring when the trees were in leaf there would be ample cover for the tents and caravans of both 21 Army Group Headquarters and those of the Supreme Commander, General Dwight D Eisenhower. He reported back accordingly and within a short time official confirmation of this was received together with instructions that the Navigation School would have to move out of Southwick House in order to make room for the Allied Naval Commander, Expeditionary Force (ANCXF) Admiral Sir Bertram Ramsay KCB and his staff.

Moving the Navigation School presented no particular problem, the RN College, Greenwich being suggested as its temporary home, but what of that hive of high priority industry the AITC? It was fortunate that it was virtually a self contained unit in the former stables and when Admiral Ramsay was consulted and informed of the effect which any interruption in training would have on the preparations being made to equip the fleet being assembled to join that of the US in the war against Japan in the far east, he readily agreed to the AITC remaining *in situ* provided it did not interfere in any way with him and his staff. So far so good, but there were many problems to be overcome in preparation for the influx of visitors and in meeting their requirements. First the supply of electric power was inadequate, though it had already been boosted to meet the needs of the AITC. The water supply which came from a well had to be augmented and so had the drainage facilities, which were barely adequate for the School itself. Teleprinter and telephone lines galore had to be laid and extra accommodation erected in the grounds for the naval staff and a house in the village requisitioned in which to house the Wrens. The author called on Admiral Ramsay at his London headquarters and suggested to him that he should assume responsibility for all the above work and to this the Admiral readily agreed, as all his staff were working at full pressure on the planning of the greatest amphibious operation ever attempted and did not want to be bothered with such mundane affairs. So it was. Inevitably all this work slowed down that planned to meet the expanding requirements of the AITC and at the end of February the construction work there virtually ceased. On 6 March, however, it was officially opened for training and the first course comprised officers in charge of the AIC in destroyers. The first class of the 1944 Qualifiers did their plotting course there and on 9 March the AIO committee attended a demonstration which was followed by a meeting to discuss the future. Four days later the AIO team for the cruiser *Scylla*, earmarked as Admiral Vian's flagship as Commander of the Eastern Task Force in the Normandy invasion, were given training. Shortly afterwards the Centre received a visit from the Gunnery School, *Excellent*.

The Navigation School moves to RNC, Greenwich

On 3 April, the Navigation School was moved temporarily to RNC Greenwich and was accommodated in the old Seaman's Hospital there. On 26 April, Admiral Ramsay and his staff took up residence at Southwick House to be followed three weeks later by the Supreme Commander, General Eisenhower and his staff and the Commander 21 Army Group, General Sir Bernard Montgomery and his staff, all of whom parked their caravans and tents under the now luxuriant foliage of the trees of Southwick Park with such success that an aerial photograph of the estate revealed no sign of anything but a country house set in the peaceful surrounding of the English countryside. However this concealment proved too effective for one Major General whose caravan had been hidden in the wilderness shrubbery. The Royal Marines had been entrusted with ensuring the security of the area of the headquarters and to this end had surrounded it with what seemed to be miles of barbed wire. Great was the astonishment of the General in the shrubbery when he awoke the morning after his arrival to find that he had been completely wired in. After he had been extricated, he was only mollified when told that his camouflage was so good that the Marines had failed to see him.

The Normandy invasion

Dryad's new home, Southwick House, has a place in history as the scene of the historic decision taken by the Supreme Allied Commander, General Dwight D Eisenhower, on the evening of Sunday 4 June 1944 to launch the invasion of Normandy. Even after the lapse of 33 years the details of that exciting and frustrating week-end remain fresh in the writer's memory. D Day was to have been Monday 5 June, but at a conference of Naval, Military and Air Commanders presided over by the Supreme Commander which took place in the old library during the early hours of Sunday 4 June, the weather forecast was so unpromising that it was decided to postpone launching the operation on a day to day basis. However, when at 2130 that evening, the conference reassembled, 'rapid and unexpected developments' as the Chief Meteorological Adviser, Dr J M Stagg has recorded (*Forecast for Overlord* by J M Stagg p 112) called for a reappraisal of the situation and led Eisenhower to take the momentous decision to reactivate the vast and complicated plan and carry out the invasion on Tuesday 6 June. I remember standing at the entrance while the conference was in progress and watching the trees in the copse opposite swaying to the rising wind and the clouds scudding across the previously clear sky, harbingers of the depression which the meteorological experts had forecast would travel up the Channel that night but which would be succeeded by a brief spell of better weather. At the time conditions seemed most unpropitious and the same thought was in the mind of the groups of staff officers gathered in the hall waiting the outcome of the great men's deliberations. When Stagg joined us, everyone looked at him expectantly, but only one man could make the crucial decision, Eisenhower. Moments later he appeared and strode towards the front door, then catching sight of Stagg, he smiled and said, 'we're laying it on again and please no more bad news' or words to that effect, then acknowledging my salute, he walked towards his waiting jeep, jumped in and drove off.

A further conference took place at 0415 the following morning, at which Stagg was able to confirm and even improve on his promise of a spell of reasonably good weather. It was at this conference that the final and irrevocable decision to launch the invasion was taken and the whole vast machinery moved into top gear. To all non-meteorologically minded, however, conditions during the day showed little signs of the promised improvement. That afternoon Rear Admiral (later Admiral of the Fleet) Sir Philip Vian, Commander of the Eastern Task Force, came to pay a final visit to Admiral Ramsay and I accompanied him to the door as he left. We

Admiral Sir Bertram Ramsay, Commander in Chief, Allied Navant Expeditionary Force (ANCXF) with his staff (l to r) G E Creasy, M L Mansergh, W F Tennant, ANCXF, C H Petrie, J W Rivett-Carnac.

looked up at the still overcast sky. 'I don't know what you think,' he said to me with a laugh, 'but it looks to me like bloody nonsense' and with that he got into his car and was driven away. Even General Eisenhower felt it necessary to seek further assurance from the indefatigable Stagg who to his intense relief was able to give it.

Clearing the approaches to the French coast

Accurate navigation was essential to the operations of the 255 minesweepers and dan layers who cleared the channels through the minefields in the path of the forces taking part in the invasion of Normandy and by the midget submarines detailed to mark the beaches in the British-Canadian sector. It is a tribute to the skill of the navigating officers of these small ships that all the flotillas laid the terminal buoys of their swept channels within one cable of the planned position and within a few minutes of the time laid down.

Lieutenant Commander Oliver Dawkins RNSVR one of a class of six RNVR and three RNR officers who did the first N* course at *Dryad* in June 1943, was the Navigating Officer of the *Algerine* class minesweeper, *Vestal,* leading ship of the group ordered to sweep a channel for Assault Force G. He has written the following account of that part of the operation (From his memoirs *Pilot's Progress* p 117 et seq (typescript), reproduced by kind permission of the author): 'We arrived at our first position exactly on time and turned south. I asked the bridge to pass the word back to the sweeping deck, "stream taut wire." Soon the recorder on the bulkhead in front of me was clicking away merrily measuring our slow advance towards the coast of France. The Decca plot and Robbie's scanner all agreed perfectly. With the tide on our beam I found we were edging to the east. I reported this to the Captain on the bridge voice pipe, and heard him give an order for the flotilla to alter course together to the westward. We all moved over ready to start the sweep at the point planned.

'Now it was time to drop the first lighted buoy. I gave the order "stand by" and then "let go." Way back astern of us it marked the entrance to our channel, and the bridge reported that it was sitting up straight and flashing the right colour sequence.

'The Captain came down the ladder to have a quick look at the plot. The tide was much stronger than any of us anticipated. Accurate information of the speed and direction of the tidal stream was a little sparse. I was now relying entirely on the Decca dials to show the immediate drift out of line. The Captain was a bit puzzled. Was I sure the "gas meter" was giving the right answer? We checked back with all available information. Back up the ladder he went. I had to call for yet another alteration to the westward to keep our line straight at this very slow sweeping speed . . .

'One of the MLs ahead protecting our bow from shallow set mines, pulled out of line. It was bad weather for his very light sweeping gear. Maybe he parted his wire or cut a mine set to stop us at the edge of the minefield. It was getting very hot in the charthouse. The wind was still fresh and the movement of the ship much more than we would choose for good sweeping . . . The familiar noise of a distant exploding mine came once . . . twice. Someone had put up a couple. That was two ships saved . . . The Captain came to the bridge voice pipe. I could hear him crunching a dry biscuit. He sounded a bit tense . . . I tried to reassure him that all our fixes and plotted positions agreed, and suggest a new course five degrees to starboard. The tide had slackened. We reduce speed by half a knot . . . I called up to the Captain that we were ahead of our ETA.

' "Look here, Pilot, if I reduce speed any further we shall not be able to sweep anything" grumbled the Captain down the voice pipe.

'With the tide now quite slack, we were steering the true course for Gold Beach. My eyes were sore and tired . . . I checked the position once more on Robbie's plot, read off the measured distance over the sea bed on the taut wire, looked again as it began to clatter round at a furious speed. *HMS Friendship* our next astern must have caught our wire in his sweep as he turned out of line to the west. A few seconds of wild clatter, then it parted and silence.

' "That's one less dial to check" said Robbie.

'The east tide set was beginning, which meant we had to change sweep wires to the opposite quarter. Solemnly we turned together to steam back down the lane we had just searched.

'After a bit of slanging on the compass platform and argument about the position of the last lighted dan buoy, the dial needles stopped and started slowly moving in the opposite direction. Uncanny — it seemed as if we had some wire overhead like a tram that not only showed us the direction but the speed at which we were steaming, to make good the course over the ground. Again we turned south and veered our starboard sweeps. The tail end trawler laying the dan buoys signalled that he was mixing it with the first of the landing craft. The Captain came down to inspect the plot.

' "We seem too damn close, Pilot. I can see the French coast quite clearly. Which of your many calculations puts us nearest to the guns on Pointe de Ver?"

'Together we checked the last fixes on my chart, showing clearly how we had reversed in a tight circle, back tracked, turned 180° to continue from the other side of the lane without missing a yard of unswept water.

'Slowly we creep southwards to the end of our lane. So still and quiet on the bridge that I can hear someone by the voice pipe sharpen a pencil. Exact moment now to lay the dan buoy, then turn 90° to port and search the area for the bombardment ships to anchor . . . Our whole flotilla is now facing east. Surely the broad silhouette of our hull must be visible to those guns ashore. Still not a shot is fired.

'I had been in the charthouse now for 15 hours plotting and fixing. Robbie now made his final check with the GEE plot. Scratch (Secretary) came in with the result of his night's work on the ARL wheelhouse plot. I looked once more at my dials on Decca. We had found the right beach, the troops would go ashore at the right spot.'

Combined Operations Pilotage Parties (COPPs)

The part played by (N) officers in the various amphibious assaults which took place during the war deserves special mention and in particular those who were members of what was known as Beach Reconnaissance Assault Pilotage Parties (Commandos) but which, because of the highly secret nature of their work were designated Combined Operations Pilotage Parties or COPPs. The officer responsible for their inception was Lieutenant Commander (N) (now Captain) Nigel Clogstoun-Willmot DSO DSC RN (Retired) who, after twice volunteering for special service, was appointed Navigating Officer to the Force Commander of an assault force assigned to carry out a raid on the island of Rhodes in the spring of 1941. In a letter to the author, Willmot says, 'despite air reconnaissance it was plain that disaster was on the cards since no one could tell what the beaches were like (bars etc) and the charts differed in places by a mile from one another. I felt that someone who knew what he was about should have a look-see and draw up sailing directions, sketches etc. The Army also were keen to know about exits and to be landed accurately. Most landing craft being armoured had not even got an accurate compass.

'The security angle appalled the Commander in Chief (Admiral Sir Andrew Cunningham) and his staff but eventually everyone was impelled by the logic of the matter to agree. So together with a Captain of Commandos (Roger Courtenay) and with the help of a submarine, canoes, and swimming we paid visits to Rhodes and examined the inclination of the beaches (including that in front of the hotel being used as the Axis headquarters) and the flower beds. Being March we were very cold and wet having no modern swimsuits at that time. It was very successful but the Germans invaded Greece and the assault was cancelled.'

Subsequently Willmot became involved in training RNVR officers in the navigation side of assaults and in planning, as well as experiments in beach reconnaissance. He found himself for a time (N) of an RAF Long Range Intelligence

Unit attached to a Long Range Desert Group, an unusual assignment which, he says, was foretold by a Sikh fortune teller in Ceylon way back in 1930.

The full story of the further exploits of Clogstoun-Willmot and his teams is told in two books (*Survey by Starlight* by Lieutenant (N) Ralph Stanbury and *The Secret Invaders* by B Strutton and N Pearson, both published by Hodder and Stoughton) and it is one of which the branch may well be proud.

Mr G R Talbot who left the Hospital Service to join one of the COPP units writes, 'after qualifying as an N, my temporary naval service was conspicuously more outstanding for the things we trained to do (or nearly did) than for the things we actually achieved.' He recalls 'a fruitless rush to India to prepare the projected landings in the Andaman/Nicobar Islands; a rush back to join an S class submarine to survey Rhodes harbour which was cancelled as they got into their canoes; back to Cairo then off to do the Anzio beach-head survey; then assistance to the American forces advancing up the west coast of Italy until Civitavechia fell, followed by attachment to Tito's Partisans for three to four months which included numerous surveys and pilotages for the Partisans under the command of Commander (later Rear Admiral) Morgan Giles GM; then on to the recapture of Greece and on up the coast to Salonika and back to Athens for the civil war and the casualties which resulted. Quite a full year' he adds, 'although quiet compared with the Health Service nowadays.'

The AITC carries on

While all the epoch-making events related earlier were taking place in the main

Harbour defence launches preceeding Bangor class minesweepers sweeping channels for the invasion forces.

building at Southwick House, the work of the AITC in the converted stables carried on. After a brief shutdown for maintenance at the beginning of April, training was resumed. The Centre now included a mock-up of the Operations Room in the new battleship, *Vanguard* and one of a weapons class destroyers was nearing completion. On 3 May the Deputy Controller, Vice Admiral C E B Simeon CB accompanied by the Naval Secretary, Rear Admiral (later Admiral Sir Cecil) J Harcourt CB visited the AITC and were clearly convinced of the future importance of the organization to all ships of the fleet.

On 26 June 1944, three weeks after the historic decision to launch the invasion had been taken by General Eisenhower in the library of Southwick House, Lieutenant Commander M E Butler-Bowdon joined the AITC as a relief for Lieutenant Commander Tibbits. 'I soon learnt', he writes, 'that the whole of the front part of the house was out of bounds except with all sorts of special passes and we could only enter by the back door. There was a sentry across the passage leading to the dining room barring access to the front of the building for non-pass-holders. Tibbits showed me the existing mock-ups which included a destroyer's Operations Room called Hotspur in the south-west corner of the stables on the ground floor. It contained an ARL table wired up to move at own ship's course and speed while at the end of the first floor passage reached by an outside staircase from Hotspur was another ARL table and numerous gadgets which were known as the Cookhouse because with these, various situations could be conjured up for passing to the models. The Cookhouse was manned by Wren Plotters with an officer in charge.

After a visit by the Director of Electric Engineering, Sir James Pringle, on 15 June, two weeks later a special demonstration was laid on for the representatives of his department which was now located at Bath. Then on 20 July, Admiral Sir Bruce (later Lord) Fraser (of North Cape) Commander in Chief designate of the British Pacific Fleet visited the Centre accompanied by the ACNS(W) Rear Admiral Wilfred Patterson, and expressed considerable interest in the models and their equipment.

On 3 August, Lieutenant Commander Tibbits, having completed his turn over to Commander M E Butler-Bowdon (he had been promoted on 30 June) and who had with such marked success and in the face of many difficulties, created the Action Information Training Centre out of a pile of old buildings, went back to sea as (N) officer of the battleship *Anson*. It is impossible to speak too highly of his achievement. When he handed over, exactly one year after the original board decision to build had been given, a total of 1,616 officers and men had undergone training or visited the AITC. Amongst the visitors were 10 flag officers and two Commodores. The staff now consisted of two Lieutenant Commanders, seven Lieutenants, one Electrical Lieutenant, one Headmaster Lieutenant, and two Third Officer WRNS together with nine ratings, and 30 Wren plotters, aircraft directors, radar mechanics, and administrative staff.

Radar Plot Ratings

As has been mentioned, it had become evident that the training of Radar Plotters should be extended to include surface plotting and on 1 June 1944 proposals to transfer the training of these ratings from Yeovilton to the AITC were put forward by *Dryad*. The branch, which had been created in 1940 was, at that time, only open to hostilities only ratings and responsibility for their training had been vested originally in the Captain of the Signal School, *Mercury*. In 1941 a new school, *Valkyrie* at Douglas in the Isle of Man was commissioned and equipped for training them in part I of their syllabus (radar), part II (air plotting) being carried out at Yeovilton. In 1943 responsibility for their training was transferred to the Captain Radar Training, *Collingwood*, and the branch was split into two categories, viz Radar Plotters (RP) and Radar Control (RC). It was not, however, until November 1944 that board approval was given to a docket raised by DTSD supporting *Dryad's* proposals. This decision which became effective on 1 November 1945 marked an important turning point in the history of the (N) branch since, for the first time, it became responsible for the training and welfare of a branch of ratings.

Expansion of the (N) branch in the Admiralty

With the establishment of a material section of the (N) branch early in 1944 and the need to supervise the fitting of AIO entailing the re-arrangement of bridge layouts and much close supervision and inspection, it was necessary to have the staff to carry out these duties and a steady trickle of appointments ensued. Soon the three small offices tucked away in a corner of the area occupied by a sprawling Hydrographic department on the second floor of the Old Admiralty building were bursting at the seams. In a docket HO 207/44 dated 27 June 1944 D of N pointed out that unless given extra office space, he would be unable to implement the Board decision which approved his material section. Dusty storerooms unoccupied for years were cleaned and brought into use; then on 3 July he was informed that the new section would have to move to Cadogan Square, a decision which was wholly impracticable. However, the situation was saved when it was decided that the Hydrographic department, with the exception of the Hydrographer himself and a small operational chart section, should move to Taunton. This enabled the Navigation branch to move into much more spacious quarters and remain together.

Departure of Admiral Ramsay (ANCXF) and his staff

On September 8, Admiral Sir Bertram Ramsay and his staff vacated Southwick House and moved to France. Before his departure Admiral Ramsay handed the author a letter in which he expressed his thanks to the officers and ship's company of *HMS Dryad* 'for the manifold kindness and unfailing help' which he and his whole staff had received during their four and a half months stay in *Dryad* and in conversation he remarked on the splendid work of the (N) officers in the marking submarines, the minesweeping flotillas, and the assault groups on whom so much depended. He bequeathed to the Navigation School the famous wall map on which the movements of all forces taking part in the invasion of Normandy were plotted, which adorns the east wall of the former drawing room, and he also gave us the flag which he had worn during his stay. It is thanks to my successor, Vice Admiral Sir Charles Norris, that the famous D Day wall map is so well preserved.

Realising its great historic value and liability to damage, he sought official approval for the construction of a glass case to protect it, but strange to relate, this was not forthcoming until, with the concurrence of the Commander in Chief, Portsmouth, he made a personal visit to the Admiralty and requested a written statement relieving him of all responsibility for the preservation of this unique monument to a wonderful and successful feat of arms without parallel in our history, unless immediate approval was given to his request. His forthright attitude had the desired effect and for this all members, past and present of the (N) and (ND) branch will always be grateful.

The map reset to show the position of the various forces at H hour on D day was unveiled on 7 August 1946 by Rear Admiral (later Admiral of the Fleet Sir) George Creasy who had been Admiral Ramsay's Chief of Staff. After Captain Norris had welcomed the distinguished allied audience attending the ceremony and emphasised 'how intensely proud all in *Dryad* are to house and cherish these valuable relics of the last war' he invited Admiral Creasy to unveil it. Before doing so the Admiral made a short speech in which he recalled the circumstances attending on the launching of the invasion and went on to say, 'I think that we can justly claim that this house was in fact the literal pin point of the invasion operation and that here flourished in its richest and highest form that splendid spirit of international and interservice co-operation and understanding, as Captain Norris has so aptly described it, on which the success of the whole operation essentially depended.'

Presentation to General Dwight D Eisenhower

Although it means running ahead of the narrative, it seems appropriate to round off the story of *Dryad's* close connection with the Normandy invasion by recording two events which took place subsequently. As General Eisenhower was unable to be present at the unveiling of the D day wall map, a recording was made of the ceremony and ultimately found its way to the British Joint Services Mission in Washington DC when the author was serving there as Chief of Staff. On instructions from the Admiralty, I arranged to call on the General who was then President of Colombia University, New York, and he kindly invited me to lunch. After I had made the presentation, he announced that he had invited two other Generals to join us but unfortunately neither of them was able to accept and so we would be lunching *a deux*. It was fascinating to hear this great man's views on many facets of the war in which he played such a prominent part.

General Eisenhower revisited *Dryad* on 6 August 1963 in connection with a D day film being made by the CBS network to mark the 20th anniversary of the invasion and he reminisced in front of the wall map for about an hour. He was shown the plaque in the former library which commemorates the historic decision described above.

Normandy invasion painting

A painting by the well known marine artist, the late Mr Norman Wilkinson CBE PRI, made from sketches which he made when embarked in a destroyer of the covering force on D Day, was subscribed for by officers of the branch and unveiled by Admiral Sir John Frewen GCB on 9 May 1965 in the presence of the artist, Lady Ramsay, and some 170 subscribers and their wives. The historic painting covers the west wall of the ante room in which the D day wall map is preserved. The artist generously donated to the School the original sketches from which it was made.

The spoils of the invasion advantage the AITC

On the departure of the 'visitors' the Navigation School inherited, not only some 100 Nissen huts but also a vast quantity of equipment in the way of furniture, desks, bedding, office equipment, stationery, in fact everything which was in short supply after five years of war. It proved to be a most welcome windfall. Not long afterwards, the staff and pupils exiled to Greenwich returned to the fold and gradually the School's navigation side returned to normal. The AITC now had full rein to develop and an increasing number of officers and men underwent courses there. Commander Butler-Bowdon continued the good work of his predecessor and in a letter to the author recalls the reluctance of some officers to accept the new doctrine.

'In lecture to senior officers about the use of the bridge operations room, I suggested that the important thing was for them to be where they could best make use of all the information available and this meant remaining there until the last moment and perhaps in certain circumstances engaging the enemy from there where they could make better use of the picture which radar was now able to provide. There was some shaking of heads and often murmurs of, "always fight my ship from the bridge, old boy." '

The next addition to the mock-ups was a cruiser type bridge operations room and it was soon evident that further additions to the staff would be necessary. Hearing that the torpedomen were somewhat put out that they had not been entrusted with the development of AIO, Butler-Bowdon journeyed over to Roedean, near Brighton whither the Torpedo School, *HMS Vernon,* had been evacuated after being bombed out of Portsmouth, and returned with a definite promise of a Torpedo Officer to add to his staff. He gradually collected representatives from all the specialist branches except the Engineers and Surveyors. However, it was not always easy to reconcile the different points of view as Captain Colin Shand recalls. 'I had an office containing a motley collection of Lieutenant Commanders from Whaley, *Vernon, Dolphin,* Leydene, and an aviator and the rows and arguments which occasionaly arose over the conflicting views of *Dryad* and the those of the gunnerymen, torpedomen, signalmen etc often grew to riotous proportions. It was sometimes necessary to quell the riot and settle the argument once and for all and for this purpose I kept in the bottom drawer of my desk, a golden top-hat (left over from some pantomime I suspect). When donned, the motley crew fell silent (or were supposed to) while – like the Pope pronouncing infallibly *ex cathedra* – I gave the gospel according to *Dryad* which was then adopted as the official policy.'

The training schedule now included all the Qualifiers courses who in 1944 numbered eight and 10 respectively, nine Fighter Direction Officers, five First

The Supreme Allied Commander, General Dwight D Eisenhower, with Admiral Sir Bertram Ramsay, outside the entrance to Southwick House.

Class Ship course officers, and three who took the (D) course. Of the above one was RAN, one RCN, one RNZN, and three RCNVR. All Sub Lieutenants doing the Pilotage course were also trained in the AITC, and any Commanding Officers who wished to send their prospective AIO crews for pre-commissioning training were welcome to do so. Every opportunity was taken to send the Wren plotters to sea in ships within the Solent — Spithead defences so that they could see for themselves the turning circles of ships of different classes because in the Cookhouse they tended to ignore this factor; it also provided them with the chance to see the equipment they were using in its proper surroundings.

By early 1945 syllabuses of training for the RP branch had been finalized and courses were in full swing. In addition to the cruiser and destroyer models there was now one of a carrier. Non-substantive badges for the branch had been designed, approved, and sealed. It is of interest to note that the Royal Australian Navy was also busy setting up an AITC in Australia.

In the field of equipment the results of five years of intensive war development were bearing fruit and much new equipment was beginning to appear in the fleet. New radar sets of greatly increased power and discrimination were coming into service and the first airborne early warning sets and auto radar plots had been developed. Some fleet escorts were being equipped as radar pickets to extend the surface warning cover of the fleet on the lines which US Third/Fifth fleets operating in the Pacific had found to be necessary. All these developments greatly increased the load both on training and ship-fitting and the staff at *Dryad* and in the D of N's Department in London found themselves fully extended.

By the end of 1944 it was patently obvious that as a result of the growth of the AIO and the responsibility for its development which the (N) branch had assumed, the Navigation School would never be able to return to its former home in the dockyard. After the death of Colonel Thistlethwayte, the Southwick property had passed to his nephew, Mr Borthwick-Norton and about this time an enquiry was received from the latter's solicitors asking when the Admiralty intended to start restoring the property to its original state, in accordance with the terms of the lease. Having regard to the alterations and additions made to accommodate ANCXF and his staff, to say nothing of the conversion of the stables to meet the needs of the AITC, this was going to be a very expensive operation. The author discussed the matter with the Director of Navigation who was of the same opinion, but the wheels of officialdom grind extremely slowly and it was not until 1948 that negotiations for the purchase of the property were begun.

On February 8 1945 the author was relieved in command of *Dryad* by Captain (later Vice Admiral Sir) Charles Norris who, once the war was over, by courtesy of the new owner of Southwick Park, was able to enjoy the shooting which had given Admiral James so much pleasure.

Intake of Qualifiers during the war years

During the war years 1939 — 1945 inclusive the intake of officers who qualified in (N) was as follows:

1939	17	(including 2 RAN and 1 RIN)
1940	12	
1941	16	(including 1 RAN, 1 RCN, and 2 Thai Navy)
1942	13	
1943	16	(including 1 RCN and 1 RNZN)
1944	17	(including 1 RAN)
1945	22	(including 1 RAN, 4 RCN and 2 RNZN)
Total	113	

In addition to the above, a number of courses were held for Reserve officers who were granted an (N*) qualification. A total of 22 officers were granted a First Class Ship qualification. Out of the total of 113 Qualifiers five reached flag rank (See Appendix III).

The first year after the war, 1946, was a bumper year with a total intake of 70 officers, seven of whom were from the RCN and two from the RAN. Of these 26 qualified (ND) and 31 (D) — 13 fell by the wayside. The large intake is accounted for by replacements of RNVR officers by those of the RN. Included amongst the (ND) qualifiers was Lieutenant (now Rear Admiral) B G G Place VC who had gained this distinction in command of midget submarine X7 during a hazardous and successful attack on the German battleship *Tirpitz* in Kaa Fiord on 22 September 1943.

ND memorial book

A book containing the names of all the officers of the branch killed on active service during the two world wars was dedicated at the Southwick Parish Church of St James-without-the Priory Gate on 11 November 1953 in the presence of Admiral of the Fleet Sir Henry Oliver and a large number of brother officers of all ages. The ceremony was conducted by the Chaplain of the Fleet, the Venerable Archdeacon F N Chamberlain. The lambskin vellum sheets on which the names were inscribed were the gift of Captain Sir David Tibbits DSC and they were illuminated by an Admiralty draughtsman, Mr Crowcher, who had been brought up in one of the lodges at the entrance to Southwick Park. The covers were made from oak taken from the old brewery staircase, displaced when the AITC was constructed. They were fashioned and carved by joiner Albert Kerry who was serving in *Dryad* at the time.

Chapter V

THE EVOLUTION OF AIRCRAFT DIRECTION

'Show me the way to go home, I'm tired and I wanna go to bed'

Old musical hall song

'There are in the world a great variety of spoken sounds and each has a distinct meaning. But if the sounds of the speakers voice mean nothing to me I am a foreigner to him and he is a foreigner to me'

I Corinthians XIV verse 10, J B Phillips Translation

Note The author is indebted to Captain Charles Coke DSO and Commander David L Pollock RNVR, both leading pioneers in the development of fighter direction in the RN, for the substance of the last part of this chapter.

In the previous chapter, mention was made of how the need for fighter protection for shipping arose on the outbreak of war and how the development of radar led to the ability to direct aircraft and so greatly improve our chances of intercepting those of the enemy. After its brief and costly brush with the German Luftwaffe during the Norwegian campaign, the Home Fleet, once its main base at Scapa Flow had been made secure and provided with adequate AA defences, did not become seriously engaged with the formidable German Air Force until the latter began to attack the convoys to North Russia in 1942. In the Mediterranean, however, as has been mentioned, the fleet was constantly engaged with the Italian Regia Aeronautica from the time that Italy entered the war in June 1940.

Unfortunately the control of the air over the fleet by naval fighters came to an abrupt end on 10 January 1941, when the carrier, *Illustrious* was heavily attacked and severely damaged by aircraft from Fliegerkorps X of the Luftwaffe which had been moved to Sicily. Although she was replaced for a period by the carrier, *Formidable,* the Luftwaffe succeeded within six months in making the eastern Mediterranean untenable for major fleet units, and inflicted heavy losses on the ships engaged in operations in the Aegean Sea in support of Greece and subsequently in the evacuation of Crete.

Many causes contributed to this sudden change of fortune but first among them were the great superiority of the German aircraft over the carrier-borne fighters both in performance and numbers, and the complete inability of the methods of fighter direction then available to counter the tactics of the highly trained German squadrons with the experience they had gained during the Battle of Britain.

It became clear that a new appreciation must be made if ships of the fleet were to be able to operate within range of German aircraft. Large numbers of modern single-seater fighters operating simultaneously from several carriers in company were a first essential. Secondly radar and its use and application needed radical improvement far beyond anything previously known at sea.

It is of interest that the final stages of the 1940/41 period in the Mediterranean were witnessed by observers from the US Navy who were able to profit from the lessons thus learned when they returned to their own country in devising the great aircraft direction organization referred to later which played such an important part in the war in the Pacific and which made much use of methods initiated by both the RN and the RAF.

1941 - 1942

A new and more determined effort was now made to meet the setbacks encountered during the previous six months. In addition to the introduction of single-seater Sea Hurricanes and Gruman Martlets, radio-telephone (R/T) communications with fighters was standardized, a longer range and lower scanning air warning radar set, Type 281 was fitted in some ships and a start was made with the selection and training of fighter direction officers.

The advent of single seater fighters brought additional problems over homing. Although these aircraft were fitted with beacon receivers, pilots never found them wholly reliable and the less experienced ones came to rely on homing vectors to bring them back to the ship. With no facilities for fixing aircraft beyond accurate plotting, a heavy additional responsibility thus fell on the fighter direction officer.

The establishment of the Fighter Direction Centre at Yeovilton

In May 1941 on completion of a spell of duty in the carrier *HMS Ark Royal* attached to Force H in the Mediterranean, Lieutenant Commander (later Captain) Charles Coke proposed to the Naval Air Division of the Admiralty the creation of a School of Fighter Direction, the need for which had been forcibly demonstrated to him whilst serving in the *Ark Royal*. After overcoming the opposition which all new suggestions inevitably encounter he was appointed to the Royal Naval Air Station at Yeovilton to put his ideas into practice.

'I first spent a week at the Controllers' Training Unit at Fighter Command (of the RAF)' he writes, 'and then I went to Yeovilton to set up the School. The first requirement was a radar set, but we had none and could not expect any authority to deprive the front line of so important a piece of equipment for the benefit of a Training School. However I sought out the RAF officer who controlled the supply of radar sets for the Air Force and I persuaded him to lend me a set from Branscombe Down, about 50 miles from Yeovilton. I took a party of ratings

'The Squadron Navigating Officer' by Sir Muirhead Bone. (Commander C J Wynne-Edwards DSC* RN)

there and we managed (although we had never seen such a thing before) to dismantle the set and bring it back to Yeovilton in three lorries. It was erected and, after repairs and maintenance, it worked. With this radar set and with aircraft from the Fighter School, we had the minimum equipment necessary for live interceptions, using plotting equipment which we designed and made ourselves.

The Fighter School, however, could not spare enough aircraft for training FDOs and so a simulated or dummy system of teaching interceptions was essential. I adopted a ground training system which I had seen used by Fighter Command and which I modified to suit naval purposes. It involved the use of tricycles on the flat ground of the airfield, each fitted with an aircraft compass to give the course to steer, and with an aircraft radio set for communication. A metronome mounted on the handlebars enable the rider to control the tricycle's speed whilst a slit cut in a wooden shield on the front of the machine gave him the same angle of view as that of a pilot from an aircraft. The function of the radar was simulated by two men with azimuth bearing plates, whose lines of sight to the centre of the airfield area were at right angles. These took bearings of each tricycle in turn and transmitted the information to the fighter direction position. Thus the officer under instruction had the position of the various tricycles/aircraft plotted for him and could order the courses and speeds necessary to make an interception.

But there was difficulty in getting the equipment required. A demand on naval stores for six tricycles elicited the reply that tricycles were not a store article, though the compasses would be supplied, and as regards metronomes, one was allowed to an Admiral's band and two to that of a Commander in Chief, what could I possibly mean by ordering six?

In the event the tricycles were bought from Messrs Walls, the ice-cream vendors, who had closed down for the war, and the metronomes from the rather surprised owner of a musical instrument shop in Taunton.

At first this simulated system was ridiculed by all, and many an embryo FDO expressed himself bored with pedalling a tricycle throughout a hot summer afternoon. (Unless, of course, one of our two Wrens was pedalling a tricycle/bomber, in which case the fighters often pedalled faster than they were ordered to!). Nevertheless the system did indeed provide splendid elementary training at no cost whatever, and it was soon accepted.'

After a brush with the Director of Radio Equipment without whose authority the system had been installed and who demanded its immediate dismantling, which caused Coke to follow Nelson's example of the blind eye, he continues his story.

'The first course began in July 1941 and the second at the end of August. The pupils on these courses were mainly enthusiastic RNVR officers who had already been directing fighters at sea and who wished to qualify and to improve their skill (in particular one can mention David Pollock who brought with him some of his friends and who did much to help progress with fighter direction). Their standard was excellent, but thereafter it was exceedingly difficult to obtain officers with the very quick mind which the job demanded. Moreover I constantly received appeals from sea for reliable FDOs to replace the temporary and unqualified ones in whom the pilots had little confidence.

'I put the problem to Admiral Boyd, just home from commanding the carriers

The control tower of the Aircraft Direction Centre at Yeovilton.

in the Mediterranean and he in turn persuaded the Fifth Sea Lord, Admiral Sir A L St G Lyster, to call a meeting to discuss the provision of FDOs. As a result I was given the choice of the newly qualified officers leaving *King Alfred.* With the help of the Instructor Commander there, likely candidates were interviewed from the 70 or so who passed out each week, and I had no further difficulties. Indeed the standard remained high and the fourth course included a university lecturer, a future Olympic gold medalist for dinghy sailing, the headmaster of a public school, an actor, and a doctor, all highly intelligent RNVR officers.

By September ideas and practices had crystalized enough to enable a pamphlet to be produced defining standard practices for use in the fleet. This was clearly an important step forward as standard codes enabled any ship with radar to direct any fighters sent to protect her, no matter their origin.

In the autumn of 1941 a mock-up of a ship's Fighter Direction Position was built in the control tower at Yeovilton and this enabled the pupils, many of whom had scarcely any acquaintance with the sea, to obtain a much clearer picture of what to expect. We also gave fighter direction training to the front

Part of the original Walls ice cream fleet, (left) on display and (right) a wartime shot of Lt Commander C P Coke RN (ONCO) under direction aboard his trike.

line fighter squadrons passing through Yeovilton during their working up period.'

On taking up sea appointments, in many cases the newly qualified FDOs had little more than lecture notes of the equipment they would require, but with instructions to fit out Aircraft Direction Rooms in their ships to the best of their ability. There were no staff requirements or schedules of equipment, but a helpful Admiralty issued the ships concerned with orders which were magnificent in their simplicity — Full facilities for fighter direction are to be fitted!

Commanding Officers, Torpedo Officers, Radar Officers, Signal Officers, and ships artisans all lent a hand and those carriers which were being re-fitted in the US had the advantage of being able to draw on American supplies. Admiral's sea cabins were hurriedly transformed into Fighter Direction Rooms with sufficient space for two officers and a rating to work; visits to New York produced more efficient high frequency R/T transmitters, inter-office loud speakers (intercoms) and much else that was new to HM Ships. Shortly before Christmas 1942, three fleet carriers happened to be together at Norfolk, Virginia and a comparison of their equipment revealed a considerable variety of method but many of the better ideas of each were standardized.

In December 1941, while awaiting a new appointment, Lieutenant Commander (later Commander) A T Fleming applied for a fighter direction course and subsequently relieved Lieutenant Commander Coke in charge of the FDC at Yeovilton when the latter went back to sea as Staff Officer Operations to Vice Admiral Sir Lumley Lyster who was about to hoist his flag in the carrier *Victorious*, as Vice Admiral Aircraft Carriers. 'I was soon able to see that important improvements had been achieved at sea since I left the *Ark Royal* 18 months before,' writes Coke. 'The FDO was now a qualified man and no longer an amateur consultant. Radar, and especially people's understanding of it had improved (though in 1943 a General wearing a VC and two DSOs who was dining with Lyster, turned to me and said, "now tell me, what exactly IS radar?"). Many more fighter pilots had confidence in the system and were willing to co-operate and the supply of crystal-controlled, push-button HF radio sets in many fighters enabled the pilot to be in instant voice contact with the FDO.'

Operation Pedestal

In August 1942 the hardest fought convoy to Malta, Operation Pedestal, provided a severe test of fighter direction. Three carriers were included in the convoy's powerful escort force, *Victorious, Indomitable,* and *Eagle,* while the *Furious* carried a squadron of Spitfires for the reinforcement of Malta. 'Carriers had not previously operated their fighters in company,' remarks Coke, 'so a means by which they would be able to do so had to be worked out. Admiral Lyster, who was an exceptionally gifted and practical seaman, devised an almost circular screen inside which each carrier would operate independently as far as possible, the whole force being turned into the wind only when absolutely necessary. There were special arrangements for screening a carrier which was forced to break through her screen.

'The fighter direction organization for Pedestal was based on the following principles:

'In quiet periods, each carrier in turn was to do a 12 hour stint as duty carrier and to keep a small fighter patrol in the air with others at readiness.

'Radio and radar silence was to be broken only when it was known that the enemy was aware of the convoy's presence. It was not always easy to be certain of this.

'When the force came under attack, the VAA would co-ordinate the effort of all carriers. (I achieved this by installing an aircraft radio set on the flag deck of each carrier and piping it down to the FDO. This provided an essential command wave).

'The above principles were purposely designed to be loose in order to give flexibility, and in the event, though the convoys came under very heavy attack, and received considerable damage, they worked well and set a pattern for the future.'

Although the equipment and the efficiency of the fighter direction organization at sea had steadily improved, the conditions in which the personnel manning it were obliged to operate left a lot to be desired. The shortage of personnel in most ships was such that officers and men were watch and stop on. Often for days on end they remained at their posts in poorly ventilated and cramped compartments living on bully beef sandwiches brought to them when a member of the team could be spared to fetch them. Their devotion to duty deserves high praise.

Further development of the Fighter Direction Centre

On taking over the FDC at Yeovilton, Fleming was thankful to find that approval had been given to Coke and the FDOs at sea to correspond direct with him so that, as he says 'there was an unimpeded exchange of information, ideas, questions and answers.'

After the loss of the *Audacity* (the former German merchant ship *Hannover* which had been fitted with a flight deck and carried six Martlet fighters) the first of the invaluable auxiliary or escort carriers, her FDO Acting Temporary Sub Lieutenant John Parry RNVR who in private life was a Cambridge don, joined the staff of the FDC. According to Fleming he possessed, 'the clearest brain and greatest economy of language I have ever met' and received a belated MBE and accelerated promotion to Sub Lieutenant RNVR for his part in bringing about the destruction of two FW Condor aircraft before his ship sank.

'In those days,' continues Fleming, 'the FDO used to work on a 30 inch plotting diagram in the charthouse, assisted by a plotting rating and a radio operator. The chaos which ensued when hostile aircraft were detected and the Admiral, Captain, Commander (Flying), and not least the (N) officer all wanted a look-see, can well be imagined.'

'In addition to training, our job at the FDC was to find some way of compressing the lavish lay-out of an RAF Fighter Command operations room with its AA fire control liaison, into such space as could be made available in the island structure of a carrier and devise the necessary internal communications. Fortunately we had an early break-through when visiting the Radar Establishment at Malvern we saw two boffins working on an idea of displaying information in a darkened control room by means of fluorescent grease pencil marking on a glass screen edge-lit by ultra violet light. We suddenly realised that we could fit a vertical glass display board and feed it with information on one side leaving the other clear for the FDO and his intercept officers, except for the filter officer who had to keep the evaluated plot.'

During the early part of 1942, three fleet carriers, *Indomitable, Illustrious* and *Formidable* were in the Indian Ocean while the fleet carriers *Victorious* and *Furious* were with the Home Fleet. Those in the Indian Ocean had particularly good opportunities for working up in the period of relative calm which followed the withdrawal of the major units of the Japanese fleet into the Pacific. Numerous exercises in the co-ordinated defence of a fleet by two or more carriers were carried out and much learnt of practical Fighter direction. Similar exercises were carried out under the more restricted conditions available in the Home Fleet.

Experience soon showed that the facilities which had been based on single carrier operations in the Mediterranean were inadequate. Filter plots comparable with those used by the RAF had to be separated from the intercept plots and provision had to be made in carrier flagships for a Fleet FDO in a position where he could follow the course of an attack and have a separate RT line of communication to other carriers.

Minor adaptations and the fitting of a vertical plot against a bulkhead were carried out by the ship's staff in *Illustrious* while at Colombo and a more elaborate lay-out based on current RAF practice in England, was fitted similarly in *Victorious* while in home waters. In the absence of staff requirements at that time, improvements were largely the result of private enterprise, the enthusiasm and co-operation of ship's staff, and the goodwill of commanding officers.

'We were under tremendous pressure,' says Fleming, 'to get some form of operations room into the carriers about to take part in operation Pedestal'.

100

'One single nissen hut and one room in the control tower on the aerodrome at Yeovilton were quite inadequate. We chucked our army protectors out of Speckington Manor in which we put our offices, lecture rooms and radio station and acquired the farmer's large stone barn and cider press as four walls and a roof to hold mock-ups of operations rooms in which we could try out our ideas and carry out training . . . Luck was on our side when we found a civil contractor with labour available to do the job provided we got Admiralty approval within 48 hours!, after which he would have to release his men.

'Time was too short to use the proper service channels and it was with some trepidation that I awaited a visit from the Board of Admiralty in early autumn. However, Pedestal had proved the point and our cynicism in naming the two aircraft carrier operations room layouts *Impossible* and *Impracticable* was unfounded as they were adopted for *Indomitable* and the new light fleet carriers.'

Although some war experience was gained during the invasion of Madagascar, it was not until Operation Pedestal in August 1942, that these preparations were fully tested. A large number of interceptions were carried out successfully and many hostile aircraft were shot down – 36 were destroyed by *Indomitable's* fighters in one day – but the price was too high. Many ships of the convoy were lost, the carrier *Eagle* was sunk and *Indomitable* was damaged. It was clear that although there had been a marked improvement in the standard of fighter defence, we were a long way from achieving even local air superiority. Better fighter aircraft and better fighter direction were urgently needed. So far as the latter was concerned there were obvious shortcomings in personnel, equipment and space.

A perspex air plot in the operations room of a modern warship.

The broad beams of the naval air warning radar sets quickly produced saturation whenever a large number of aircraft were in the sky, with the result that enemy aircraft could slip through undetected and lost fighters could not be identified and homed. Better arrangements for filtering and tracking were essential as also was some form of PPI presentation. Low scanning radar and height finding were still inadequate to enable the interception of squadrons with any knowledge of the limitations of our radar sets.

The fatigue of concentration in a hot climate for days on end imposed too great a strain on officers and men to enable them to maintain the standard of warning necessary to allow the remainder of the ship's company to be kept at a relatively low state of readiness. Once again the attack was outstripping the defence. If fleets at sea were to be able to fulfil their classic role within range of air attack, a reassessment of the whole concept of fighter direction was needed. However it required a serious set-back involving grave losses in ships to give such development the required priority and even so the few available scientists were hard put to meet the demand.

1942 - 1944

Equipment. Before Operation Pedestal those fighter direction officers who had seen RAF control stations in action were well aware of the deficiencies in the naval organization. Reports had been made from sea advocating something more like the RAF sector station but incorporating more accurate control on the lines of the RAF GCI station. In some carriers, an attempt had been made using ship's staff to make good the deficiences, but the days of makeshift were passing and the time had come for properly designed equipment and planned lay-outs.

The Air Warfare and Training division of the Admiralty was ready with plans based on RAF practice and the experience of fighter direction officers at sea and anxious to put them into operation. A prototype lay-out was hurriedly installed in the carriers *Victorious* and *Formidable* before they left the UK to provide air cover for operation Torch, the invasion of North Africa in November 1942. The lay-out allowed for a Senior FDO responsible for the whole organization, a main air display plot maintained by an officer and some ratings who were engaged exclusively in plotting and filtering, and two intercept positions at which officers carried out individual interceptions. Although as the result of experience, minor improvements were made and more space and better ventilation provided, this lay-out remained the basis for all subsequent ones throughout the war. In December 1942 when the *Victorious* was temporarily assigned to the US fleet in the Pacific, the prototype lay-out with which she had been fitted for Torch was quickly adopted as a pattern throughout the US Navy.

By the beginning of 1943 the importance of fighter direction was fully recognized both in the Admiralty and at sea and also the fact that it required more serious co-ordination and direction than it had hitherto received. As a result the Director of Air Warfare and Training (DAWT) was made responsible for drawing up staff requirements for all types of ships and the Director of Aircraft Carrier

The navigating officer of the carrier HMS Victorious wearing an aviator's helmet, enabling him to take sights without disturbance from the noise of aircraft.

Requirements (DACR) was made responsible for the provision of equipment and fitting out.

One of the most noteworthy improvements made about this time was the introduction of the vertical internally lit display screen which could be clearly seen by all concerned. A similar advance was made in communications, both internal and external. It was essential to keep the noise level in the fighter direction room as low as possible since the FDO must be able to communicate instantly with the Captain, the Commander (Flying) and other officers. Voice-pipes had proved useless and were replaced by telephones and talk-back systems. There will always remain a doubt, however, in the minds of many wartime FDOs whether the sound-powered telephones with which they were supplied were really the most satisfactory available as they were not comparable to the GPO type used by the RAF for similar purposes.

As equipment became standardized, so too came better and more adequate RT communication systems. The Type 57 set, with which FDOs generally had to make do, was not designed for intensive use. Some ships had managed to procure superior American sets but these were not popular with the communications staff who had to maintain them. The introduction of VHF for all communication with fighter aircraft was a great step forward. When *HMS Indomitable* completed her refit early in 1943 she was equipped with four HF and four VHF transmitters for the exclusive use of the FDO. Although a generous allowance by earlier standards, by 1945 even this scale was inadequate. There were many difficulties to be overcome such as interference between sets and internal ship's noises and although these slowed down progress, with patience and skill they were overcome in time.

Associated with the standardization of equipment was the adoption by all services of the allied standard phonetic alphabet and standard fighter direction code. Ease of communication is a valuable asset in war and the value of a self evident code was demonstrated later in 1943 when a crippled fleet carrier on passage from Malta to Gibraltar was able to control fighters for her own protection involving 11 different services and six different nationalities.

Finally came progress in radar presentation. In 1942 the *Illustrious* had been refused permission to fit an RAF PPI on the grounds that the broad beams of Type 281 would create saturation. Trials, however, showed that although the broad beam gave a result inferior to the narrower beams of the GCI sets used by the RAF, practice enabled a fair interpretation to be made, intercept officers reading their own PPI were able to obtain a better and quicker appreciation than they could from a plot told by the ordinary scan. More plots could be told from a PPI and more raids plotted and intercepted. This led to the adoption by the navy of the skiatron for general use for intercept plots, though officers who had worked in the RAF GCI stations preferred the PPI.

Skiatron and PPI presentation brought night fighter control within the reach of HM Ships and trials using the former were carried out by *Indomitable* in the Irish Sea in the spring of 1943, using RAF aircraft. The results although not up to GCI standard, were promising, but another year was to pass before the necessary equipment became available.

Personnel

The progress made during 1942-43 with the provision of better equipment, created a need for better trained officers and men to use it.

As equipment became more sophisticated and the theory and practice of plotting and controlling aircraft improved, the demand from sea for more thorough training became increasingly insistent. Pilots, quite understandably, could not have confidence in officers who had little experience of service at sea or in the air. The length of the course was gradually increased and ultimately became four months. The corner of the control tower at Yeovilton in which it all began, had been replaced by Speckington Manor in 1941 where there was ample space for mock-ups and training did not interfere with the work of the air station. In the autumn of 1943 Lieutenant Commander (later Rear Admiral) F B P Brayne-Nicholls, who had spent a short while on the staff of the AITC, *Dryad,* was transferred to the FDC at Yeovilton. 'As far as I know,' he writes, 'I was the first Navigating Officer of an airfield.' His task was to prepare syllabuses for Radar Plot ratings in air and surface navigation. At that time there were usually between 60 and 80 officers under training with an instructional staff of about 20, not including the Wrens who played an invaluable part in the training.

As soon as the training of officers had been regularized and FDOs had been granted the status of a specialist (F) branch, the training of ratings followed. Although the need for these was fully recognized at sea, the general shortage of manpower and a certain reluctance on the part of the Admiralty to initiate a new branch, delayed the inception of training. Prior to the autumn of 1942 the FDO in a ship had to accept any ratings whom the Commander could be prevailed upon to spare; hence the efficiency of each ship's organization depended largely on the competence of such ratings as the heads of departments saw fit to spare and the ability of the FDO to train them.

This haphazard method of selection and training was incompatible with the priorities and standard of training which Operations Pedestal and Torch had shown were now mandatory. Without waiting for Board approval, but with the blessing of the Fifth Sea Lord, volunteers for training as Air Plotters were called for from sea and the depots and a hutment School was established at Speckington as well as a small Training Centre at Twatt in the Orkneys. By the end of 1942, a separate air plotting training scheme was in operation and ratings who completed the course were granted the non-substantive rate of Air Plotter and paid accordingly.

The first ship to have a complement of Air Plotters was *Indomitable* on completion of a refit at Christmas 1942. By the summer of 1943, a steady flow of ratings was passing through Speckington and ships commissioning or completing refit acquired some. These ratings subsequently became the Radar Plot ratings mentioned in the last chapter.

Operating experience

During the second half of 1942 and the first half of 1943, a period of reconstruction and improvement supervened to be followed by one of trial and action. The organization was certainly more efficient than it had been hitherto. Seafire aircraft were now in service with the fleet and the new escort carriers were being commissioned. A number of battleships and cruisers had a fighter direction organization of some sort and were capable of controlling a few aircraft and intercepting isolated raids. However, a set back occurred during the invasion of Sicily when *Indomitable* was hit by a low flying aircraft. From the point of view of fighter direction, the incident served to demonstrate the urgent need for a low-scanning radar and the importance of a flexible centralized fleet air reporting organization. In fact two battleships and a cruiser, all of which were fitted with a type of low-scanning radar, obtained plots of the approaching unidentified aircraft but the orders in force did not allow of radio silence being broken to report a single unidentified aircraft.

A further reminder of the navy's shortcomings occurred shortly afterwards in the Aegean when a number of cruisers fitted with the obsolete, pre-1942, system, found themselves incapable of controlling RAF aircraft under the difficult conditions then pertaining in those waters and heavy casualties resulted. It was obvious that a full and up-to-date fighter direction organization was needed in all capital ships and cruisers and not just in carriers.

Meanwhile under the arduous conditions in which the convoys to and from north Russia were obliged to operate, the inclusion of escort carriers was paying big dividends not only in thwarting the attempts of the Luftwaffe to attack the convoys but also in the adaptation of fighter direction methods to the direction of aircraft against U-boats using DF as the primary source of information. This led to the term 'fighter direction' being changed to the broader one 'aircraft direction', but before the change took place the following incident occurred:

'At one stage of the war in 1943, intense north-south air patrols over the western part of the Bay of Biscay by VLR aircraft of Coastal Command working with a killer squadron of fighters were having great success against U-boats on passage to and from ports in western France. So much so that at one time there were believed to be nearly 100 of them waiting to get in or out. A cruiser patrolled in the deep field to the west to cover the frigates against a counter attack by German destroyers based in French ports.

'The natural German reaction was to send out fighter patrols consisting of six Ju88s or Me110s and these in turn inflicted heavy damage on our Liberators and Sunderlands.

'Coastal Command suggested that the cruiser, when proceeding to or from its patrol area, should be routed so as to pass fairly close to the French coast during daylight with an escort of six Beaufighters or Mosquitos on three hour reliefs, and this was arranged.

'After one unsuccessful run, *Sheffield* was proceeding southwards in this way and well into the Bay when at 1500 the six Beaufighters scheduled to relieve at that time failed to turn up. Feeling somewhat naked so near to enemy airfields, the cruiser continued on her course and at 1800 a group of aircraft was detected by radar approaching low from the north and six Mosquitos arrived exactly on time. As they were orbitting the ship to identify themselves another group of aircraft was detected 15 miles due west and tracking east. The FDO in *Sheffield* just had time to pass a vector to the Mosquitos when six Ju88s appeared returning to base from patrol in the Bay. The delighted Mosquitos delivered a dashing attack and pieces of Ju88 fell around the cruiser before the battle was lost in the clouds.

'Around 2100 that night the *Sheffield* received a signal from the Commander in Chief Plymouth, 'congratulations on your brilliant fighter direction. By Mosquitos five Ju88s certain, one probable; by Beaufighters four Me110s certain, one probable, one possible.' In puzzled modesty the cruiser continued with her patrol.

'On her return to Plymouth a week later, her Captain was greeted with many expressions of surprised gratitude, and hearty congratulation. He put a face on it as long as he could but set about to discover the truth. The Beaufighters which should have contacted him at 1500 had proceeded to a position 60 miles north of the rendezvous and although not sighting the *Sheffield*, doggedly continued to orbit that spot for three hours. However they picked up the vector passed to the Mosquitos and assuming the *Sheffield* had used the wrong callsign, steered west and within 30 seconds of the latter's attack on the hapless Ju88s, encountered a squadron of Me110s with the result stated above. The chances of war are hard on the loser.' (*ND Bulletin*, December 1955)

1944 - 1945

The year 1944 will always be remembered for the greatest amphibious operation of all time, the invasion of Normandy. Although in this operation carriers were not employed, battleships and cruisers were provided with enlarged teams and acted as links in the air reporting organization. The landings in the south of France, however, gave the RN its first real opportunity of controlling a large number of aircraft from several carriers during offensive operations against enemy held territory but the lack of opposition on the scale expected prevented the acquisition of experience in maintaining a sustained defence against heavy attack. All the same these operations together with a study of reports received from the US Navy regarding operations against the Japanese in the Pacific, revealed weaknesses in the organization which needed to be remedied before the British fleet could join its ally in those waters.

During 1944, the ships earmarked to form the British Pacific Fleet were taken in hand and fitted with improved and standardized radar equipment suitable for fighter direction which was now available in quantity. Although the Type 277 centimetric set, adapted from its original AS function was not as good as the American SM/SP set, it gave the fleet a reliable low warning set to a range of about 20 miles. Skiatrons and PPIs were now standard fittings and air conditioning was installed. An invaluable exchange of ideas between the RN and the RAF took place and led to the conversion of *HMS Boxer* for the control of fighters during a combined operation.

Training continued apace and Speckington was turning out between 20 and 30 officers a month on completion of a four-month course. As mentioned in Chapter IV the training of Air Plotters was extended to include surface plotting and their name was changed to Radar Plotters. Despite the increased training facilities now available both in *Dryad* and at Speckington, complaints were received from sea with increasing insistence that the synthetic training available at these establishments was no substitute for practical interception exercises with aircraft. Only nature could produce the vagaries of weather and radio and radar conditions which a FDO might have to face at sea. To meet this criticism and provide accommodation and training for the ever-growing fleet requirements, the construction of the Royal Naval Air Direction Centre at Kete in South Wales was begun in 1944, but the war ended long before it could be completed.

As we have seen, the amalgamation of aircraft direction methods with those used for surface plotting led to the formation of the action information organization and the absorption of the Air Plotters into the Radar Plot branch, It also led directly, as will be seen, to the merger of the fighter direction and navigation specialist branches after the war.

The Pacific campaign

The Pacific campaign fully justified the allied expenditure of effort and manpower in the field of aircraft direction. The US Navy, reinforced in 1945 by a British task force comprising most of the more modern major ships of the RN, operated what in effect was a sea-borne air force in support of the operations of the US Army and Air Force based on the Phillipines and Okinawa and which ultimately led to the defeat of Japan.

The following notes made by Lieutenant Commander (later Sir) Richard

Thompson RNVR the FDO in the *Victorious* during the last two strikes against Japan, illustrate the pitch of efficiency which had been reached.

'Thursday, 12 April 1945. There are good days as well as bad and this for us was a good one. A beautiful intercept on a crossing Dinah this morning, a thrilling chase and a splash at the end of it — 35 miles. Good one on a second Dinah and she was too quick and we could not catch her; a third at 52 miles and four Oscars — too fast, but a fine painstaking intercept; a fourth on four Zeros all (shot) down at 40 miles and a fifth on two Oscars — 30 miles — both down, and another damaged.'

'Shortly after the signal had been received to cease hostilities against Japan and in fact was still flying in the flagship of the British Task Force, *King George V* of which the author was in command, a kamikaze aircraft, which had succeeded in evading the combat air patrols, was detected just as it was about to start its death dive on some luckless ship in the force. David Pollock, the FDO was on the Admiral's bridge when the report was received over the loudspeaker (his look of horror was captured by a photographer standing near) he contacted the ADR, an interception was made by two US Corsairs in the vicinity and we thankfully watched as the flaming bandit splashed down half a mile astern.'

Commander Pollock's conclusions

Although for reasons of space, it has not been possible to reproduce *in extenso* Commander Pollock's valuable report on the development of aircraft direction, his concluding remarks are as follows:

'With the entry of the Third fleet into Tokyo Bay, the risk of attack from the air was at an end, and with it was gone something of the fascination which for five years had provided an absorbing interest to a number of officers and men, the great majority of whom were temporary wartime substitutes for fully trained RN personnel. They had had opportunities for enterprise, inventiveness and responsibility which were not given to many junior officers or men in the other branches of the service. Despite the many disappointments in the various phases of the war, the sense that something was achieved in the end and that the foundations of an organization have been built of an enduring service to the RN, is its own reward.

'If any lesson is to be learned from the story of the growth of aircraft direction as part of the defence of ships at sea, it must surely be the old and well established doctrine that each new weapon produces its counter-weapon. If the navy is to be able to defend itself from air attack, progress in methods and equipment must be far-sighted and continuous and not dependent upon the pressure of failure or impending disaster.'

In a letter to the author, Commander G R M Going DSO whose war record betokens a charmed life and an astonishing capacity for survival, writes:

'The credit for this valuable achievement (related above) which the US Navy was so quick to copy and overreach, lies first with Admiral Boyd and two outstanding observers, Commanders Kenneth Short and Charles Coke and also with a team of outstanding RNVR officers recruited by Commander David Pollock who had been SOO 2 in the Mediterranean to Admirals Lyster and Boyd. They had

Commander David Pollock RNVR.

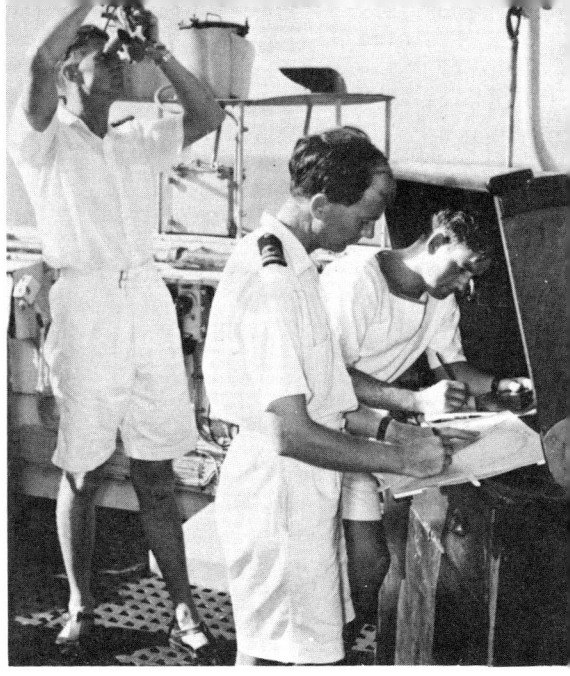

The navigating officer of HMS Albion, ~~changing~~
~~*stations using the relative plot on the PPI.*~~
Ian Mackay, taking sight using the
'Rapid Astn' method.

all been friends since their varsity days and were already successful in civil life as
well as being outstanding 14 foot International dinghy sailors.

Their initiative, drive, and capacity for mastering the Admiralty system got
aircraft direction officers appointed to ships in the fleet, started a School, launched
a specialization and recruited a very high standard of RNVR officer to man it —
all in under two years!'

The Royal Naval Air Direction Centre, Kete

Although not commissioned until after the surrender of Japan, it seems appropriate
to include in this chapter an account of the Royal Naval Aircraft Direction Centre
which was built at Kete in Pembrokeshire as a replacement for Speckington Manor
which lacked the facilities needed for a successful operation of radar. Commander
G R M Going who had returned home at the end of 1944 after being relieved as
Senior FDO and SOO 2 in the Eastern Fleet was given the task of supervising the
completion of the new station. 'Kete was unique from the start,' he writes,
'situated 14 miles from the nearest town, with but one pub in between, and
right on St Anns Head, it was the nearest thing to a ship ashore you could get.
The radar coverage was clear as far as South America and the buildings and equipment, though austere, were well suited to the job. To say it was bleak would be
an understatement and we had a duty gale emergency party equipped with pickets
and frapping lines to secure the roofs of the buildings in bad weather.

'The complement was as unusual as the site. We had 225 Petty Officers and ratings, 170 Wrens whose quarters were segregated by a three-wire fence, a staff of some 60 officers and instructors and a capacity for 130 officers and RP ratings under instruction.'

Kete was first occupied by a commissioning party of some 60 officers, ratings and Wrens on 6 August 1945 and training began on 10 September. During the next 12 months some 500 officers passed through the station and six long F courses were held, together with five Air Traffic Control courses and about a score of short courses laid on for Admirals and foreign radar officers. The most up-to-date radar and radio sets were installed including an RAF Type 70, at that time the latest in Air Warning equipment. Information from these sets was fed into the model building via an aircraft direction building where safety tracks of all airborne training aircraft were kept.

The model building contained a demonstration mock-up of an aircraft carrier's action information organization, complete with compass platform, bridge plotting room, operations room, and radar display room as well as models of the installations in an escort carrier, a battleship, and a frigate. On days when flying was not possible the models could be fed with synthetic radar. Aircraft co-operation was provided by Seafires, Mosquitos and Fireflies of 790 Squadron based at the RNAS Brawdy which together with the RNADC formed one command known as *HMS Goldcrest*. Later when the air station was closed down in February 1948, the latter commissioned as an independent command known as *HMS Harrier*.

In addition to the radar, RT, and model rooms, the Centre was equipped with seven class rooms, a library and information room, an aircraft recognition centre, an ARL automatic plotter room with live tables, a building containing six PPI trainers and one for ground interception training of which the famous tricycles referred to above, were a part. The amenities were well catered for and included a gymnasium equipped with two 35 mm projectors, a NAAFI canteen, sports grounds and an ex-German yacht which was moored in Dale roads.

'The remarkable thing,' writes Commander Going, 'is that the station settled down remarkably well and became at once a happy ship which I understand it remained to the end.'

Captain R D Butt CBE who joined Kete in 1947 as a Lieutenant of two years seniority writes, 'there were about 45 RN students divided into three courses and their seniority ranged from one year in as a Lieutenant to Lieutenant Commanders of several years seniority who had commanded their own ships. There was a good sprinkling of ex-aviators and submariners including Godfrey Place VC. We were housed in dormitories of about 10 students in each hut and the principle recreations were beer and the AD Wrens.

'The training consisted of technical radar lectures to teach us as much about radar as the (N)s knew about their compasses; endless model exercises based on the great carrier battles of the Pacific war; synthetic interceptions using a primitive electric trainer; direction of converted Wall's ice cream tricycles to intercept each other on the lawn and a limited amount of live training. The aircraft for the latter was an early make of Fairey Firefly operated from Dale and as the aircraft were single engined and very worn out, they always operated in formation, two as a target, two as combat air patrol fighters.

110

'As the Kete radar was also old and difficult to maintain and the weather uncertain, the number of occasions when four aircraft, the radar, and the weather were all OK simultaneously, were disappointingly few. There was also instruction in the art of visual direction and this was great fun; one stood on the roof with a radio set and directed a fighter on to a low flying shadower by eye.

'We also flew in the back seat of the fighters and learned quite a lot about air tactics and the planning of maritime air operations. Also attached to Dale was a Naval-manned ex RAF GCI Station where selected newly qualified FDOs were taught the more skilled art of night fighter control using air to air radar fitted fighters and a flying classroom Avro Anson suitably equipped.

'The Kete course lasted about seven months and during our last week we were told, first, that specialist pay had been abolished, and secondly, that we would be cross-trained as (N)s. I remained grateful to Kete, it taught me a lot about operating aircraft and provided me with a wife from amongst the AD Wrens.'

The training of Radar Plot (RP) Ratings

The history of RP training is a long and complicated one and it is not intended here to do more than record the milestones in its development. As stated in Chapter IV with the amalgamation of the (N) and (D) branches *Dryad* became responsible for the training of a large proportion of the Royal Navy's seamen, but since during the first years of war continuous service ratings had been barred from qualifying as radar plotters, when the war ended there were only 199 CS ratings with this qualification of whom only four were RP1s. At the same time there were 4,782 hostilities only (HO) ratings, the majority of whom had an RP 3 qualification. It was estimated that the number needed to man the post war fleet would be of the order of 4,000 of whom 16% would be PRIs and RP1s, 18% RP2s, and 66% RP3s.

When hostilities ceased there were no less than seven naval establishments in addition to *Dryad* engaged on RP training, but two of these closed down in 1946 and the training of RP2s was transferred to *Dryad* from RNAS Yeovilton. The plan was to establish an RP School at each home port but as it was impracticable to construct new buildings at that time, suitable old ones had to be used. In the case of Chatham, Admiralty House and Garrison Point were selected, Kete did duty for badly blitzed Plymouth ratings, and at Portsmouth, Fort Purbrook on Portsdown Hill, four and a half miles from *Dryad* was chosen. The work of conversion of the Fort was delayed by the severe winter, however by the end of March work went ahead and by August sufficient sets were functioning to enable classes to start, but fitting out was not completed until May 1948 and live training did not begin there until August.

At the end of 1947 about 2000 of the 3800 HO ratings still serving were demobilized, and although by that time nearly 1000 active service ratings had been trained to take their place, the shortage was still acute. Plans to make good the deficit received a setback when on 30 September 1949 the Chatham RP School, *Wildfire*, at Sheerness was closed down for reasons of economy.

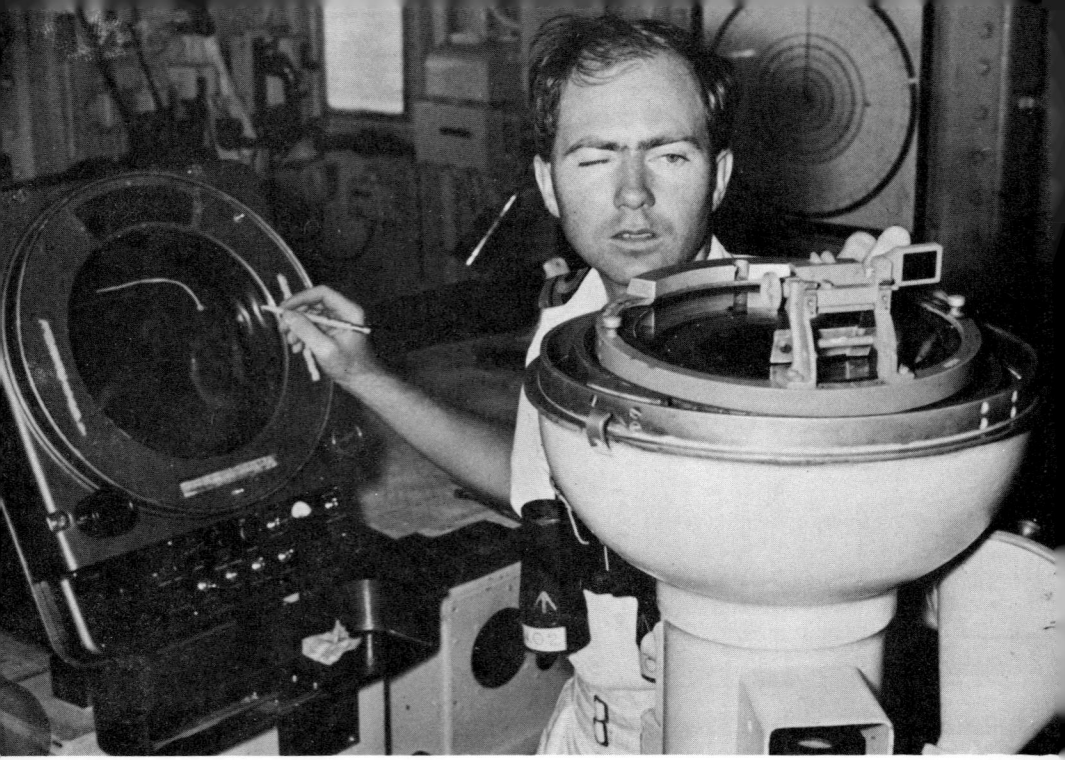

The 2nd navigating officer, HMS Albion, changing stations using the relative plot on the PP1.

A situation report on the RP branch for 1 December 1950 showed the progress to make good the back-log.

	Boatswain PR	PRI	RP1	RP2	RP3	Under training
Required	58	28	186	742	1820	—
Available	2	13	111	905	2033	213

In order to get more RP ratings to sea, in 1953 the Admiraly ordered a cut of 15% in the shore training of junior rates, but a further problem arose the following year when 1260 trained men were released from the branch. The majority of these were seven-year men and this produced a shortage of 2nd and 3rd class rates. *Dryad* too was suffering from a shortage of class rooms and accommodation which adversely affected the ability of the establishment to cope with the increased amount of training now required.

With the increasing complexity of the equipment being fitted in HM Ships the demand for a great number of the higher rates grew and in 1957 the Admiralry allowed an RP1 rate to be included in the complement of private destroyers and frigates. This provided another headache for the drafting authorities since a large number of those with higher rates had only another two years to serve so that in 1958 the situation regarding PRIs was still difficult.

Early in 1959, a new scheme of training in connection with specialist qualifications was introduced whereby a seaman rating began his SQ training immediately on completion of his new entry training and before going to sea. This meant that those who opted for the RP branch joined their ships with a knowledge of the theory of radar, voice communication, reporting, the local operations plot, and air plotting and so were better able to play a part in the complex task of fighting their ships.

Although by June 1961 the situation regarding PRIs and RP1s had somewhat improved, the shortage of RP1s continued, but by now the facilities available in *Dryad* had improved and it was found possible to increase the number of RP2 classes to make good the deficiency.

Another step towards the ultimate goal was taken in 1962 by placing increased emphasis on pre-commissioning and command team Training for which the steadily improving facilities in *Dryad* were admirably suited.

Poor recruiting during the next five years added to the difficulty of reaching the authorized numbers in the various categories of the RP branch and the table below gives the state of the branch as of 30 June 1968.

SQ	Borne	Authorized	+ or −
PRI	111	111	—
RP1	341	367	-26
RP2	1017	1255	-238
RP3	1941	2221	-280

Fort Purbrook closed down

As part of the six-stage development plan for *HMS Dryad* initiated in 1964, stage three included the construction of a radar block to be begun in 1965 for completion in 1966. In the event it was not until 1968 that the transfer from the old victorian fort to the new building began and the white ensign which had flown over the former for 20 years was hauled down on 19 December of that year.

Plan Opstrain

The following year, 1969, the authorized number of PRIs was increased to 130 in order to provide one for every *Leander* class frigate and advancement within the RP branch received a filip with the introduction of new regulations requiring at least first and second class specialist qualifications for confirmation as Petty Officer and Leading Seamen respectively. But great changes were in the offing and in 1973 a plan known as Opstrain was produced and implemented the following year. Under this plan the training of all seamen officers and men became centred in *Dryad*. This was followed on 1 January 1975 by the formation of a ratings operations branch and as a result the sub-specialist branches open to seamen were changed to radar, missile, sonar, and electronic warfare plus three smaller sub-branches: minewarfare, diver, and survey recorder while the old RP qualifications lapsed. The new syllabuses for these courses began in *Dryad* in the autumn of

1974 when the role of the School was changed to that of maritime operations of which more anon.

Navigator's Yeomen

In 1957 approval was given for private destroyers and frigates to carry a qualified Navigator's Yeoman irrespective of whether or not a qualified (ND) officer was borne. Suitable candidates were selected provisionally in *Dryad* and *Harrier* from ratings with an RP2 qualification. These ships were also to be allowed an RP1 in view of the increasing complexity of the equipment with which they were being fitted.

In 1963 AFO 888/63 introduced a new system of manning and training for Navigator's Yeoman duties but the change did not come into force until 1965 when the original RP basics selected as suitable became available for training and drafting as RP3s and for Navigator's Yeoman duties. The course for the last named lasted two weeks and was basically a chart correction and deck watch course, any further training required being given at sea.

RP Wrens

In the summer of 1940, marked by the famous evacuation of Dunkirk, Wren plotters first made their appearance in the Dover Command, being personally selected by the Flag Officer, Dover, Rear Admiral (later Admiral Sir) Bertram Ramsay, where they recorded the movements of the channel convoys and their escorts. By the end of the year there were 46 of them distributed amongst the home commands. By 1941 Wren Officer plotters made their appearance and from then on the whole branch expanded both numerically and geographically so that by 1942 there were Wren Officer and rating plotters as far afield as Capetown, Alexandria, Melbourne, and other ports abroad.

On page 225 of her book *Blue Tapestry* the wartime Director of the WRNS, Dame Vera Laughton Mathews DBE writes, 'all up the east coast, known as E-boat alley, the plotters' work was of the highest operational importance. I was told by the Chief of Staff at Chatham that when the enemy E-boats were "heard" the keeness and speed with which the Wrens plotted the position and the signals were got out to the motor gunboats made a difference of 10 miles to the pursuing MGBs. It was stated that Wren plotters had undoubtedly saved hundreds of ships and thousands of men's lives by their accuracy and swiftness in detecting and reporting enemy movements.'

Shortly after the invasion of Normandy was launched, the Portsmouth — Southampton area became one of the targets for the V1 flying bombs and the calm and efficient way in which the Wren Officer plotters in the war room at Southwick House recorded their movements until they had either exploded in the city or passed safely overhead was most impressive to watch. Never once did I notice any sign of nervousness or panic although Southwick House was in the direct line of fire.

However these courageous young ladies were not the direct forerunners of the RP Wrens who started life in 1943 as aircraft direction Wrens affiliated to the extant fighter direction branch. They were employed in the first AIO shore model ever built, that of an aircraft direction room of a headquarters ship, which was construction at Speckington. When the ADC at Kete was opened in 1946, they moved there taking their trikes with them, the function of which has been described earlier.

Unlike the Wren plotters who were disbanded at the end of the war, the RP Wrens, like the RP ratings, remained in business when hostilities ceased and continued to play a most important part in the development of the AIO and shore training associated with it. In 1961 they numbered 153, comprising 1 CPO, 10 POs, 23 Leading and 119 Wrens.

On 12 March 1960 to compensate for the closing down of the ADC at Kete, a synthetic trainer known as the Harrier trainer was officially opened at *HMS Dryad* and manned largely by RP Wrens from Kete. It was six years, however, before they had their own quarters in *Dryad* — Pinsley House — which was opened on 8 July 1966 by HRH Princess Marina, who appropriately arrived by helicopter.

In addition to acting as pilots on the simulators, staff Wrens man positions such as detectors, trackers and analysers in the radar display rooms and positions in the models such as assistant fighter controllers and height-finders. *Dryad* is now in its own right the home of the RP Wrens branch and besides performing very important duties they add a touch of female elegance and glamour to an otherwise all-male domain!

Chapter VI

POST WAR YEARS – FORMATION OF THE ND
BRANCH and THE DEVELOPMENT OF HMS DRYAD

'Ideals are like stars; you will not succeed in touching them with your hands. But like the seafaring man on the desert of waters, you chose them as your guides, and following them you reach your destiny'

Carl Schurz 1859

Admiral of the Fleet Sir John H D Cunningham GCB, MVO

At the annual dinner which, in 1948, took place on 22 July, the opportunity was taken to unveil a portrait of one of the most distinguished members of the (N) branch, Admiral of the Fleet Sir John Cunningham, which had been subscribed for by officers of the branch, the artist being Mr J B Souter. Vice Admiral J E T Harper who was a member of the staff in 1906 when Sir John qualified and whose connection with the battle of Jutland was mentioned earlier, unveiled the portrait which hangs in the main entrance hall at Southwick House.

Shortly after this event, Sir John relinquished the post of First Sea Lord which he had held since 1946 and the following exchange of messages took place:

From *HMS Dryad:* 'On behalf of the ND branch may I wish Lady Cunningham and yourself every happiness in the future and long life to enjoy your leisure after so many years of arduous and distinguished service. We hope to have the honour of seeing you at the annual dinner for many years to come.'

From First Sea Lord: 'Lady Cunningham and I thank you and through you all in ND branch for the very kind wishes contained in your signal. I look back with the keenest pleasure to my connection with navigation and wish all possible good fortune to ND officers past, present and future.'

A brief biography of the former First Sea Lord, who died on 16 December 1962 at the age of 78, will be found in Appendix III.

All of One Company – The formation of the ND branch

With war over in Europe, it became of increasing importance to ensure that by the time peace came in the far east and reservists started to return to civilian life, permanent provision should be made for the future organization of fighter direction. Moreover, it was not at that time transparently clear to all concerned that the whole of the action information organization must be welded into one entity as soon as possible. All incoming information from whatever source, must be rapidly processed and collated so that it could be presented to the command in the

116

quickest and most digestible form. All out-going directives or orders, whether to ships or aircraft, must emanate from the command through the medium of one comprehensive system.

As we have seen from the previous chapter, when the war ended action information concerning aircraft and their direction was almost wholly separated from that concerning surface ships and submarines, though the methods employed had much in common. In all carriers and many other ships fitted for aircraft direction, the ADR was physically separated from the operations room. However, it was perfectly natural that there should be grave misgivings in the Fleet Air Arm about suggestions that the direction of airmen in the air should be undertaken by officers other than those trained under their aegis. Equally there was opposition from some (N) officers to the idea that this new art should be grafted on to their traditional profession and that they should assume parental responsibility for what appeared to be a monstrous and demanding cuckoo in their comfortable nest.

In December 1945, Captain R W Ravenhill CBE, DSC relieved Rear Admiral Benn as Director of Navigation at the Admiralty and in the spring of 1946, Captain Wynne-Edwards, the Deputy Director with special responsibility for co-ordinating developments in connection with the AIO, at the former's suggestion, prepared a paper making detailed proposals for the amalgamation of the navigation and fighter direction branches which the Director docketed and which, in due course, received board approval (CW.26236/46). The board decision was made known to the fleet in an AFO part of the opening paragraph of which reads: '. . . having regard to the trend of development of the Action Information Organization, further consideration has been given to the future responsibilities of Navigating and Fighter Direction officers, and Their Lordships have decided that these two branches shall be amalgamated into a new specialist branch to be known as the Navigation Direction Branch (ND) with headquarters in *HMS Dryad*. This amalgamation will take effect from 1 July 1946 on which date all specialist navigating officers and fighter direction officers will come under the aegis of the new branch.'

The method of training ND officers was to be carried out on the lines previously practised by the (N) branch, that is by means of a Qualifying course followed by a period of sea training and an advanced course. The Qualifying course was planned to last 34 weeks, of which the major part would be spent in *HMS Dryad* but eight weeks were allowed for instruction in practical air interceptions at the new ADC at Kete and in the specially equipped control ship *HMS Boxer*. On passing out, an (ND) officer would be qualified for appointment to a small ship as Navigating Officer and to an aircraft carrier as an Intercept Officer. Young officers already qualified in (N) or (F) were to undergo suitable conversion courses to qualify as (ND). At the end of two years' sea-going experience, specialist officers would return to *Dryad* for an advanced course lasting 11 weeks on the successful conclusion of which they would acquire an (ND†) status and be considered fully qualified to carry out all the duties of the branch.

The question of the complementing of the branch was fully dealt with in Wynne-Edwards' paper. It recommended that there should be two Qualifying courses a year, each consisting of 11 officers to build up to a total of about 243 officers below the rank of Commander. With a view to the inevitable retrenchment in the Admiralty staff following the end of the war, it was suggested that certain duties carried out by the Director of Air Warfare and Flying Training the Director of Air Organization and the Director of Airfield and Carrier Requirement should be transferred to the Director of Navigation and Direction and that the last named's staff should be augmented accordingly.

Publication of the ND Bulletin

The first issue of a new publication known as the *ND Bulletin* appeared towards the end of 1946. It was an Admiralty publication and issued as a Confidential Book and sponsored by the Director of Navigation and Direction, Captain Ravenhill. In the foreword he states, 'the main object of the *Bulletin* is to keep the fleet informed of the work of the ND branch and to stimulate interest and discussion of navigation direction matters.' Certainly the 55 pages of the first issue covered a wide range of subjects illustrating the extent of the responsibilities now carried by the branch. The first two editors of the *Bulletin* were Lieut-Commanders E M Penton and R A F Heap, both Navigating Officers, the third was Lieut-Commander R Dyer, a (D) officer and the fourth and last was an (N) officer, Lieut-Commander J D D Moore DSC who held office for the remaining 13 years of the *Bulletin's* life. The 39 issues form a valuable record of the ND branch during the period covered and the author is greatly indebted to the editors and contributors whose work has proved so helpful to him in his task.

In 1947 the security rating of the *Bulletin* was downgraded to Restricted and publication continued until December 1968. In June 1952 the editor, David Moore, published the following comparative picture of *'Dryad* then and now' of which the following is an extract:

'The writer had the good fortune to join the instructional staff at *Dryad* in 1945 just after V E Davy, and a curious pot-mess it was. The wardroom was always bursting with people of both sexes and of all shapes and sizes. Half the mess scarcely knew the other half because there were two sides of the house one being the Nav House transplanted and the other the AITC. Luckily there were enough people in the latter who were recent members of the former to provide a bridge which eventually contributed greatly to the integration of the two halves. Needless to say an enlightened policy of general post within the establishment was being pursued with this object in view and it was no fault of the majority, who had temporary commissions that they tended to know those who worked on their side of the house much better than those who didn't.

'Time passed and the balance of numbers tipped in favour of the straight stripers. Restlessness at the cleavage between the two sides increased and a nameless prophet called a conference and integrated the whole machine with such foresight that his plan is only altered in minor detail today. With extraordinary little friction, the new machine began to turn over at once, and at least one person who rejoined the staff after an interval of two years was struck more forcibly by the smoothness of its running and its close similarity to the original conception, than by almost any other feature of *Dryad*.'

Important adjuncts to the Navigation School from the beginning of its existence ashore were the sea-going tenders, for as Admiral Sir Henry Oliver once said, 'the sea is a vast affair and you cannot learn it in college, you should be brought up to it.' However cogently the basic principles may be taught in a classroom, there can be no substitute for practical experience at sea, the same applied later on in the matter of aircraft direction.

During the inter-war years the School tenders consisted of three former mine-sweepers, HM Ships *Alresford, Saltburn* and *Carstairs*, all of which were specially fitted out for instructional purposes. During world war II, they were used for local defence and the following story from Commander R E C Dunbar shows that the old ladies still had some fight in them.

'At the time I joined *HMS Alresford* On 11 September 1940' he writes, 'our duties were to take out classes for pilotage instruction about three times a week and every other night we were AA guard in the Nab channel and usually anchored off St Helens. A few days before I joined, my predecessor, Commander Rudyard Helpman, was on this patrol and hearing aircraft approaching, ordered "enemy aircraft — red 30 — angle of sight 30° — fire!" and to his surprise scored a direct hit with the first shot from the old 12 pdr gun which was the ship's only armament. During the time when the German invasion was expected, we anchored every night in St Helens Roads and we seemed to be "the hope of the side." I asked the Chief of Staff how we should deal with the invasion fleet when it arrived and he repeated to me Nelson's famous dictum, "no man can do wrong if he lays his ship alongside one of the enemy".'

When hostilities ceased in 1945 the *Alresford* was put on the sale list and was bought in 1947 by Belgium for mercantile use. Her place was taken by *HMS Rochester*, a sloop of 1105 tons built in 1931. For a year she did duty as the only tender, but she had had a hard war and commitments were increasing so in 1946 she was joined by *HMS Starling* (1350 tons) built in 1942, a ship with a famous reputation gained under the command of that ace of U-boat killers, the late Captain F J Walker CB DSO*. During the winter of 1947/48 the *Rochester* was reduced to a care and maintenance party but in August 1948 she was manned again and served for another year until relieved in October 1949 by *HMS Redpole*, a sister ship of the *Starling*.

For the next decade these two ships did yeoman service and an example of their performance can be seen from the figures for the *Redpole* in 1954:

12 Advanced (N) course officers
7 Long (N) course officers plus nine from NATO countries
101 Sub Lieutenants
80 Dartmouth Cadets
34 Upper Yardmen

The ship was at sea for 127 days in the year either in the Isle of Wight area with Sub Lieutenants or further afield with the Advanced (N) and Qualifiers classes. In addition both ships embarked their full share of day trippers in the form of Seaman Boys and Combined Cadet Force Cadets.

On 6 November 1959 the *Starling* paid off, the ceremony being attended by

Captain Walker's widow and many of the ship's previous commanding officers and others who had served in the wartime support groups. She was relieved by *HMS Wakeful* (1710 tons) which was commissioned on 3 November and given an additional role as ASWE trials ship. On 15 July 1960 the *Redpole* was relieved by *HMS Carron* (1730 tons). Owing to their greater size, the new tenders were unable to work in some of the very confined waters frequented by their predecessors but their movements still provided students (and their commanding officers) with those anxious moments which teach the enduring lessons of pilotage.

In the spring of 1963, as a measure of economy, the *Carron* was paid off thus putting a considerable strain on the remaining tender, *HMS Wakeful.* The Dartmouth Training Squadron was called upon to help, but this was not really a satisfactory solution, and as a result of strong representations, in the autumn of 1965 *HMS Ulster* (1710 tons) after suitable conversion joined the *Wakeful* as a sea-going tender to the ND School. Soon afterwards the tenders attached to the various training establishments were pooled, and in consequence they worked for several masters. The following extract from an article in the *ND Bulletin* for December 1967 shows with what these ships now had to contend. The tender concerned was *HMS Ulster,* and the contribution was written by her Captain, Lieut-Commander A N H Weekes R.N.

'Each week up to 48 juniors (O) are embarked from the new entry establishments and the consequent weekly class change complicates her navigational training programme. She also carries up to 32 SSM(E)s from *HMS Sultan* who due to the compactness and complexity of their syllabus can be of little assistance to a reduced and overworked engine room department . . . The number of different types of course which visit *Ulster* runs into double figures. Most come for a week or less; chief among these are the RN Sub Lieutenants during their fourth year courses, there being at least six courses every year with 15 to 17 officers each. This not only stretches the wardroom facilities, but reduces the amount of training that can be given to any particular officer to a barely acceptable minimum. Other short courses such as embyro SD List officers, instructor officers, RNR Subs or those from foreign Navies, tend to have smaller numbers and thus more individual attention during sea training . . . Amongst her other jobs *Ulster* is often used as the Rubber Frigate for commanding officers designate. These officers live onboard for anything between one and four days and practise ship handling whenever nothing else is going on. This kind of training has never yet needed more than the usual number of fenders, but it does require the ship's captain to have nerves of steel.'

The *Ulster* was 23 years old when she was assigned to training duties and it was not long before she began to show the signs of age. At the end of 1972 she was relieved by *HMS Torquay* (2150 tons) a *Whitby* class frigate completed in 1956.

HMS Boxer

Although not a tender to *HMS Dryad,* a ship which played an important part in the early years of ND and AIO training was *HMS Boxer* (5410 tons full load) an LST built in 1942 which, after much active service in the Mediterranean was converted in 1945 to an aircraft direction ship to take part in the war against Japan. Hostilities ceased as she was entering the Suez Canal so she was recalled and in 1946 was converted to a training ship for Electrical Officers in radar operation and maintenance and for (ND) officers and RP ratings in action information, plotting and interception. She was fitted with four massive masts to carry every type of aerial then in operational use and with a carrier type aircraft direction room and a cruiser-type operation room. She was a strange looking but most useful ship and continued as a training ship until 1955; amongst her commanding officers was Captain C J Wynne-Edwards DSC*.

The ND Division of the Admiralty in 1950

In Chapter IV it was related how the Director of Navigation finally suceeded in detaching his department from that of the Hydrographer and gained independent status as a result of his increased responsibilities in connection with action information and the advent of radar. Then in July 1946 these responsibilities were further augmented by the amalgamation of the N and D branches. With the subsidence of the turmoil of war it seems appropriate to record the way in which by 1950 the department had increased from its pre-war complement of one Captain and three Commanders. The growth of the family tree is shown below.

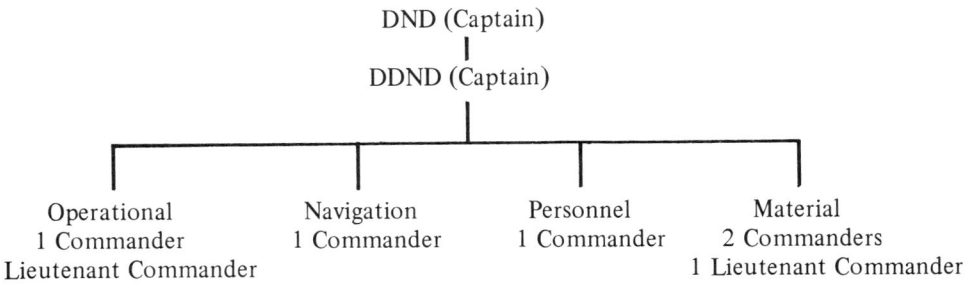

It will be seen that the number has more than doubled since the pre-war days; eight civilians were also employed and, in addition, one Commander was attached to the division for the rewriting of the *Admiralty Manual of Seamanship.*

It is unnecessary here to enumerate the long list of duties carried out by each member of the staff; suffice it to say that they covered all aspects of navigation, AIO, direction, and warning radar, both personnel and material. DND was also responsible for naval life saving and certain aspects of fleet replenishment at sea.

From being a somewhat obscure and isolated department it had become one which had more outside contacts than possibly any other of the naval staff. The list of committees on which DND was represented was extensive and there was continuous routine liaison with the Naval Electrical department and those of the Naval Construction and Gunnery divisions. A close liaison had been established with the Ministry of Transport and Trinity House.

Appointment of (N), (D) and ND Officers

On 1 July 1946, the Captain *HMS Dryad* had become the nominating authority for all (N), (D) and ND officers. At the same time (D) officers came under the aegis of the Naval Assistant to the Second Sea Lord instead of NA2SL (Air). During the war the number of qualified (N) officers increased from 150 to about 500 due to the employment of retired officers and by the addition of a number of RNR and RNVR officers who qualified (N*). One of the latter, Lieutenant A C Coging RNR, who took the course in 1944, was appointed to the Woolworth carrier *HMS Reaper* which was ordered to join the Pacific Fleet. He had previously been 'makee-learn' (N) of a corvette and a sloop and he recalls that when taking his leave of the Captain, *HMS Dryad,* he was warned to be 'bloody careful' when navigating a much larger ship than any he had previously served in. 'I joined the *Reaper* in the Forth,' he writes, 'and we went right round the world outwards through the Panama Canal and home through the Suez Canal. We did a lot of hard work in the Pacific at the end of the war, ferrying troops, ex-prisoners of war, stores and so on. In Hong Kong we finally got the news that we were going home and arrived in the Clyde in March 1946.' His Captain, well pleased with this successful feat of navigation presented him with a silver cigarette box suitably inscribed. When he returned to *HMS Dryad* and recounted his experiences, the appointments officer exclaimed, 'you went round the world and through both Canals! Trust the RNR to have luck like that.

Another N* officer, Lieutenant Commander W A J Cunningham VRD RNR DL was appointed in March 1945 to the Admiralty cable ship *HMS St Margarets* and sailed to join the fleet train of the British Pacific Fleet on 3 July 1945. However Japan surrendered before the ship reached her destination and she was diverted to Freemantle, West Australia. After five weeks enjoyment of the delights of Perth, she was sent to Colombo and ordered to repair the telephone cable between India and Ceylon where it crosses the Palk Strait. 'Despite the torrid conditions on the ninth parallel,' he writes, 'we found the damaged cable and repaired it without incident; my only recollection of the operation, apart from its novelty to me as a layman, is of the enormous insects which passed over the bridge causing the unwary to duck as from birds.'

It was estimated that 250 ND officers would be needed in the post war fleet requiring a yearly intake of two courses of about 11 officers each, but until this number could be provided, the gap was filled by (N*) officers who volunteered to remain on as long as required, and by an intake of some 20 Lieutenants (A) who volunteered as (D) officers on a four-year extended commission. However the appointment of more (D) officers in the fleet became a matter of increasing urgency and a board of enquiry was set up presided over by an officer qualified in both (N) and (D).

Introduction of sub-specialization

By the latter half of 1951, five years of marriage between the (N) and (D) specialists had shown clearly that an officer could not become a complete master of both, so it was decided to introduce sub-specialization, that is to say a Qualifier could become ND (N) or ND (D). During the four years 1947-1950 a total of 108 officers had qualified ND of whom 35 subsequently qualified as N† and 27 as D†.

By 1953 sub-specialization having proved itself, various adjustments in the length of the (N) and (D) courses were made. By including in the general ND course all those sections common to both (N) and (D) such as warning radar and AIO, it was found possible to lengthen the time spent by the (D) course at *HMS Harrier* by a week and increase the time spent at sea by the (N) course to include a week's survey as well as three weeks' pilotage. The (N) course received similar treatment.

The little 'd' scheme

A shortenened form of (D) course for junior officers as well as reserve and national service officers was introduced in 1954 in order to give greater flexibility in the complementing of ships to meet the requirements of the AIO and to enable the size of the ND(D) specialization and in particular the number of ND(D) officers in each carrier to be reduced. When the scheme was introduced it was made mandatory for an officer before being selected to specialize in ND(D) to have served for two years as a 'd' officer.

However two years later, in 1956, it was found that the two year obligation was proving too restrictive, so it was cancelled, though the 'd' scheme continued. It was emphasized that those who did the 'd' course were free either to return to general service after completing one commission in this capacity or to go on and qualify as ND(D).

Captain R D Butt CBE's experience

'In 1951, when serving at the RN Air Station Ford,' he writes, 'having qualified as (ND†), I was invited to state which side of the fence I wished to be put. I had done one job as (N) of a frigate, one as intercept officer in a carrier and a combined ND advanced course. I applied forthwith to revert to (N) as I could see little prospects ahead in the (D) world except endless sea jobs in carriers, with many years to wait for my turn to be senior (D) officer, whereas as an (N) officer I would get more variety and a charge job at once. But (N) was over-subscribed and I was compulsorily reverted to (D). However, I went as Senior (D) of a cruiser sent to Korea which was some consolation. By 1953 it was found that the balance of (N)s and (D)s was incorrect and I got a further opportunity to revert to (N) which I seized and was accepted, against the advice of my Admiral (a former (N) specialist!). However, I'm glad I did as it helped a lot in my three subsequent sea jobs in command.' He subsequently commanded *HMS Dryad* from September 1967 to August 1969 and was the first qualified (D) to do so.

Plans for the future of HMS Dryad

Meanwhile, with the ending of hostilities the action information training centre in the former stables of Southwick House was absorbed into the establishment as an integral part of the training equipment needed to fulfill its role as the ND School. As was to be expected, in the immediate post war years, development was restricted by financial considerations and by the need to repair bomb damage. It was not until the end of 1950, for example, that a new carrier model was completed.

As mentioned in Chapter IV, although as a result of its use as a headquarters for the Normandy invasion, the School inherited a lot of temporary buildings, mainly nissen huts, it was obvious that in the course of time these would have to be replaced by more permanent structures, but before this could be entertained, a plan based on the future needs of the school would have to be prepared, but what was the future of the school? At that time no one could have foreseen its growth to the vast establishment it is today with a ship's company of almost 2000 and some £70 million worth of equipment.

Limited improvements

In 1950 a notable deforestation took place in the vicinity of Southwick House; this became necessary because of the need to accommodate an increased number of staff and pupils. Arrangements were in hand to light the main driveway at the eastern end of which a guard house had been erected and decorated with the ship's crest. Behind the guard house the new quarterdeck had been levelled and surfaced, the area in front of the house being renamed the forecourt. A car park, canteen and cinema had been constructed in buildings inherited from Operation Overlord.

Within the house efforts were being made at redecoration, but financial stringency was a stumbling block. Mrs E H Martin had presented the school with a portrait of Nell Gwynn by Sir Peter Lely in memory of her husband, Captain Evan Hamilton Martin and this was given pride of place over the main staircase. A handsome georgian cut-glass chandelier purchased by the mess gave atmosphere to the main hall.

Horticultural activity around the house was in full swing with new flower beds created along the south side. Minor improvements had been made in the officers' and ratings' quarters both of which were still wartime buildings. A first class galley fitted with modern equipment was providing the best meals in the command. The recreational facilities, though still meagre, comprised some hard and grass tennis courts, a soccer ground, a rugger ground and a concrete cricket pitch, plus a 0.22 rifle range.

Despite two years of negotiations, the Admiralty did not yet own Southwick Estate so the master site plan which envisaged enlarging the house to at least twice its present size and constructing a dining room capable of seating 150 officers, with cabins, classroom and offices elsewhere, as well as permanent brick buildings for ratings, a swimming bath, a theatre, new instructional models, garages, new roads, and even married quarters, remained but a dream!

Nevertheless in spite of the difficulties, steady, if slow progress was being made. The building used as an information room was being converted into a chapel and space was being levelled to provide more grounds for soccer, rugger and hockey, while the senior and junior ratings canteens were being redecorated and made more attractive.

The old cinema in 1961.

Southwick House in 1968.

The purchase of Southwick House

As mentioned in Chapter IV, negotiations for the purchase of Southwick House from its new owner, Mr Borthwick Norton, began in 1948 but it was not until 7 July 1950 that the conveyance was signed. The price paid for the house and 295½ acres of land surrounding it was £40,000. Although the late Admiral of the Fleet Lord Cunningham of Hyndhope, First Sea Lord at the end of the war, when he first heard of the suggested purchase is reputed to have told Admiral Sir Geoffrey Layton, Commander in Chief Portsmouth, 'tell the Captain of the Navigation School to take his navigators back to the dockyard — what does he think they are doing inland, so far from the sea?' or words to that effect, it was probably the best purchase the Admiralty ever made. There was ample room for expansion and this enabled *HMS Dryad* to keep pace with modern training requirements and amenities and especially to undertake the increased responsibilities needed as the central training establishment for navigation and direction leading eventually to its present role as the School of Maritime Operations.

Funeral of His Majesty King George VI

The funeral of His late Majesty King George VI who died on 6 February 1952 involved *HMS Dryad* and the RP branch in their first major ceremonial duty in London. A detachment comprising three officers and 94 ratings formed part of the Portsmouth battalion under the command of Captain G W Hawkins of *HMS Siskin*. The *Dryad* contingent was assigned to a section of the route taken by the cortege covering a part of Whitehall from Derby Gate and King Charles II Street to a point half way to the Cenotaph.

Rebuilding begins

In 1958 the foundation stone of a new aircraft direction tactical trainer to the

125

north west of the main building and known as the *Harrier* trainer was laid by Captain Charles P Coke DSO then commanding the carrier *HMS Victorious*. Soon afterwards work began on Park House designed to accommodate Chief and Petty Officers and a new carrier model named Arcturus. There was then a pause while a five year development plan was drawn up and approved, the time-table for which was as follows:

Stage	Task	Start	Complete
1	*Junior Ratings blocks (2)*	*June 1964*	*December 1965*
	Wrens block	*June 1964*	*January 1966*
	District heating	*June 1964*	*December 1965*
2	*Office and instructional block*	*July 1964*	*January 1966*
	Works compound	*July 1964*	*April 1965*
	Estate compound	*July 1964*	*April 1965*
	Officers garages (50 per cent)	*July 1964*	*July 1965*
	New road	*July 1964*	*July 1965*
3	*Cinemasium (including tennis courts, .22 rifle range, road and roundabout)*	*March 1965*	*May 1966*
	Officers' cabin block (including garages 50 per cent)	*December 1964*	*February 1966*
	Motor transport building	*December 1964*	*July 1966*
	Radar block	*March/April 1965*	*May 1966 (+ time for installation*
4	*Southwick House, modernization*	*October 1965*	*September 1966*
5	*Ships company galley/dining hall (including CPOs garages)*	*April 1966*	*June 1967*
	Parade ground	*December 1966*	*December 1966*
	Combined tactical trainer	*April 1966*	*March 1968 (+ time for installation)*
6	*Sick bay*	*June 1967*	*June 1968*
	Tactical school	*January 1968*	*May 1969*

The plan received the blessing of Their Lordships and the Droxford Rural District Council in 1963 and for the six years 1964 to 1969 *HMS Dryad* was never free from the noise of pneumatic drills and the roar of builder's lorries, but in the minds of those called upon to endure the discomfort was the knowledge that they were witnessing the construction of a training complex superior to any other of which the RN could boast.

In 1966, the newly completed administration and instructional block was opened by Dame Beryl Oliver, widow of Admiral of the Fleet Sir Henry Oliver and named Oliver block in memory of her famous husband and founder of the School. The following year a major addition was made to the building programme by the inclusion of a four storey building to house the most sophisticated equip-

Oliver Block.

ment yet designed for synthetic training. The building known as the Cunningham block was scheduled for completion in 1968. 'A visitor to *HMS Dryad* can hardly miss the Cunningham building a-glow in its exterior pattern-work of thermal insulation; the white plastic laminate with which the walls of the upper storeys have been faced,' so runs a description of the new block in the *ND Bulletin* for December 1968, which also contained a long and detailed account of the function of the equipment installed in it.

The year 1970 saw the completion of the five (later changed to six) year development plan with the exception of the sick bay, the second officers' cabin block and the third junior ratings block. Considering all the problems which had to be overcome, this was an achievement of which all concerned could be proud.

There was considerable delay in starting with the modernization of Southwick House but, when completed in 1970, the old house had been improved out of all recognition. Instead of being a combination of wardroom, classrooms and offices it now provided officers' accommodation only. With WRNS officers on the top floor, the hall painted in pink and white, a new bar, to say nothing of a dive in the cellars and the house itself coated with a pleasing shade of greenish cream, it stands out pleasantly in the midst of the new structures which surround it. A new and more spacious dining hall was added and named after the late Admiral Sir John Frewen GCB and, adjoining it, Lake House with a total of 93 officers' cabins and Orchard House with a further 40 cabins. In 1972/3 further additions were made comprising two houses, one for the Captain, *HMS Dryad* and the other for the Captain of the Tactical School. Work began on a second tactical trainer, the enlargement of the boiler house, oil fuel storage capacity, and extension to the heating

Entrance to the Harrier Building

duct network to supply the new trainer and the sick bay, (renamed medical and dental centre).

Revision of the structure of the ND branch

In April 1956 a working party was convened to study the future requirements of the ND branch and the changes necessary to enable it to fulfill its commitments in the fleet, taking into account the vastly different background and the reduced number of general list officers becoming available, following the reduction in the size of the armed forces on which the Government had decided. It was also necessary to widen the scope of employment for special duties list officers, ie those promoted from the lower deck. The result of this study was published in AFO 1188/57 which gave details of the entry, training, and employment of both officers and men in a new ND structure. It was decided that initially all officers in the ND branch would qualify solely in AIO and aircraft direction. Although sub-specialization in navigation would follow for certain officers at a later stage, it was also decided that greater emphasis should be placed on the fact that basic navigation is, and indeed always has been, part of the stock-in-trade of every seaman officer. Further it was decided that, with the necessary training and experience, the navigation of small ships could also be undertaken by officers of the special duties list. However, before these proposals could be fully implemented, they were overtaken by subsequent events which are dealt with later.

Meanwhile let us leave the "powers that be" in Whitehall to wrestle with the problems of the ND branch, and let us join the flagship of the East Indies

Squadron lying in the harbour of Trincomalee onboard which a surface plotting exercise is about to begin. The (N) and (D) officers are hovering over the LOP in the operations room where everything is ready, headsets donned and chinagraphs poised.

The bitter end

'Exercise will begin in one minute's time − out,' and then came another signal passed by light from one of the Indian Navy's ships present, 'regret am unable to take part. My Type 86 US.'

'Well,' said (N), 'let's get 'em over here. They can man up the BPR − use it as another ship.'

'But protested (D), 'they'll never make it in time − not now.' The exercise in fact had started.

'Nonsense,' rejoined (N), 'they'll be here in a quarter of an hour.' So the invitation was drafted and sent.

'Now have everything ready for them in the BPR won't you,' said (N), 'I'm just off ashore to NHQ. Don't scrub the plot, because I'd like to see it when I get back.'

So the exercise proceeded in the placid way of all surface plotting exercises, (D), however, thinking dark thoughts about the ND merger. Towards the end, the

A view of the Dryad Club from Oliver Block.

incident of the Type 86 all but forgotten, the operations room door swung open and a swarm of ratings with jolly brown faces was ushered in accompanied by an officer. Aghast (D) saw how many there were, far too many for the BPR and with only 10 minutes to go, the exercise was beginning to run down. Having brought them here, no doubt against their will, thought (D), we must do something with them. Let them man up the operations room too; we'll prolong the exercise a little.

So the senior RP 1 took half of them to the BPR whilst the others had headsets clamped on them where they stood. Chinagraphs were pressed into their hands and they were pushed, protesting loudly in Hindustani, towards the plot, and told to plot. Alas they would not plot. They wrote down everything they heard. 'Plot', they were urged, 'look like this.' They were shown again and each one drew a plot just like the one shown them, then continued writing busily.

The exercise took on a new, chaotic lease of life, the general harassment being increased by an attempt on the part of the visiting officer to negotiate for the purchase of a Burberry and some shoes from the slops.

(D) had darker thoughts about the ND merger, but finally the exercise came to a confused and jabbering halt. 'Pass any comments on this channel – over' and then he was shown a signal, passed by light. It read 'Your so-and-so M(uch) R(egret) U(nable). My motor boat US.' (D) took the visiting officer aside. 'Who' he asked, with foreboding 'are you and your men?' They were a party of telegraphists on a sight-seeing tour from a different Indian ship!

(From the *ND Bulletin* of December 1954, contributed by Lieut-Comder (D) G H Ellison)

The axe

The subject uppermost in the minds of most members of the branch in 1957 was the impending reduction in the strength of the RN upon which the Government had decided. In the event the cuts made were not as large as had been feared and amounted to 30 out of 130 (N) officers and nine out of 90 (D) officers. Of these 15 (N)s and five (D)s were outside the zone for promotion. Out of 70 Commanders five (N)s and two (D)s were asked to retire.

The closing down of HMS Harrier and the RNAS Brawdy

Another casualty of the axe was the aircraft direction training centre, *HMS Harrier*, at Kete to achieve a saving of some 500 personnel. The blow was countered to some extent by the recent availability of the air defence tactical trainer (ADTT) which reduced the need for live direction training ashore. The closing of the ADTC displaced a large number of RP Wrens since *HMS Harrier* had one of the largest Wren complements of any shore establishment. In fact there were times when the female population outnumbered the male and as a result, quite a high proportion of RP

HRH Princess Marina with the C in C, Admiral Sir Frank Hopkins and Captain M S Oliphant, commanding HMS Dryad, arriving to unveil the new WRNS quarters at Pinsley House.

The operations room in a Whitby class frigate in 1959.

Wrens were converted from pedalling trikes to pushing prams as the wives of ND officers and RP ratings.

The closing down of *HMS Harrier* was closely followed by that of the RNAS Brawdy from which, ever since 1950, the firm of Airwork Limited had provided the aircraft needed for live interception at Kete. It operated 12 Sea Mosquitos supplied by the Admiralty while the firm provided five pilots (most of whom were former members of 790 Squadron which had previously provided the targets operating from first Dale and then Culdrose) and carried out the necessary maintenance. It was an unusual arrangement but it worked well from the start. The task of providing live direction training was now transferred back to RNAS Yeovilton, thus the wheel had come full circle.

Various trophies and other items from *HMS Harrier* whose name was so closely linked with that of *HMS Dryad,* were transferred to the latter including the stained glass window from the chapel and the sum of £413 of non-public funds which was used to form the Harrier Trust Fund the interest from which is used for the benefit of ND and RP personnel.

Implementing the new structure

It took sometime to implement the changes enumerated above. The last of the old style ND (N) courses, QN23, of eight officers including two RCN, completed in June 1958 of whom seven subsequently qualified (N). The last of the ND(D) courses, QD21, of four officers including one RAN and one RCN completed in September 1958, but in order to maintain an even flow of qualified (N) and (D) officers to the fleet it was necessary for some of the officers completing the ND course to qualify immediately in either (N) or (D) instead of first going to sea as an ND officer. Thus course ND 1 of seven officers was followed by course N1 and course ND 2 of five officers by course D1, completing in October and November 1958 respectively.

The first course for Sub Lieutenants (SD) PR began in January 1958 and those who qualified went to sea later that year.

Liaison between HMS Dryad and the US Navy's CIC Center

As mentioned earlier, the US Navy very quickly accepted the idea of aircraft direction and from it and general war experience in the Pacific, evolved the combat information center (CIC) corresponding to the RN's AIO. The first CIC School opened at St Simon's Island about 15 miles from its present site at Glynco, Georgia. In 1948 it was moved to Glenview, near Chicago, but returned to new quarters at Glynco in 1955.

The first RN exchange officer to be attached to Glynco took up his appointment in February 1957 and at the same time a US N officer joined the staff of *HMS Dryad* whereby both Schools were able to exchange ideas and maintain a direct link with each other through their respective naval authorities.

It came to someone in *HMS Dryad* that it would be a nice idea to present its American oppo with a shield bearing the *Dryad* crest and motto and suitably inscribed. Captain David Tibbits DSC, then in command of the ND School, approved the idea and the presentation was made by the Chief of Staff to the Admiral, British Joint Services Mission in Washington DC, Commodore David Goodwin DSC, on 11 August 1958. By a fortunate coincidence, Captain Tibbits was on leave in Bermuda at the time and thanks to the US Navy who sent an aircraft to pick him up, he was able to be present. As the originator of the AITC nothing could have been more appropriate.

A return visit was made by the Captain, 10 officers and three senior ratings from Glynco between 1 and 5 December 1960 at which a further exchange of gifts was made. The US visitors received a gavel and anvil made of *Victory* oak and a complete set of cricket gear and in return presented *HMS Dryad* with a mounted model of a WV2 aircraft, framed photos of the CIC School, and two palm trees from Georgia.

Liaison with other ND Schools

HMS Dryad, as might be expected, established a close liaison with other ND Schools as and when they were formed. One of the first, the Royal Australian Navy's, *HMAS Watson* developed out of a radar establishment founded in 1945. In April 1951 a qualified ND officer sailed for India to establish a School at Cochin and in 1958 the Royal New Zealand Navy decided to establish its own ND School on North Head overlooking Auckland Harbour.

The 1959 review of the ND branch

The reduction in the size of the fleet which followed from the steady pruning of the RN during the late 1950s resulted in a certain cutting back in the time spent on courses and therefore in the length of syllabuses. All (N), (D) and PR officers were still required to qualify in the general duties of AIO but the cumbersome titles of ND (N) and ND (D) were abolished and only those officers who specialised in (N) or (D) were so designated.

A review of the branch as a whole made in 1959 showed that the establishment of (N) officers was well up to strength and allowed for a certain number to be given general service appointments, but in the case of (D) officers, numbers did not yet allow of this and it was still necessary to continue with the 'd' scheme. Fourteen of these were accepted in 1958 and 20 in 1959, but in July of the following year after 11 more had been accepted, the scheme came to an end. The reluctance of junior officers to volunteer for the (D) qualifications (there were only four in 1958 and 12 in 1959) was attributed to doubts whether this specialization offered a career as good as that of the others.

SD officers

Meanwhile the number of SD (PR) officers continued to grow and by early

Officer and members of the WRNS manning the Redpole trainer.

specialization in (N) or (D) they were helping to provide the flexibility in appointment which was so badly needed to the benefit of officers of both the general and SD lists. In June 1961 there were 46 names on the selection roster for Sub Lieutenant (SD) (PR) but only about a quarter of them were fully qualified and therefore eligible and the norm was one course a year of eight to nine. In 1962 the course was lengthened to 31 weeks to allow for increased instruction in radar, synthetic interception, and helicopter direction. The last named was becoming increasingly important particularly in the field of AS warfare.

In September 1963, a further change was made in the course for SD officers which was now set at nine weeks and aimed to give them a sound basis from which, after further experience at sea, they could obtain a watch-keeping certificate and play their part in the action information organization. At that time the number of these officers who had passed the specialist Qualifiers course was three (N) and 10 (D) and they were proving well able to perform those duties. SD Boatswains also were being given an increasing number of appointments as commanding officers and first lieutenants in small ships.

Equalisation of the long (N) and (D) courses

In November 1961 the long (N) and long (D) courses were made the same length, ie 32 weeks which included 14 weeks common ND course, and 18 weeks of

Scene on the bridge of the helicopter-cruiser HMS Tiger,

specialised (N) or (D) instruction. Then the following year the first step was taken in the evolution of the Principal Warfare Officer, when operational team training for all long course specializations was introduced. (G), (TAS), (C), and (ND) qualifiers were formed into syndicates and played tactical games on the action speed tactical trainer which had been installed in *HMS Vernon*. It was not until the Cunningham building was opened in 1968 that proper tactical games could be played in *Dryad*.

The record shows that in 1962 the number of officers volunteering to specialise in (N) was satisfactory, on the other hand the small number seeking the (D) qualification was giving cause for concern and the loss of the 'd' officers was keenly felt. To overcome the shortage, a number of officers entered on the supplementary list were put through a 'd' course which they completed in 1963.

The confrontation in Indonesia which lasted from 1963 to 1966, during which a large proportion of the fleet was concentrated off Malaysia, put a heavy strain on the attenuated numbers in the ND branch.

FAMILY FAILINGS

It's the Alpha Bravo Charlie of the Navigator's trade
That you always choose a harbour for which pilotage is paid
Then you fix it with the plumbers that the ship is trimmed down aft
And you slip a gin to Chippy to add something to the draught

Though QR's are damned dogmatic on the fate of unclaimed tots
And in theory that's the reason why the scupper-piping rots
Nonetheless it's common knowledge from the wagons to the boats
That when no one else is looking they go down the Boatswain's throats.

Gold for Wreckers; booze for Boatswains; have Directors got no vice?
Has the daily talk of Angels left them singularly nice?
No! – for marriage is their weakness, and they take it as they please,
As is proven by the large and growing brood of little d's.

Contributed by Commander A R B Sturdee DSC, to
the ND Bulletin of December 1956

The last of the Boatswains

In 1948 the Admiralty decided that as Boatswains were the only Warrant Officers without an alma mater that it was in every way appropriate that *HMS Dryad* should fulfill this role since, as was mentioned in Chapter III, the Navigation School was responsible for their training. This meant maintaining the roster as well as the general supervision of the course they were now required to undergo. At that time there was a wide diversity of jobs for these officers such as dockyards, boom defence, training establishment in addition to serving in ships at home and abroad. They also assumed responsibility for diving, hitherto the prerogative of the gunnery branch and those with the requisite experience were granted the suffix QDD (Qualified in deep diving).

All Boatswains were made honorary members of the wardroom mess in *HMS Dryad* and encouraged to visit the establishment any time they were in the port.

In the middle of 1951, there were more appointments for Boatswains than there were officers to fill them. The strength at that time was 145 (including those promoted to Lieutenant) plus 10 QDDs and 20 were recalled from retirement to make good the deficiency.

In 1949 the title of Warrant Officer had been changed to that of Branch Officer, then in 1957, with the change in the officer structure of the RN, they became Special Duties (SD) officers. In 1962 as a result of the technical changes which had taken place in HM Ships generally, it was decided that no more seamanship Boatswains would be qualified and on 9 March 1970 to mark their 500 years of service to the RN the Boatswain branch presented to *HMS Victory* a carving in the form of an inkstand made from oak from that famous ship and depicting the many forms of seamanship. It was accepted by the Commander in Chief Naval Home Command, Admiral Sir John Frewen GCB. By 1975 the number of seamanship Boatswains still serving had dropped to 30 and the last of them will retire in 1984. However the title of Boatswain (PR) continues.

Transfer of the Seamanship School to HMS Dryad

Perhaps it was something of a paradox that simultaneously with the phasing out of the Seamanship Boatswains it was decided that *HMS Dryad* should become responsible for the general supervision of all seamanship training in the RN. As a result the Portsmouth Command Seamanship School situated at Flathouse was added to the expanding responsibilities of the ND School where the rewriting of the *Seamanship Manual* was already in hand. However although the teaching of navigation and seamanship are by nature closely linked in many ways, in 1971 another transfer of responsibility took place, this time to *HMS Excellent*, the Gunnery School. Three years later when the Operations branch was introduced, this peripatetic child was placed in the care of *HMS Vernon,* the Torpedo School. The reasons for these changes are complicated but updating of the seamanship manuals is now the responsibility of the naval staff authors (civilians) who are accommodated in *HMS Dryad.*

Chapter VII

THE DAWN OF THE COMPUTER AGE

'The old order changeth giving place to new'
        The passing of Arthur-Tennyson

'But the age of chivalry is gone. That of sophisters, economists and calculators has succeeded; the glory of Europe is extinguished for ever.'
        Reflections on the French Revolution Edmund Burke

Admiral of the Fleet Sir Henry Oliver GCB, KCMG, MVO, LLD

Throughout his long and distinguished career and afterwards the founder of the Navigation School, Admiral of the Fleet Sir Henry Oliver, maintained a close and personal interest in its progress and welfare. From time to time he was visited by successive Captains of the establishment with messages of congratulation and good wishes as the years passed, until on 22 January 1965 our remarkable founder celebrated his one hundredth birthday. On that day he received more than 200 separate expressions of congratulation headed by one from the Lord High Admiral, Her Majesty the Queen, and to mark the occasion at noon a deputation headed by the Vice Chief of the Naval Staff, Vice Admiral Sir John Frewen, accompanied by the Captain, *HMS Dryad*, Captain D B N Mellis and the Director of Navigation and Tactical Control, Captain D N Forbes waited on him and presented him with an address which read as follows:

'We, serving officers of the Navigation Direction Plot Radar and Boatswain Branches, and officers of other branches serving in *HMS Dryad,* wish to convey to you our consciousness of the great debt owed to you by the Royal Navy in general and *HMS Dryad* in particular for your long and greatly distinguished service to our country before, during and after the Great War; and of our pride in you as the senior serving officer of the Navigating Branch, that tree planted by you whose fruit we are. And we take this opportunity, on the 37th anniversary of your promotion to the rank of Admiral of the Fleet and on the eve of your one hundredth birthday, to send you our heartfelt wishes for your continued good health and happiness.'

The Hydrographer of the Navy, also waited on him with some fair charts drawn by Sir Henry's own hand and some of the early surveys he had made. The Chief of the Defence Staff, Canadian Armed Forces sent the following message:

On the occasion of your one hundredth birthday, officers past and present of the Royal Canadian Navy who have been honoured to train and serve in the Navigation specialist Branch which you founded some 62 years ago, extend their most sincere congratulations and assurances that they will continue to do their utmost to uphold the well established principles of the Branch.'

Other tributes were received from the Royal Australian and Royal New Zealand Navies and the United States Navy and a number of messages were sent through the Captain, *HMS Dryad.*

Inevitably the long voyage had to end and to the great regret of all Navigating officers past and present on 15 October 1965, in his 101st year, Sir Henry died. A memorial service was held in Westminster Abbey on 16 November at which ND officers of the RN, the RAN and the RNZN acted as ushers. In his memory the new Instructional and Administrative block, then under construction at *Dryad,* was named Oliver block.

Flag appointments held by former Navigating Officers

It is interesting to record that in 1966 no less than eight Flag appointments were filled by former Navigating Officers viz, Commander in Chief, Home Fleet, Flag Officer Second in Command, Home Fleet, Flag Officer Medway, Deputy Supreme Allied Commander Atlantic, Admiral Superintendent, Portsmouth, Senior Naval Member of the Directing Staff, Imperial Defence College, Flag Officer, Royal Yachts, and Assistant Chief of the Naval Staff (Warfare). No better testimony is required to the firm foundations laid by Admiral of the Fleet Sir Henry Oliver.

Chief Petty Officer A N Bunce MBE

In Chapter III mention was made of the valuable services rendered to the Navigation School by the Chief Quartermaster, Chief Petty Officer G D Glover DSM who died in harness in 1932. His successor was an equally remarkable man, Chief Petty Officer A N Bunce MBE who retired at the age of 75 on 18 December 1967 after 35 years continuous and outstanding service to the School.

Arthur Newman Bunce joined the RN as a Boy 2nd Class in 1909 at the age of 17½. By 1913 he had qualified as an Able Seaman and a Seaman Gunner and in July 1914 was the trainer of a 12 pounder gun in the battleship, *Dreadnought.* It was in this ship that an incident occurred which was to affect his whole life. When up aloft to house the topmast for passing under the Forth bridge, a red hot cinder from the funnel lodged in his eye. Painful as it was, he did not report sick, for the annual gunnery prize shoot was due and as trainer of his gun, he was not going to miss such an important event. His crew duly won but soon afterwards World War I broke out and 'Joe Bunce was not going sick when the country was going to WAR' as he put it. By November he was permanently blind in that eye but no one but he knew of it. He served in the *Dreadnought* throughout the war becoming a Leading Seaman in 1916 and a Petty Officer in 1918.

After the war, the first scheme for promotion from the lower deck was introduced and Bunce was immediately put forward as a candidate. Alas a medical exam was necessary, his injury was discovered, and the MO told him that not only could he not become an officer but that he would have to be invalided. Undismayed, Bunce proposed a deal with the Doctor — if the latter would say nothing, he, Bunce, would give his word that he would withdraw as an officer candidate and never again get involved in a situation requiring an eyesight test. The MO agreed and despite many subsequent attempts by senior officers to persuade him to apply for promotion to Commissioned or Warrant rank, Bunce kept his word. He was rated Chief Petty Officer and was Chief Boatswain's Mate of the aircraft carrier, *Courageous,* when, in 1932, the time came for him to take his pension.

As Commander of the School at the time of Glover's decease, the author was faced with the task of finding a successor. Fortunately a member of the Staff at the time Lieutenant Commander (later Captain) T K W Atkinson (who was to lose his life as King's Harbour Master, Singapore when it fell to the Japanese in 1942) knew of Bunce's sterling qualities and that he was just about to take his pension. He was interviewed, offered the post, and accepted. From the moment he joined, we knew we had found the right man. Assisted by the two Chartroom attendants, Hopkins and Porter, Bunce quickly made the job his own. When war came in 1939, such active service ratings as were employed at the School were relieved by naval pensioners and Bunce became their leader. As Sergeant of a unit of the Home Guard he and his men went into action in 1941 when the School was bombed and, when later the move to Southwick House took place no one dreamed of interfering with his side of the business. All he wanted was for space to be allocated in which to house his charts and set up the various navigational instruments used for instruction.

When it became necessary to move the Navigation School to the old Sailors Hospital in the grounds of the RNC Greenwich in 1944, thanks to Bunce's efforts the transfer of equipment was achieved without a hitch and the same when the return to Southwick took place later in the year. After the war his position was recognised, somewhat tardily, by making him part of the official complement in the grade of Civil Employment Officer, but he continued to control the Chartroom which also served as his office until, with some reluctance on his part, he occupied a room of his own in the newly constructed administrative block.

In 1953 his outstanding service was recognised with an award of an MBE and few of Her Majesty's loyal subjects have appreciated the honour more. When the time came for Bunce to retire, a farewell luncheon in his honour was held at *Dryad* on 16 December 1967 at which the Commander in Chief, Portsmouth, Admiral Sir John Frewen GCB, the senior serving (N) specialist, presided and the Captain, of *Dryad,* Captain D S Tibbits DSC, made the principal speech. Fifty three officers attended including six former Captains of the establishment, 10 former Commanders and six former First Lieutenants. Some 218 officers contributed to a farewell presentation which consisted of a television set, a painting of *Dryad* by Lieutenant Commander Hugh Knollys DSC, and a cheque. Captain Tibbits ended his speech with these words:

'Depending on the period in which we have served at *Dryad* we recognise this master hand as belonging to 'Bunce' or to 'Mr Bunce'. Either way, he has become an institution and in retirement he will be a legend — remembered for all time, where Ns and Ds and NDs meet, for his unerring judgement and timing, as a

RP ratings under instruction in HMS Dryad in 1968.

brilliant staff officer, but above all for his loyalty, example and friendship.'

The computer age

The war was responsible for significant advances in many fields of scientific endeavour and it ushered in what is often referred to as 'the computer age' the impact of which on the work of the ND Branch must be recorded.

Radio aids to Navigation

Before the introduction of radio aids to navigation, the Navigating Officer was obliged to rely on dead-reckoning supplemented by astronomical observations to determine his position when out of sight of land. The accuracy of this position depended on a correct assessment of the ship's speed, leeway, tidal streams and currents. If obliged to make a landfall in poor visibility, he had to rely largely on soundings and fog signals and in fog the only indication of the presence of another ship in his vicinity was the sound of her fog signal. Today, thanks to the many forms of radio aids available, he has been relieved of a great deal of anxiety when navigating under adverse conditions, and considerably less use is made of astro-navigation.

In 1939, the only radio aid in general use was Medium Frequency Direction Finding, (M/F D/F) but by 1946 a number of different systems had been introduced as a result of requirements generated during the war. In May of that year the first International Meeting on Radio Aids to Marine Navigation (IMRAMN) assembled in London under the chairmanship of Sir Robert Watson-Watt with Mr Horton, Chief Scientist of the Admiralty Signal Establishment as vice chairman. Amongst the members of the UK Delegation were the Director of Navigation and Direction and the Director of Radio Equipment, as well as the Captain Superintendent and members of the scientific staff of ASWE. Most of the world's maritime nations were represented.

The conference lasted 10 days and agreement was reached on a number of desired technical developments. One of these was the Chart Comparison Unit which enabled the picture obtained by radar to be compared with the chart of the area and thus automatically indicate the ship's position in pilotage waters. Trials with an experimental set fitted in one of the Navigation School tenders, the *Starling,* were carried out in 1947.

The second meeting of IMRAMN took place in New York between 28 April and 5 May 1947 and was attended by 120 delegates from 31 countries. Although there were some minor disagreements, 28 clauses covering the broad developments of radio navigational aids in the future were adopted unanimously, a success attributable to the lengthy and detailed work done by the sub-committees. In due course the Ministry of Transport played an increasing part in the development of radio aids to Navigation, a description of each of which is given in the *Admiralty Manual of Navigation.* This publication originally sponsored by the Director of Navigation and Direction is written by the Naval Staff Authors attached to *HMS Dryad* and from it the following table is taken.

CLASSIFICATION OF RADIO AIDS

Function	Distance from nearest danger Miles	Accuracy required as %ge of distance from nearest danger	Urgency	Systems available
Ocean Aid	*Over 50*	*± 1 per cent*	*15 mins*	1 *MF/DF (shore-based)* 2 *Loran L* 3 *Consol* 4 *Decca* 5 *Omega**
Landfall Aid (L) **Coastal** **Navigation (C)**	*Between 50 & 3*	*± ½ mile* *± 200 yds*	*5 mins to ½ min*	1 *MF/DF shipborne &* 2 *Loran (L and C)* 3 *Consol (L)* 4 *Decca (L and C)* 5 *Radar*
Pilotage Aid	*Less than 3*	*± 50 yds*	*Instantaneous*	1 *Decca* 2 *Radar*

* French system under development — see below
Note Consol cannot be used inside a range of 25 miles from the transmitter.

142

The Omega system listed in the table above has the advantage of being world-wide and like Loran and Decca it is hyperbolic. When completed, it will employ eight transmitting stations located in various parts of the world, only seven of which were in service in 1977. It has an accuracy of two miles by day and four miles by night. Despite a number of initial setbacks, it is considered that there is a good future for this system and it is being widely fitted in the RN.

Radar

The employment of radar as an aid to navigation was well established before the end of World War II and it is now widely used not only for determining a ship's position in coastal waters but also for monitoring the movement of traffic in congested areas like the Straits of Dover and in rivers such as the Thames. Mention has been made of the Chart Comparison Unit and allied to this is what is termed 'blind pilotage' by which the Navigating Officer makes use of radar and radio aids to conduct a ship along a prearranged track in pilotage waters. This may be useful in low visibility when shore marks cannot be distinguished. Giving rein to his imagination in the *ND Bulletin* for June 1951, Lieut-Commander J D D Moore DSC, contributed the following as a glimpse of the future.

' "Lock into Shore Control," said the Captain and I promptly pressed the button and heard with relief the answering signal. I estimated that we were within 10 miles of the Nab Tower but the fog was so thick that we could scarcely see the jackstaff.

' "Locked in Sir" I reported and the Captain remarked that if I wished to go below and shift into plain clothes, he certainly for one would have no objection.

' "I'll go down to Pilotage Control, Sir," I replied rather with the air of one who desires to appear keen inspite of a marked inner sense of redundancy. However the miracle in the Pilotage Control Room revived my spirits and I will attempt to describe it.

'On the bulkhead the huge television screen clearly showed the ship as a scale model about three inches long outlined in light. She moved slowly over the illuminated surface of a much magnified large scale chart of the Portsmouth approaches. Lines of bright light snugly fitted into the coastline revealed how the PPI pictures of the various shore radars had been combined and matched precisely to the chart. Further inspection revealed points of light at the charted positions of the buoys while here and there, other model ships moved about leaving luminous trails behind them.

'The presence of these other ships gave no cause for anxiety because the wheel and the engine and revolution telegraphs were now being worked from shore through remote radio control, and should any other shipping approach, the necessary alterations of course would be made by the shore control direct. In fact the ship was now in the hands of operators ashore and since all other shipping in the port was likewise being conned from ashore in accordance with a planned traffic movement system, it was most unlikely that any other vessel would come near. If she did, then any emergency could be appreciated and action taken more rapidly by the skilled navigator and helmsman ashore than it could be from onboard. According to the new regulations shore control

The enclosed two-tier bridge fitted in a missile armed destroyer.

assumed full responsibility for the safety of the ship from the moment of locking in.'

Satellite navigation

The further developments which have taken place since the end of World War II have resulted in a new type of radio aid – satellite navigation (SATNAV). The current SATNAV known as Transit makes use of five satellites in circular polar orbit at a height of 600 kilometres above the earth, each taking about 106 minutes to complete an orbit. The path of each satellite is monitored by three stations located in the USA and the parameters of its orbit are transmitted by the stations to a computer carried by the satellite which stores this information. In this way each satellite's orbit relative to the earth is known exactly at all times.

The satellite transmits its identity, the parameters of its orbit, up-to-date ephemeris information and a time signal every two minutes. From this information, combined with doppler ranging, a ship fitted with a special receiver and a computer can deduce her position with an accuracy of the order of 250 metres. Apart from the considerable cost of the system, there are certain technical requirements which must be met in order to achieve such accuracy. The ship's speed must be known within 0.2 knot and her course within half a degree, but given these conditions, it is the most accurate world-wide method of position finding known today. A new type of satellite system, known as Navstar is under development which, it is hoped, will further increase the accuracy whilst reducing operational costs.

Ships Inertial Navigation System (SINS)

An aid to navigation of a different kind, the development of which was spurred on by the advent of the nuclear-powered true submarine in the Ships' Inertial Navigation System. The principle on which it is founded is not new. In 1852 the French scientist Foucault had shown by means of a pendulum that the rotation of the earth could be detected without reference to heavenly bodies and later repeated this demonstration using a gyroscope. This opened up the possibility of establishing a reference direction fixed in space (defined for example by the spin axis of a gyroscope) without the need for external observation.

In 1873 an article in *Nature* explained that if the earth's gravity vector could be defined in relation to two references fixed in space, the geographical position could be found. 'But,' the writer concluded, 'such delicacy of equipment is not to be be hoped for.' However the great advances made in recent years with precision engineering, metalurgy and electronics have now made this possible.

In 1923 Dr Schuler had shown that a pendulum could be used to define the true direction of the vertical, even on a moving vehicle, provided that the pendulum had a period of about 84 minutes. Although it is impracticable to make a conventional pendulum with so long a period, it is possible, nevertheless, by combining an accelerometer and a gyroscope, to make a synthetic pendulum having the required property. Given then gyroscopes and accelerometers of adequate accuracy, we may establish the requisite reference axes in space and also the direction of the true vertical, and hence find our position.

This is the principle of the present day Inertial Navigation System. It is based on the accurate measurement of the moment of inertia or acceleration in the North-South and East-West planes. It employs three gyroscopes, each with its axis parallel to one of the planes of movement (N - S, E - W, and vertical) and two accelerometers (N - S and E - W) mounted in a three point gymbal assembly to allow for the rolling, yawing and pitching of the ship. By integrating the accelerometer outputs we get N-S and E-W velocities and a second integration gives distance travelled in the N-S and E-W directions. In the construction of a synthetic Schuler pendulum the torque applied to precess a gyroscope is made proportional to the integrated accelerometer output which is proportional to the velocity. By performing a second integration the position is established.

Although the inertial systems in use at sea today have reached a high standard of technical achievement, they are subject to certain sources of cumulative error; hence whenever an opportunity occurs, it is desirable to check the position by other means. The first SINS were produced in the USA in the late 1940s but the Admiralty Compass Observatory has since developed those in use in the RN's nuclear-powered submarines and some surface vessels.

Despite the fact that SINS provides both an accurately stabilised horizontal platform and a gyro compass, it is still necessary to fit separate gyro compasses which are more robust than the delicate instruments of which the former is composed. Great improvements have been made in these and the liability to wander in high latitudes, which was a feature of the earlier compasses, has been reduced considerably. By the simple expedient of removing their north-seeking characteristics they can be turned into a directional gyro compensated only for movement in the vertical plane. The compass then becomes a free 'directional' gyro.

Submarine polar navigation

The *USS Nautilus* was the first submarine to transit the North Pole during an arctic voyage in 1958. The following year *USS Skate* was the first ship to surface at the pole. The RN did not commission its first nuclear-powered submarine, *Dreadnought,* until April 1963 and it was not until eight years later that an attempt was made to emulate the achievement of the two US ships.

In preparation for the voyage, the *Dreadnought's* standard navigational equipment consisting of one SINS Mk 1, one Mk 23 compass, and one Arma-Brown Mk 1. Model 5 compass was supplemented by a Mk 19 compass which was installed in the radar office from which much of the normal equipment had to be removed. This last is a sophisticated gyro compass which, in addition to giving very accurate azimuth, also provides roll and pitch information for ship's attitude purposes and for the stabilisation of weapon systems. The Sperry Mk 19 is made in the USA but a British-designed Naval Compass Stabiliser Mk 1 (NCS1) has been developed to use in the RN).

Another significant factor on this voyage was the presence onboard of Mr W L Thomson, a scientist from the Admiralty Compass Observatory, whose contribution to the success of the voyage, though difficult to quantify, was certainly great.

The ship sailed from Faslane on 20 February 1971 and arrived off Spitzbergen on the morning of the 26th, then surfaced and proceeded northwards up the coast. Late that afternoon as it was obvious that she was approaching the ice edge, she dived and set course for the Pole.

The main navigational problem with which she was confronted stemmed from fact that since all gyro compasses depend for their north-seeking qualities on the tilting motion of the horizontal component of the earth's rotation which at the pole is zero, they cannot be used to direct a vessel during her final approach to that position. Even the highest quality gyro compass will lose its north-seeking ability within a few degrees of the pole, and it then becomes necessary to employ other techniques to obtain a heading reference. The SINS equipment can be made to operate in a directional role to latitude $90°$ and, to a lesser extent the Mark 19 compass can be similarly used. These then together with the log form the basis for dead reckoning in extreme latitudes. Radio aids can be used to check the position and submarines are also fitted with a periscope sextant incorporating an artificial horizon which proved very useful, but observations taken with a hand held sextant are liable to suffer from abnormal refraction and the effect of the intense cold on the sextant as well as from the lack of a good horizon.

In a letter to the author Commander A G Kennedy who was in command of the *Dreadnought* during her polar voyage, remarks, 'we reached the north pole at 0800 on March 3, but due to the very heavy ice condition, which at times was more than 100 feet thick, it was difficult to find a polynya (window) suitable for surfacing. One was eventually found that afternoon, and having cleared the ice from the top of the conning tower, we stepped out into a clear, cold arctic night with a temperature of 37°below zero. We stayed in this position until 0200 the next morning when, having completed various tasks, we dived and headed south along the Greenwich meridian. All courses from the pole being south it is important to know along which meridian the ship is heading.'

The Navigating Officer of the *Dreadnought* during the voyage was Lieut-Commander C L Napier.

Qualified (N) Officers in submarines

The *Dreadnought* was followed, after an interval of three years, by the first of five Fleet submarines, *HMS Valiant,* and it was decided that four of the submarine officers detailed to serve in these ships (they are still 'boats' to the submariners) should take the (N) portion of the ND Qualifying Course. However with the commissioning of the first of the ballistic missile-armed submarines, *Resolution,* (7500 tons) on 2 October 1967 and in view of the sophisticated navigational equipment installed in her, it was decided that all submarines of this type should carry an officer specially qualified for the navigational task peculiar to these ships. An (N) officer was appointed to the staff of the Chief Polaris Executive, whilst a member of *Dryad's* staff doubled as Staff ND Officer to the Flag Officer, Submarines.

In October 1976, *Sovereign,* the second ship of the *Swiftsure* class of Fleet submarines, repeated the *Dreadnought's* polar exploit by surfacing at the north pole. The scientist, Mr W L Thomson, who had taken part in the latter's polar voyage was on board the former ship to supervise and advise on the navigational equipment carried.

The tender HMS Ulster.

Captain Tibitts, commanding HMS Dryad, with Rear Admiral Frank L Johnson US Navy.

ND Trials and Development Section

The wider responsibilities which devolved on the Director of Navigation and Direction in 1945 were mentioned earlier and are set out in detail in Appendix IV. They covered not only advice on the arrangement and lay out of bridges and charthouses, but also that of Operations Rooms and Plotting Rooms as well as for the trials of new plotting equipment. It was soon evident that the ND Branch needed a Trials and Development Section similar to those attached to the other Seaman sub-specialist branches. The post war climate of economy and personnel problems delayed the creation of such an organisation until 1948 when it was set up officially in *Dryad* and added to the responsibilities of the Captain of the establishment, but led by a Commander ND who was accountable to the Director of Navigation and Direction. The first Commander (X), as he was known, was Commander (N) E F S Back DSC. Aided by a team of ND 'application' officers at the Admiralty Surface Weapons Establishment, the ND (X) Section played a key role in guiding the AIO into the computer age and in designing new Operations Rooms and hardware as well as reconciling and co-ordinating the varying requirements of the users with ship designers in the Ministry of Defence.

The ND Books and Instructional Publications Section

As mentioned in Chapter VI, in 1950 the ND Division of the Admiralty had acquired an additional Commander to rewrite the *Seamanship Manual*. The Division, in fact, was responsible to the Board for the 'preparation and periodical revision' of not only this book but also of five others together with any additional books 'which come within the responsibility' of the branch. It soon became evident that the ad hoc method of appointing an officer to deal with a particular requirement was no longer acceptable and that a permanent organisation was needed. Accordingly a 'Books and Instructional Publications Section' was established in *Dryad* in 1952 under Lieut-Commander R Dyer. As the number of books needed to cover the various activities of the AIO increased, the practice of employing active-service officers exclusively as authors was seen to be unsatisfactory so they were replaced gradually by retired officers and others with the necessary experience who were employed on a permanent basis in a civilian capacity.

The first two officers to be appointed as civilian authors were P M Whatley and J D D Moore both retired Lieut-Commanders (N) who joined the section in the late 1950s. The last named, as head of the BIP section, directed its work and promoted its expansion to meet the needs of the AIO for the next 20 years as it moved into the computer age. Each ADA system called for a set of volumes to describe its capabilities and limitations for the benefit of its users, including code books listing the manual injections which the operators might need. The section expanded and by 1968 when the Naval Staff was reorganised as described below, the staff of the Director of Navigation and Tactical Control as he was then styled, had six civilian authors working in *Dryad* and was responsible for the production of some 50 volumes which they had written and which had to be kept up to date.

The *Admiralty Manuals of Navigation and Seamanship* are on sale to the public and have been acclaimed throughout the world as authoritative textbooks. They are used not only in warships but by the merchant navies of many foreign countries. The latest edition of the *Seamanship Manual* written by Whatley and Moore with the assistance of a former Boatswain, Lieutenant (SD) W D Hughes has sold more than 100,000 copies to the public besides those required for the Royal Navy.

Automation

The fundamental changes in the structure and training of the Seaman Branch which are about to be described, was due to the great advance made during the 1950s in computer technology. The scientists working for the Admiralty were not slow to appreciate that the introduction of this technology would lead inevitably to a revolution in the methods of controlling weapons being developed for use in maritime warfare. In particular it was foreseen that in the field of Action Information, the application of this new technology, now known as automation, would necessitate a completely fresh approach. The problem which the Action Information Organisation was intended to solve was basically that of data processing, *ie,* the sorting and filtering of the flood of information obtained from a warship's sensors, mainly radar and sonar, and its presentation to the command in an intelligible and concise form thus enabling the ship's armament to be directed and controlled to the best advantage.

Not only was the digital computer, on which automation is based, ideally suited to the solution of such data-processing problems, but it also provided a means for the automatic control of the weapons systems, if this seemed to be desirable. However the adoption of automation in the AIO presented a challenge, because while making full use of the computer's problem-solving capability it was essential to ensure that the Captain and ship's officers remained firmly in control of the tactical handling of the ship in battle.

The leading figures in advocating this new approach were Dr R Benjamin BSc (Eng), PhD, ACGI, FIEE, then working in the Admiralty Surface Weapons Establishment at Portsmouth and close to Southwick Park, and Commander P W Holt (ND) (N†). In 1959 the first named demonstrated to the Admiralty naval staff that it was feasible to introduce automation into the AIO and he gave the outlines of a system which later became known as Action Data Automation (ADA). Since the end of World War II, the RN had made considerable progress with data processing in the AIO, notably in developing improved methods of presentation on cathode ray tube displays based largely on analogue computers. A system known as the Comprehensive Display System was already at sea in the carrier *Victorious,* so Dr Benjamin's proposals came as no surprise to the naval staff and it was not long before board approval was given to the development of ADA. To ensure close collaboration between the design and the user sides in the RN and between both these and the electronics industry which would have to produce the required equipment, was now the main aim.

The development of ADA

The instructions given to a computer to enable an operator to control and use it to the best effect are called programs and the whole activity of designing, making and using them is called software as opposed to the computers themselves, their circuitry, control consoles and ancillary equipment which is known as hardware. It was in the field of software that the ND Branch was called upon to give a lead. It was essential to make sure that the work of the programmers took into account the needs of maritime tactics and that their use and control would be easily understood by ship's Operation Room teams. The idea was that these last would control the ship's sensors, data processing and weapons by means of manual injections (pressing the appropriate buttons) while seated at consoles, in accordance with a prepared code or directory designed to cover all their requirements.

To implement this, Dr Benjamin and Commander Holt persuaded the Admiralty to establish an organisation known as 'The ADA Rule-Writing Group' (ARWG). Led by Commander Holt, it comprised officers from all the specialist branches (ND, Air, Gunnery, Torpedo, Anti-submarine and Communications). Working closely with the programmers employed by the Ministry of Defence, they success-fully tackled all the problems as they arose and the first complete ADA Weapons

system was installed in the second batch of County class, missile-armed destroyers, the
the delivery of which was made between 1966 and 1971.

Creation of a Centralised Appointing System

On April 1 1965 another break occurred with a long established custom when the
Captain, of *Dryad*, ceased to be the appointing authority for (N), (D), (PR)
and (B) officers. A centralised appointing system was set up in the Ministry of
Defence to handle all officers' appointments. However the long standing personal
link between the Captain of the School and the Specialist officers trained there
was not entirely severed since he continued to be consulted by the new Director
of Naval Officers' Appointments who had a specialist representative of the
branch on his staff. Moreover officers were encouraged to keep in touch with
the Captain of their 'Alma Mater' *Dryad*.

Courses for Merchant Navy Officers

The appearance on the maritime scene of supertankers drawing between 50 and
60 feet and the increasing number of collisions being recorded led to the introduction
in 1966 of courses for senior Merchant Navy Officers which led to the establishment
of an interesting liaison and exchange of ideas to the mutual advantage of both
services.

The phasing out of the Aircraft Carriers

In 1966 the Government pronounced a suspended sentence of death on the RN's
remaining aircraft carriers and it was clear that this much contested decison would
affect the future of the (D) specialists. However as was pointed out at the time,
fighter control though highly important, was only a small part of a (D) officer's
expertise and it could be assumed therefore, that his skills would be as much in
demand in the future as they had been in the past. Instead of being largely locked
up in carriers they would be available for appointments in other modern ships
in the fleet in which the Action Information Organisation was certain to remain
the nerve centre of operations.

The abolition of the Director of Navigation and Tactical Control

The practical effects of the introduction of automation into the Action Information
Organisation, by which the direction and control of a ship's weapons system were
centralised within the Operations Room, were becoming apparent. The existing
division of the Seaman Branch into sub-specialised branches, each having its own
separate training scheme, was incompatible with the development of the comprehensive control of weapons systems and the speedy response to all forms of attack
which were now available.

As a consequence of this it was evident that a reorganisation of the naval staff
had become necessary and in 1968 this took place. As a result the 55-year-old post
of Director of Navigation was swept away after 23 years of independence and grow-

ing responsibility. He was not the only casualty. Accompanying him to the chopping block were the Directors of the Gunnery, Torpedo, A/S Warfare and many other associated Divisions. The object of the exercise was:

a To bring the naval staff more closely into line with the organisation of the central staff in the Ministry of Defence, thus facilitating the exchange of information.

b To match the organisations of the other services.

c To functionalise

Two new Directorates were created ie Naval Operational Requirements (DNOR) and Naval Warfare, (DNW) each consisting of some 22 officers representing a cross-section of specialisation and sub-specialistion, to take over the work formerly performed by what were known as The Tribal Chieftains. Captains of each sub-specialisation were to hold functional posts within the new Directorates, one of whom on DNW's staff was to be a Captain ND (N†) who, working through his Director, would act as the adviser on Navigation to the Admiralty board in such matters as collisions and groundings etc.

Revision of the ND Course

The year 1969 saw a revision of the ND course which was shortened from 18 to 12 weeks. The first of the new style ND courses began in September of that year and the new syllabus roused considerable interest at the other seaman sub-specialist schools and came to be regarded as a suitable basis for future Operations branch officers, the introduction of whom was then under consideration.

The Principal Warfare Officers (PWO) and the Centralisation of Shore Training

After much discussion between the seamen sub-specialist schools the aims of all long courses were changed to reflect:

a Training as an Operations Room Officer.

b Training in a particular sub-specialisation.

and after a long term trial in the Fleet, it was decided in 1972 to change the title of Operations Room Officer to that of Principal Warfare Officer. This decision followed logically from the re-arrangement of general naval training in four centres which had been foreshadowed in the 1970 defence estimates. One of the centres was to be *Dryad* which was to become the one for Tactical and Operational Training. To implement this decision, it was necessary for the ND School to absorb parts of the Joint A/S School, of the Torpedo School, *Vernon,* and of the Gunnery School, *Excellent,* as well as the Communications School, *Mercury,* though it was not intended that the last named should move from its existing site at Leydene.

Thus by 1970, as one of the seaman sub-specialist Schools, *Dryad's* main professional courses were those for qualifying Navigation and Direction Officers who received the more theoretical aspects of their training dovetailed with the essence of the job, *ie*, practical work at sea or directing live aircraft, both fixed wing and rotary, at the RN Air Stations at Yeovilton and Portland. Other officer courses included familiarisation for Acting Sub-Lieutenants, embryo and substantive Special Duties List Officers, Instructor Officers about to take up a sea appointment, and foreign officers. The scope of the training, however, was not limited to the more conventional users. It covered the training of Helicopter Control Officers and ratings, Hovercraft navigators and pilots, masters of Merchant Navy tankers (who take a refresher course in blind pilotage) and a number of short familiarisation and acquaint courses. In all some 98 different courses are provided in *Dryad,* an indication of the variety of the task.

Because of the excellent practical operational facilities available, the demand for Command Team training increased as the number of trainers and models grew. A trainer is a computer controlled simulator which can generate controllable threats in the form of ships, aircraft and missiles which are displayed as simulated radar echoes in a number of life-sized mock-ups of ships operations rooms known as models. It is therefore possible to exercise a ship's operation team from the Captain to the most junior Radar rating in a reasonably realistic situation. The exercise is controlled by an officer known as the Trainer and when it is over, an extensive post-mortem takes place at which mistakes are pointed out and views are aired. To keep pace with changes in ships and equipment, new models are constructed from time to time.

TRAINERS (CUNNINGHAM BUILDING)

ADA Trainer	*Computer Room, Planning and Tape Preparation Room,*	*Tactical Trainer*	*Tactical Block (Tactical school, Offices).*

TRAINER CREWS

ADA Monitoring Officers and Trainer Crew   *Tactical Monitoring Officers and Trainer Crew*

MODEL OPERATIONS ROOMS

ADA GMD Model   *20 General-Purpose Cubicles*
Future ADA Models
                             2 MHQs

Move of the Tactical School to Southwick

As part of the plan for centralised training announced in 1970, the Tactical School was to move from its home in the former Royal Military Academy at Woolwich to a new building in *Dryad.* This had been allowed for in stage six of the development plan and was completed in February 1970; the first tactical course was held there the following June.

Temporary Halt in (N) and (D) specialisation

Almost unnoticed in the general upheaval which followed on the decision to introduce the PWO was the related one of the abolition of sub-specialisation for general list officers and for a time it seemed as if the long and historic line of (N) officers was about to die out with the course due to finish in May 1972. However wiser counsels ultimately prevailed and in July 1973 a new type of sub-specialist (N) course was introduced, known as the Principal Warfare Officer (Navigation) [PWO (N)] Course. It comprised seven officers including two from the RAN and lasted 12 weeks, three of which were spent at sea. At the same time an Advanced (N) course lasting five weeks was re-introduced.

Training for the (D) Specialisation also ceased in May 1972 but the continuing need for aircraft controllers for which an output of about 24 a year was requested, was met by a course at Yeovilton, responsibility for which was transferred to the Flag Officer, Naval Air Command, but the Captain of *Dryad* remained responsible for the operational performance of aircraft direction.

Visit of HM the Queen

On 20 July 1973, Her Majesty the Queen honoured *Dryad* with a visit. She was received by a royal guard drawn up in front of Oliver block and visited the Redpole and Harrier trainers, where a multi-threat game was in progress. She was then conducted through the Purbrook block where a number of students were being instructed in radar reporting, plotting and blind pilotage. She next visited the Cunningham block where the Director of the Tactical School explained the features of a game which was in progress, after which she boarded a land-rover and toured the establishment ending up at the Wrens block where she was taken up to the roof for an overall view of the park. She then returned to Southwick House and visited the ante-room containing the famous 'D' Day wall map and also the ward-room.

Establishment of the School of Maritime Operations

The last link with the past was severed when on 15 October 1974 the School of Navigation and Direction became the School of Maritime Operations, though the parent ship name of *Dryad* was retained. In effect this made *Dryad* the alma mater of Principal Warfare Officers rather than exclusively that of the PWO(N). This change of role reflected a logical evolution from that point in time when the (N) Branch first interested itself in the Action Information Organisation, Aircraft Direction and the Radar branch. With the dawn of the computer age in maritime warfare the need and the opportunity arose to integrate the fighting skills within ships teams and to match the training effort to the future needs of the fleet. In the new organisation the Captain of the School of Maritime Operations became the single authority responsible to the Commander in Chief, Naval Home Command for the basic training of Seaman officers and Operations branch ratings in anti-submarine warfare, above water warfare, electronic warfare, action information organisation, aircraft control, communications and navigation.

The Queen has a point explained to her during her visit to HMS Dryad in 1973.

As the result of a comprehensive review of officers' training, a complete progressive system has been evolved from Sub-Lieutenant to Command in which the centralisation of warfare training in *Dryad* is destined to play the major role. It is expected that this will lead to better preparation for qualification for a Bridge Watchkeeping Certificate and the gaining of the knowledge necessary to qualify as a Principal Warfare officer. SMOPS is also closely concerned in the preparation of officers for command.

HMS Dryad as seen by John Winton (reproduced from *The Naval Review,* October 1975 by the kind permission of the author, John Winton, and the editor, Vice Admiral Sir Ian McGeogh KCB, DSO, DSC.)

'Those who knew *Dryad* in the late fifties, say, when there was the country house, the stables, the pig farm and some rows of unmentionably squalid huts, simply would not recognise it now. *Dryad* is big and getting bigger all the time. It is a concrete, glass and steel complex with a campus like a modern university. One great glass and concrete block houses the School of Maritime Operations and another one right next door the Tactical School. There are brick blocks full of radar sets and concrete blocks full of computers (one of which, incidentally has been programmed to be unbeatable at draughts).

'There is a seven storey Wrennery, and an indoor riding school near completion and a Cinemasium (cinema cum gymnasium). There is some energetic gardening; lines of new trees and beds of mahonia and Rose of Sharon and potentilla and some interesting plants like tall gladioli. They have a green house and a swimming pool and squash courts. They have nothing as mundane as a sick bay; they have a Medical and Dental Centre. And there are dozens more buildings for eating in and cooking in and living in and drinking in and listening to lectures in and watching TV in. They seem to have been building new blocks of something as fast as they can go for years. Coming from the world outside, where there are some chilly winds of austerity blowing, it is an odd experience to see such ample signs of material prosperity. Where one wonders are all those defence cuts one keeps reading about?

'Touring *Dryad,* one walks feeling slightly disembodied along silent air-conditioned corridors. Somebody knocks at a door. A face appears. Silent scrutiny. Door opens. More corridors. Somebody pins something like a sawn off Biro to your lapel. At the top of a breathless flight of stairs a dishy red-head Third Officer WRNS magically materialises waiting to shake hands. More silent air-conditioned corridors and then suddenly — an authentic ship's Operations Room. It is all there — rows of orange radar screens, red lighting, scrambled broadcast voices all talking refined Serbo-Croat, officers walking restlessly too and fro, pausing to clap despairing hands to foreheads, exclaiming 'death where is thy sting?' The next room is jammed full of Wrens, wearing headphones, bashing buttons on consoles, typing at space age typewriters, knitting or just sitting. Next is an auditorium fitted out like a 21st century parliament. One man standing at a lectern in front of a display of lights and symbols that come and go, is addressing the others. His voice is stern, admonishing. From time to time one of the listeners seizes a hand microphone in front of him and hotly contradicts the speaker. Never have I seen so much concentrated cerebral activity, so many frowning furrowed foreheads, so many furiously puffed cigarettes.

'In yet another room, a dozen or so trainee plotters are learning how to set down a simple anti-submarine tracking incident. An instructor flits from side to side, seeing that they have all got their plotting tables switched on right scale, right time etc. Pick up a pair of headphones, half expecting to hear the day's recipe or the latest test match score but there is only a lugubrious voice repeating the same set of numbers over and over again. Ask the nearest plotter what he is doing. He turns out to be a guttural Geordie with an impenetrable accent. His neighbour is an equally monoglot Scot. (This tends to confirm one of my favourite mental visions: a Recruiting Officer to any boy with an especially marked speech idiosyncrasy, "come along my lad, we need you as a Communication number").

'What you might well ask, is going on in *Dryad?* The main cause of the turmoil is the advent of a gentleman called a Principal Warfare Officer, PWO for short, pronounced Peewo . . . In the late 1960s admirals doing sea inspections discovered that seamen officers of the old sub-specialisation (G, TAS, N, and C) though quite competent in their own lines of business, were not professionally versatile enough, not broadly based enough in their experience, not flexible enough in their responses, to be able to deal quickly and correctly with modern forms of attack. These attacks could come from sea, air or underwater, or any combination of all three. Moreover an attack could develop before the Captain could even be called to the Operations Room. At the same time it was felt that the depth of their specialist knowledge tended to make officers involve themselves too intimately in the nuts and bolts of their parts of ship.

'So it was decided that a new kind of multi-purpose, all-singing all-dancing officer should be trained and a new form of establishment, the School of Maritime Operations (SMOPS) set up to train him. The old sub-specialisations would be abolished. The training functions of *Excellent, Vernon* and parts of *Mercury* should, over a period of years, be concentrated in *Dryad* under the aegis of SMOPS. Hence the furious rate of building at *Dryad.*

'The Maritime Tactical School, which co-exists at Southwick with the School of Maritime Operations, shares the same facilities but is a separate entity, responsible to CINCNAVHOME (Commander in Chief, Naval Home Command). In dull moments I like to think of the Tactical School mandarins, pondering their imponderables. I am probably grossly over-simplifying, but it seems that tactics is still the art of compromise in a period of permanent political tension.

'From quite early on in its history *Dryad* used models, tactical trainers and mock-ups of ship's Operations Rooms for courses to practice on. The modern simulated exercise, a major training tool in the School of Maritime Operations has reached a highly sophisticated level, using an enormously costly investment in buildings, electronic equipment and staff. However it is quite rightly argued that to assemble the same number of ships, aircraft, submarines and missiles, both friendly and hostile, at sea, would be very much more expensive. As it is, a big exercise lasts most of the forenoon, with various incidents being injected, actions and reactions recorded, and the whole is subjected to a critical post-exercise wash-up in the afternoon (hence that parliamentary debating chamber). So that there can be no argument later about what actually happened, the state board is photographed at very short intervals of time, and the film can be run back and scrutinised later.

'The exercises could not be run without the Wrens, who perform necessary but often rather dull and repetitive tasks. Many a Wren is left all by herself in her solitary room, or Vehicle as it is called, bashing buttons, twiddling knobs, and manipulating the controls so that her simulated ship or aircraft continues to behave on everybody's screens just as the exercise planners require.

'The Wrens have also exerted a tremendously civilising influence on the place as a whole. Not so very long ago it used to take a posse of five or six beefy patrolmen to deal with the incoming libertymen roaring off from the last bus from town. Now all is quiet as a monastery cell. As somebody told me in the *Dryad* club "they've all got their little Jenny Wrens to make eyes at. Ye wouldn't believe it, they sit and make eyes at each other, even at breakfast over a soggy egg."

'Southwick does suffer from one geographical disadvantage. There is a sense of being landlocked. *HMS Dryland* as the *Navy News* cartoonist calls it, is true in more senses than pun. That great hill in front effectually shuts out sight and sound of the sea. It is logistically that much more difficult to arrange sea trips at a time when it is psychologically vital to give young men just joined a whiff of the sea. They can more easily leave the service now, only half a dog watch after they have joined it, and months in class rooms soon take the edge off their enthusiasm.'

Retrospect

Looking back over the centuries spanning the history of navigating officers in the RN, one basic factor obtrudes: the paramount importance of knowing your position at all times in relation to natural hazards and additionally in time of war, with regard to your opponent. As has been mentioned earlier, a knowledge of navigation is indeed part of the stock in trade of every seaman, but experience has shown that the safety of HM Ships at sea and of aircraft in the air can only be assured as a result of specialist training and practical experience of an art which makes a highly important contribution to the efficiency of a maritimé force.

The scientific equipment available today has made the work of the navigator, both at sea and in the air, simpler in some respects but more complicated in others, but the basic principle stated above has not changed. How nearly were the lessons of history ignored a short time ago, when the wind of change blew through Whitehall sweeping away sub-specialisation and leaving the Principal Warfare Officer as what John Winton refers to as 'a new kind of multi-purpose, all-singing, all-dancing officer.' Fortunately the counter blast from those at sea, obliged a re-appraisal of this unwise decision. The sophisticated equipment available today in modern warships and aircraft demands an even higher standard of navigation than formerly. Indeed, the navigational side of the School of Maritime Operations training is not only to continue but is to be carried out once again in *Mercury*, a move in 1977 that must surely bring a wry smile to the watching spirit of Dummy Oliver! The wheel has turned full circle since he first persuaded the powers that be, some four and seventy years ago of the importance of navigation in the Royal Navy.

'Here is my journey's end, here is my butt, and very sea-mark of my utmost sail' — Othello Act V — Scene 2

Appendix I

CIRCULAR LETTER

ADMIRALTY, 15 JUNE 1903

My Lords Commissioners of the Admiralty having had under their consideration the question of the selection, training, and advancement of Navigating Officers of the Royal Navy, have decided to carry out certain changes in the existing system as enumerated below.

1   Officers will, as hitherto, be selected from those who volunteer for navigating duties, preference being given to those who have obtained a First Class in Pilotage in the examination for the rank of Lieutenant, and who have obtained good classes in navigation and other subjects.

2   Selected candidates will be sent to a Navigation School Ship which is about to be established at Portsmouth, with a suitable staff of instructors. The course of instruction while they are attached to the school ship will last for 90 working days, part of the time being spent at sea in the ship and the remainder on shore. While going through the course they will live on the school ship. The details of this course are given in Appendix A.

After the candidates have qualified in the School they will, as far as practicable, be appointed to serve for a short period in the large ships of the Mediterranean, Home, and Channel Fleets, so as to obtain experience under the Navigating Officers in the work of a Fleet in regard to navigating duties as laid down in Appendix B. It will be necessary for every candidate to obtain a certificate from the Navigating Officer as to his qualifications, which is to be forwarded through the Captain of the ship with his covering remarks.

Upon the result of the examination in the School and the reports from the ships to which they are afterwards sent, the permanent appointment of officers for navigating duties will depend.

3   Before presenting himself for examination in Pilotage for first-class ships, a Lieutenant (N) will be permitted to attend the School for one month's study. He will be allowed to make his own choice of the subjects he wishes to study, bearing in mind that the examination will include the subjects in which he was previously examined when in the School as a Sub Lieutenant, and that an advanced knowledge of those subjects will be required. The present compass course at Greenwich prior to passing for 1st class ships will be abolished.

Navigating Officers will also be granted facilities for attending the School for a month's course of study at periodical intervals during their subsequent career.

4   The nature of the examination in Pilotage for 1st class ships will be made more searching and it will be conducted by the officers on the staff of the Navigation School Ship, partly viva voce, and partly on paper. First and second-class certificates of proficiency only will be awarded, the third-class certificate being abolished. Any officer who fails to pass at the second trial will have his name erased from the list of Navigating Officers.

The examination will be compulsory, and officers will be obliged to present themselves for examination within a reasonable time after completing three years' sea service as Lieutenants (N).

5   Navigating Officers, while borne in ships in reserve, will be given every opportunity of going through short courses of Gunnery and Torpedo in order to keep themselves efficient in these duties.

6   Lieutenants (N) will in future be placed on exactly the same footing as regards executive

159

command and ship's duty generally as Gunnery and Torpedo Lieutenants, and are not to be excused from any ship's duties except those which interfere with the special duties pertaining to them. They will be appointed and succeed to the position of First Lieutenant, if a vacancy occurs, in all ships where a Commander is borne exactly in the same manner as any other specialist officer.

A Commander when borne for Navigating duties will not be appointed as the Executive Officer.

In ships where no Commander is borne the Navigating Officer will not be appointed for First Lieutenant's duties.

In rendering the special report on the qualifications of a Navigating Officer (Article 1,035, King's Regulations) a further clause is to be added, viz:

(g) As to his capabilities as an Executive Officer.

7 Midshipmen who show special aptitude when working with the Navigating Officer (Article 1,066, King's Regulations) are whenever possible when the ship is under way to be taken off other duties, and to navigate the ship independently from the after bridge, fixing positions on the chart, etc, and bringing the result of such work to the Navigating Officer. Midshipmen who qualify in this manner satisfactorily are to be specially reported to the Admiralty.

8 The ordinary Pilotage course for Acting Sub Lieutenants, which was reduced to six weeks a few years ago, will be extended to the original period of two months. As soon as possible this course will be transferred from the RN College, Greenwich, to Portsmouth, and will then include practical instruction in, and opportunities of, adjusting the compasses of destroyers.

9 Instead of one Commissioned Officer taking sights and working the reckoning daily (as laid down in Article 1,019, King's Regulations), arrangements are to be made, when practicable, for one Junior Lieutenant or Sub Lieutenant to be taken partially off watch-keeping (keeping a dog or morning watch), so as to work with the Navigating Officer for 10 working days under way, but not necessarily all in one trip.

The officer thus told off is to be on deck when coasting, making the land, going in and out of harbour, etc, and is to be in every way encouraged to get an insight into navigating duties. If at the end of the 10 days the Captain is satisfied with his work, he will be relieved and another officer is to be told off for this duty. A special report is then to be forwarded to the Admiralty that the course has been duly performed by the officer.

Lieutenants who go through this course satisfactorily will be favourably considered for the command of destroyers.

My Lords consider that in large fleets abroad a few lectures on the subject of Navigation might with advantage be given during the winter months. By this means many officers in the fleet would acquire a better knowledge of practical navigation and would thereby be rendered more fit for command.

10 These Regulations are to come into force from this date.

By Command of their Lordships,

EVAN MACGREGOR

To all Commanders in Chief,
Captains, Commanders, and
Commander Officers of
HM Ships and Vessels at Home
and Abroad

APPENDIX A Course of instruction on shore
Terrestrial Magnetism

(a)   Compasses; including the Elementary Manual and Admiralty Manual and Admiralty Manual, leaving out the Mathematical Theory.

(b)   Effects of electrical appliances on compasses and chronometers, and the regulations affecting the same.

(c)   A visit to the Observatory at Deptford.

Navigational Astronomy

(a)   Finding the stars, use of star finder, description of different astronomical methods for obtaining positions at sea (Lecky).

(b)   Use of ex-meridian tables, azimuth tables, slide rule, new navigation (maximum and minimum altitudes), great circle tables, and instruction in all the most approved modern short and accurate methods of obtaining astronomical positions at sea.

(c)   Principles of advanced meteorology (Abercromby), winds, currents, ocean passages, revolving storms.

(d)   Artificial horizon sights and use of sextant stand (sun and star observations). Supply, management, rating and comparisons of chronometers, meridian distances. (This part of the instruction will have to run through the whole course, being dependent on the weather).

Surveying
(The whole of this Course will be carried out at the Port)

1   Elementary principles of the various chart projectsion.

2   Description and use of surveying instruments – theodolite, sextant, station pointer (including theory of). Simple optical principles of telescopes and binoculars.

3   Theory of tides (a simple explanation, such as Lecky's), causes affecting tides, use of tables, tidal streams, etc. Tide pole, erecting, watching, and recording observations. Datum mark.

4   (a)   Construction of a small plan. (This will be carried out practically preceded by an explanation of the principles involved).

(b)   Principles of triangulation, selection of stations and marks, measurement of base. True bearing by theodilite and sextant, and by sextant alone.

(c)   Correcting the angles and working out the triangulation, determining the scale, plotting the triangulation, laying off chords, use of beam compasses, brass scale.

(d)   Elementary principles of coast lining, topography, heights, etc.

(e)   Lead lines, and correction of. Sounding. How to get on a line of soundings. Reduction of soundings.

(f)   Obtaining variation by landing compass.

(g)   Drawing the plan. Title. Memoir. Information required on the plan. How to record and send in rough work.

(Note – Each candidate will plot and draw the plan, and marks will be awarded for this and the way he has kept his Field Book in the final examination).

(h)   Rapid methods of rough surveying. Examination of a shoal or suspected area out of sight of land and how to fix it. (lectures only – not to be done practically).

Ship and Fleet Work

(a)   Thorough knowledge of principles of Martin's mooring board and Battenberg's course indicator, with problems. Cruisers opening and closing a fleet, rule of the road, etc.

(b)   Principles of anchoring and mooring on other ships. Berthing a fleet; bringing a fleet into harbour.

(c)   Handling ships, action of screws on rudder, use of helm, etc. Obtaining turning circles. Explanation of system of steering gear and visit to ships in yard.

This completes the course on shore

Officers will now visit some of the leading instrument makers in a similar way to the visits paid by Gunnery and Torpedo candidates to Woolwich and the leading electrical firms.

1.   Swinging ship and adjusting compasses. Use of Thomson's Deflector.
2.   Practical pilotage; navigating a ship among shoals; fixing the ship, etc.
3.   Astronomical observations, being a practical application of the previous instruction in 'Navigational Astronomy.'

In order to fully employ the period afloat for instruction, no hard and fast rules can be laid down as to the order in which the time is to be utilized. It must be left to the discretion of the instructor. Thus, the ship might spend the forenoon adjusting compasses, do practical pilotage in the afternoon, and be outside in the evening taking twilight stars.

Marks will be awarded for the sights taken on shore and afloat during the course and for the survey. The instructor in the ship should note on the passing certificates what proficiency the candidates display during the cruise afloat in handling the ship, pilotage, etc.

An extra paper should be set in the harder subjects, and liberal marks set apart for it to encourage evening study during the course.

At the examination on the conclusion of this course marks will be awarded but no classes, those who pass the best examination being given the best appointments, any special remarks by the examining officers being noted in their favour.

APPENDIX B

Duties and responsibilities of a Navigating Officer as set forth in the King's Regulations, and in notes bearing on the navigation of HM Ships.

General principles of navigation and pilotage, including the various systems of lights, buoys, fog signals, etc.

Steering appliances of ships, steam and hand, telemotor gear.

Principles of screw propellers affecting turning of ships; action of rudder; use of helm; how to obtain turning circles; advance; tactical diameter, etc.

Principles of station-keeping and handling ships in a fleet.

A knowledge of the method of keeping store accounts.

Demands, supply arrangements, and correction of charts and all navigational publications supplied.

Use of charts and different methods of fixing positions.

Supply, use and care of navigational appliances, sounding gear, patent logs, meteorological instruments.

Appendix II

BIOGRAPHIES

Admiral of the Fleet Sir Henry Oliver GCB KCMG MVO LLD

Born at Lochside, Kelso on 22 January 1865, he joined the training ship *HMS Britannia* in September 1878 and two years later passed out in the top 10 of his term of 47 cadets. In September 1880 he joined the ironclad battleship *Agincourt,* and in January of the following year was promoted to Midshipman. Although steam powered, the *Agincourt's* screws could be lifted when under sail, this method of propulsion being preferred whenever there was sufficient wind. His next ship was the wooden corvette *Amethyst* on the South America Station in which he remained until August 1885 when, having being promoted to Sub-Lieutenant, he returned home to undergo courses at the RN College, Greenwich, having had to forego the foreign service leave due to him in order to do so. Eighteen days after the one year's course ended, he was on his way to the Pacific to join the flagship *Triumph* in the rank of Lieutenant. Financial considerations led him to apply for surveying duty and in June 1889 he joined the surveying ship *Stork* in Simons Bay, South Africa. Here he remained until the ship paid off at Malta in March 1894. Having qualified as a Navigating Officer for First Class ships and the Hydrographer having refused to promote him to Assistant Surveyor, 1st Class, he applied to return to general service and after taking a compass course at the RN College, Greenwich in the autumn of that year, he was sent to join the Second Class cruiser *Wallaroo* at Sydney, NSW of which he became First Lieutenant and (N). The ship paid off at Sydney in the late spring of 1897 and Oliver reached Plymouth in July. His next appointment was to the First Class cruiser *Endymion* in reserve at Chatham but in January 1898 he relieved the Commander (N) in the 9000 ton armoured cruiser *Blake* in the Channel Fleet. After turning over to the new cruiser *Niobe* at the end of 1898, and a period of service in South Africa during the Boer War, he was promoted to Commander and appointed (N) of the Channel Fleet flagship *Majestic* in September 1900. While serving in this capacity, Queen Victoria died and Oliver was given the task of ensuring that all the ships selected to salute the Royal cortege on passage between Cowes and Portsmouth were in their correct berth. Later that year he performed a remarkable feat of navigation which has become legendary when, in thick fog, he led the battle-squadron down the Irish Sea and anchored them in the Scilly Islands.

In June 1903, Oliver was promoted to Captain at three and a half years seniority and given the task of founding a floating Navigation School in the old sloop *Mercury* and subsequently ashore in the former Naval College christened *HMS Dryad*. On April 25 1907 he was appointed in command of the new armoured cruiser *Achilles*, then in October 1908 he became Naval Assistant to the First Sea Lord, Admiral Sir John Fisher and continued in that post until January 1912. He returned to sea in command of the new battleship *Thunderer* and as Flag Captain to Admiral Prince Louis of Battenberg during that year's annual manoeuvres. By August 1913, Oliver had reached the top of the Captain's list and was appointed Director of Naval Intelligence being promoted to Rear Admiral in December of that year.

Soon after the outbreak of war in 1914, the First Lord, Mr (later Sir) Winston Churchill sent him to Antwerp to destroy 38 German merchant ships interned there and on his return he became Naval Secretary to the First Lord. A month later, after the Battle of Coronel, he relieved Admiral Sturdee as Chief of the War Staff with the acting rank of Vice Admiral. In June 1916 he was awarded a KCB and when the Naval Staff was reorganised, later that year, be became Deputy Chief of the Naval Staff and a member of the Board. In January 1918 he was relieved and awarded a KCMG for his valuable services and in March was appointed Rear Admiral Commanding the 1st Battle-cruiser Squadron with his flag in *Repulse*. In January 1919 he was confirmed in the rank of Vice Admiral and on the dispersal of the Grand Fleet in March of that year, he took temporary command of the Home Fleet with his flag in *King George V;* when she was placed in reserve he remained in her as Admiral Commanding the Reserve Fleet.

For the next four years from August 1920 to August 1924 he occupied the

Admiral of the Fleet Sir Henry Oliver from a portrait in HMS Dryad.

Admiral of the Fleet Sir John H D Cunningham

164

post of Second Sea Lord, being promoted to Admiral in November 1923. His last sea-going command was that of Commander-in-Chief Home Fleet, which he held until August 1927. On January 21 1928 he was advanced to Admiral of the Fleet. He was the recipient of many foreign decorations including the Order of St Anne of Russia, the Sword of Sweden, the French Legion of Honour and the US Distinguished Service Medal. He was ADC to HM King George V from 1912 to the outbreak of war and in 1920 he received an honorary degree as Doctor of Law at Edinburgh University. Oliver's service to the Navigation Branch of the Royal Navy will long be remembered and he retained his interest in it throughout his long life. He died on October 15 1965 in his 101st year. His portrait by J Blain Leighton hangs in the main hall at Southwick House above a case containing his orders, decorations and medals, presented to *HMS Dryad* by his widow Dame Beryl Oliver GBE.

Admiral of the Fleet Sir John H D Cunningham GCB

Born on April 13 1885, he joined the training ship *HMS Britannia* in 1900 and the following year was appointed to the cruiser *Gibraltar,* flagship of the Cape Station at the time of the Boer War and earned the medal awarded for that campaign. Returning home in 1904 as an Acting Sub-Lieutenant he gained five firsts in his exams for the rank of Lieutenant to which he was promoted in October 1905. He was one of the 11 officers who qualified (N) in *HMS Dryad* in May 1906 and was appointed Assistant (N) in the battleship *Illustrious* and subsequently (N) of the gunboat *Hebe,* the cruiser *Indefatigable* and the minelayer *Iphigenia.* After completing a First Class Ship course in February 1910, he joined the staff of *HMS Dryad.* His next appointment was to the cruiser *Berwick* in the West Indies and he was serving in her when war broke out in 1914. The following year he joined the battleship *Russell* in the Mediterranean from which he was rescued when she sank after striking a mine off Malta in 1916. He then joined the battle-cruiser *Renown* in the Grand Fleet and remained in her until July 1918, having been promoted to Commander in July of the previous year. After a short spell in the battle-cruiser *Lion,* flagship of the Battle-cruiser force, in 1919 he joined the new battle-cruiser *Hood* as Squadron (N). In 1921 he returned to *HMS Dryad* as Commander of the School and in 1923 was appointed to *Queen Elizabeth* as Master of the Fleet in the Mediterranean. In June 1924 he was promoted to Captain and his appointments in that rank included Deputy Director of the War College, command of the mine-layer *Adventure,* Deputy Director of the Plans Division of the Admiralty and command of the battleship *Resolution,* flagship of Admiral Sir William Fisher, Commander in Chief, Mediterranean. Promoted to Rear Admiral in July 1936, the following October he joined the Admiralty as Assistant Chief of the Naval Staff and the following year, when the Admiralty regained control of the Fleet Air Arm, his title was changed to ACNS (Air) and in 1938 to that of Fifth Sea Lord and Chief of the Naval Air Services.

In August 1938 he was appointed to command the First Cruiser Squadron in the Mediterranean and hoisted his flag in *Devonshire.* Advanced to Vice

Admiral in 1939, soon after the outbreak of war his Squadron returned to Home Waters and he played a prominent part in the ill-starred Norwegian campaign in the Spring of 1940. He took charge of the evacuation of Namsos and rescued King Haakon and his entourage from Tromso.

On August 12 1940 he was appointed Naval Commander of Operation Menace mounted in co-operation with General De Gaulle to capture the port of Dakar and establish Free French control in West Africa. That the operation failed was in no way his fault as Professor Marder makes clear in his admirable account of the affair. In March 1941, he returned to the Admiralty as Fourth Sea Lord and Chief of Supplies and Transport and, two years later, in June 1943, he became Commander in Chief, Levant with the acting rank of Admiral (confirmed two months later). In October 1943 he relieved his namesake Admiral Sir Andrew Cunningham as Commander in Chief, Mediterranean when the latter was appointed First Sea Lord in place of the late Admiral of the Fleet Sir Dudley Pound. It has been said that John Cunningham's greatest achievement as Commander-in-Chief Mediterranean was in the field of allied co-operation. He was admired and trusted by the leaders of the various allied forces serving under him and he was responsible for the naval side of the operations leading up to the defeat of the German forces in Italy and the landings in the south of France. On May 24, 1946 he succeeded to the post of First Sea Lord and remained in that office until September 1948. His war service was rewarded with a GCB as well as numerous foreign decorations. He was made a freeman of the city of Athens for the part he played in the restoration of Greek independence, a fact not generally known. After an aduous period as First Sea Lord, his knowledge of the oil industry led to his appointment as Chairman of the Iraq Petroleum Company, as it then was, and he also became President of the Royal Naval Association. One of his two sons was lost in 1941 when serving in submarine P 33. His wife, whom he married in 1910, pre-deceased him in 1959; he himself died on 16 December 1962. His portrait by J B Souter hangs in the main hall at Southwick House.

Admiral Lord Mountevans of Chelsea KCB DSO LLD

Born on 28 October 1881. At the age of eight, he and his two brothers aged seven and nine attempted to run away to sea but were intercepted by a friendly policeman. Later he was sent to the training ship *HMS Worcester* from which in 1896, he entered the RN as a Mishipman. In 1900, whilst still a Sub-Lieutenant, he volunteered for and was selected as Second Mate of the whaler *Morning* which was sent out by the Royal Geographical Society in 1902 with stores and clothing for Captain Robert F Scott, who had been obliged to winter in the Antarctic when his ship the *Discovery* became trapped in the ice in MacMurdo Sound. A second relief voyage was made the following year when the *Discovery* got clear. On his return Evans was appointed to assist Captain Oliver with the founding of the Navigation School (see Chapter II). Then on April 26 1905 he joined the battleship,

London and on 5 March 1907 he was appointed (N) of the cruiser *Talbot* in the Channel Fleet. On 23 July 1908 he joined the instructional staff of *HMS Dryad* and two years later, when Scott was planning another expedition to the Antarctic which was to include an attempt to reach the South Pole, he invited Evans to accompany him as (N) and second in command of the whaler *Terra Nova*. When in January 1912, Scott was ready to start on his dash for the South Pole, Evans was in charge of the last of the supporting parties which turned back in latitude 87½°S. With him were Chief Stoker Lashly and Petty Officer Crean. 'We gave three good cheers for the southern party as they stepped off' wrote Evans, 'and then turned our sledge and commenced our lonely march to base . . . Little did we think that we would be the last to see them alive.' Evans and his two companions were lucky with the weather and got back safely though towards the end of the journey he himself developed scurvy and owed his life to the devotion of his two companions. Invalided home, he returned to duty with the RN and in June 1914 was given command of the *Tribal* Class destroyer, *Mohawk* in the Dover Patrol. In 1916 he transferred to the flotilla leader *Broke* in the same flotilla and on the night of 20 April 1917, in company with *Swift*, he engaged six enemy destroyers returning to Belgian ports after bombarding Dover. During the spirited action which followed, Evans rammed the destroyer G 42 which later sank and disabled the G 55 with a torpedo and she too foundered. For this action he was specially promoted to Captain and awarded a DSO. In October 1917 he became Chief of Staff to the Vice Admiral, Dover and in 1918 he went back to sea in command of the light cruiser *Active*. After a period on half pay following the end of the war, he was appointed in command of the cruiser *Carlisle* in China and soon added to his already famous reputation by effecting the salvage of 221 out of 350 passengers from the Chinese vessel *Hong Mo* which had run ashore in bad weather near Swatow. For his personal bravery on this occasion in swimming with a line to the wrecked ship, he was awarded Lloyds gold medal for bravery. In July 1923 he returned home to take command of the Fishery Protection and Minesweeping Flotilla and in June 1926 he took over command of the battle-cruiser *Repulse* in which he remained until his promotion to Rear Admiral in February 1928.

In May 1929 he went out to Australia in command of the cruiser Squadron there where he remained until 1931. On being relived, instead of officially visiting the ships of his Squadron to say good-bye, he entertained 2000 officers and men with their wives in a local cinema. In March 1933 he hoisted his flag in the cruiser *Cardiff* as Commander-in-Chief South Africa, having previously learned to speak Afrikaans. He came in for some criticism for the way he handled an incident in Bechuanaland when he publicly deposed the Regent Tshekedi but afterwards reinstated him. On his return to the UK in 1935, he was given the Nore Command which he held until January 1939. Three months later he was nominated Regional Commissioner for London in the Civil Defence Organisation and he held this post throughout the war. His courage and enthusiasm throughout the London blitz were an inspiration and example to his fellow workers. As Sir Harold Scott was to write to him, 'he brought to the post the directness and dash of the sailor, a power of leadership that in the difficult days to come inspired and sustained men and women all over London.' His outstanding war service was recognised by the award of a peerage. A brother officer wrote of him, 'as a man of action Teddy Evans will undoubtedly be remembered among the small band of Britain's naval leaders of our century.' He was the author of a number of books for boys and also on arctic exploration. He died whilst on holiday in Norway on 20 August 1957.

Admiral Sir Wilbraham T R Ford KCB, KBE

Born on 19 January 1880, he joined the training ship *HMS Britannia,* in January 1894 and on completing his courses for the rank of Lieutenant, in 1902 he joined the surveying service and was appointed to *Rambler* in China. On his return to the UK, in 1905 he qualified (N) in *Mercury* and was subsequently appointed to the cruiser *Eclipse* in which cadets from the RN College Osborne did their sea training. In December 1908 he joined the RN College Dartmouth as a term officer, an appointment in which his aptitude for all kinds of sport had full rein; he had won the army and navy middle-weight boxing championship in 1904 and he was a scratch golfer. On leaving Dartmouth he returned to *HMS Dryad* for a First Class Ship course and his next appointment was to the cruiser, *Black Prince* which he joined on 1 August 1911. Two years later, on 25 April 1913 he joined the battle-ship, *Swiftsure,* flagship on the East Indies Station and which after the outbreak of war took part in the attack on the Dardanelles. The following year, on 1 July 1916 he was appointed to the battle-cruiser, *Glorious,* in the Grand Fleet, having been promoted to Commander on 31 December 1914, and after the end of the war, on 14 July 1919 he was appointed Navigating Officer of the battleship, *Valiant.* After promotion to Captain on 31 December 1920 he attended a course at the Naval War College and on 1 September 1922 he assumed command of the destroyer depot ship *Diligence* in the Mediterranean Fleet which was followed by two years in command of the cruiser *Calliope* in the Home Fleet. In 1926 he joined the Admiralty as Director of Physical Training and Sports and in May of the following year he was appointed in command of the Boys Training Establishment, *Ganges* at Shotley. In 1929 he returned to the Mediterranean in command of the battleship, *Royal Oak* and the following year he became Captain of *HMS Dryad.* In 1932 he was appointed ADC to HM The King and later that year he was promoted to Rear Admiral. After a period on half pay, in 1934 he went out to Australia in command of the cruiser squadron stationed there and whilst holding this appointment, on several occasions he drew attention to that country's need of naval defence. In August 1936 he was offered the post of Flag Officer in Charge and Admiral Superintendent, Malta and in January 1937 began what was to prove a most eventful tenure of that command. When Italy entered the war in June 1940 and the island was subjected to continual bombardment first by the Regia Aeronautica and later by the Luftwaffe, he co-operated to the fullest extent with the Governor, Sir William Dobbie, in its defence. His opposite number in the RAF, Air Chief Marshall Sir Hugh Lloyd, with whom he shared a 'hole in the ground' during the height of the blitz, was to write of him 'Admiral

Admiral Sir Wilbraham T R Ford.   *Admiral Lord Mountevans of Chelsea*

Ford was a very good looking man, every inch an Admiral, of fine physique and most amusing and entertaining. There was never any doubt who was in command when he was about and he ruled the dockyard and all visiting ships with a rod of iron and he was much admired and respected throughout the Mediterranean. Duty came first in everything he did and he was devoted to the interests and well-being of everyone under his command and for that reason he was deeply loved by the hundreds of Maltese employees in the dockyard.'

On his return to the UK, he was received by HM The King who invested him with the KBE which had been awarded to him in July 1940 and the KCB gazetted in the New Years Honours List for 1942. Later that year he became Commander-in-Chief, Rosyth, a post which he held until 1944. He died on 16 January 1964 at the age of 83 and he will be remembered by all those who had the privilege of serving under him as a most courageous, kind and accomplished officer.

Admiral Sir Frederick Edward-Collins KCB, KCVO

Born on 26 December 1883, he entered the RN in 1898 through the training ship, *HMS Britannia.* As a Midshipman in the battleship *Goliath* he saw active service in China during the Boxer rising in 1900 and subsequently served for a year in the battleship *Victorious.* He qualified (N) at *HMS Dryad* in 1905 and the following year was appointed to the gunboat *Thistle* in China. While serving in her he gained the bronze medal of the Royal Humane Society for rescuing a Chinese coolie from the Yangtse in very difficult circumstances at night and with the river in full flood. After completing a First Class Ship course, he was appointed (N†) of the Second Class protected cruiser *Flora* on the China Station and two years later he returned to *HMS Dryad* as a member of the directing staff. On 19 January 1913 he joined the battleship *Superb* in the Home (later Grand) Fleet and two years later he commissioned the new battle-cruiser, *Tiger,* in the 1st Battle-cruiser Squadron. Promoted to Commander in 1917 he was appointed to the operations division of the Admiralty and in 1919 he returned to China as Squadron (N) in the flagship *Hawkins* and in 1922 his knowledge of those waters was put to good use when he was appointed Naval Representative on the Wei-Hai-Wei Rendition Commission. Promoted to Captain in December 1923, he served on the Signal Books Committee and two years later he returned to sea in command with the Atlantic Fleet. In 1927 he returned to the Admiralty as Deputy Director of Plans and in 1930 attended a course at the Imperial Defence College. His next command was the battle-cruiser *Renown* and in March 1932 he became Naval Assistant to the Second Sea Lord. In May 1935 when Admiral Sir Dudley Pound was selected to relieve Admiral Sir William Fisher as Commander in Chief, Mediterranean he took Edward-Collins with him as his Chief of Staff but due to the Italian attack on Abyssinia the change in command was deferred until March 1936. Promoted to Rear Admiral in January 1938, he was given the command of the Second Cruiser Squadron in the Home Fleet and hoisted his flag in the new cruiser *Southampton* which, in the spring of 1939, formed part of the force detailed to escort the battle-cruiser, *Repulse,* in which the King and Queen were voyaging to Canada. For this service he was created KCVO having been advanced on 16 May 1939 to Vice Admiral. Soon after the outbreak of war his flagship was damaged during an air raid on the Firth of Forth and the Squadron was reconstituted with the four ships of the *Arethusa* class with *Galatea* as flagship. In June 1940 he became Second in Command of the Home Fleet and Flag Officer Commanding the 18th Cruiser Squadron with his flag in *Manchester.* On 31 December 1940 he relieved Admiral Sir Dudley North as Flag Officer Commanding, North Atlantic at Gibraltar where he remained until September 1943 when he retired at his own request having been advanced to Admiral in January of that year. On his return home he continued to serve for the rest of the war as Flag Officer in Charge, Falmouth in his native Cornwall where he died on 17 February 1958.

Admiral Sir Henry Ruthven Moore GCB CVO DSO DL

Born on 29 August 1886, he entered the RN through *HMS Britannia* in 1902 and qualified as a Lieutenant (N) in December 1908. His first appointment was as Assistant (N) in the battleship *Albion.* The ship was at Gibraltar when in February

1909 the US Great White Fleet comprising 16 battleships, a destroyer flotilla, a depot ship, a repair ship, two supply ships and a despatch vessel called there on its way back to the US. The Commander (N) in the *Albion* was sick and Lieutenant Moore was given the task of berthing the American battleships detailed to enter harbour. He recalls that on boarding the flagship, the Admiral, Rear Admiral Charles S Sperry USN, expressed some surprise at seeing such a comparatively junior officer charged with such an important mission. However when all ships were safely berthed, his surprise gave way to admiration for the way in which the manoeuvre had been carried out. On 21 January 1911 he was appointed (N) of the light cruiser, *Adventure* and in 1913 he returned to *HMS Dryad* for the First Class Ship course. He was subsequently appointed (N) of the light cruiser *Active* and on 4 November 1915 he became (N) of the new light cruiser *Castor*, Commodore J R P Hawksley, leader of the 11th Destroyer Flotilla in the Grand Fleet. During the night following the Battle of Jutland on 31 May 1916 the flotilla was engaged by the German 2nd scouting group which managed to approach within a mile before switching on searchlights and opening a murderous fire, from which the *Castor* suffered severely and incurred numerous casualties before she could reply. However Moore managed to draft an enemy report, one of the few which the Commander in Chief received, and which indicated that enemy light forces forces appeared to be searching for the British battlefleet. For his part in the action Lieutenant Commander Moore was awarded a DSO.

On the surrender of the German fleet on 21 November 1918, he was entrusted with the task of anchoring the 50 German destroyers in their assigned berths off Inchkeith which he did as one unit.

Promoted to Commander in 1919, he joined the directing staff of the RN Staff College at Greenwich and two years later became Naval Assistant Secretary to the Committee of Imperial Defence and to the British Delegation to the Conference for the Limitation of Armaments in Washington DC. On 18 November 1924 he took up his appointment as executive officer of the cruiser *Delhi*, in the 1st Cruiser Squadron attached to the Mediterranean Fleet and which later formed part of the Special Service Squadron under Admiral Sir Federick Field which cruised round the world. In 1927 he was selected to undergo a course at the Imperial Defence College having been advanced to the rank of Captain in 1926, and was subsequently appointed Deputy Director (1930-32) and Director (1932-33) of the plans division of the naval staff. Then he returned to sea in command of the cruiser *Neptune* in the Second Cruiser Squadron of the Home Fleet. In 1936 he became Chief of Staff to the Commander in Chief, Home Fleet, Admiral Sir Roger Backhouse, with the rank of Commodore 1st Class. He was ADC to HM the King from 1937-38 and on promotion to Rear Admiral in 1938 became Chief of Staff to the Commander in Chief, Portsmouth. In 1939 he took command of the 3rd Cruiser Squadron in the Mediterranean Fleet and the following year he returned to the Admiralty as Assistant Chief of the Naval Staff (Trade) a newly created post which emphasised the important part which the convoy organisation was playing in the war at sea. In 1941 he relieved Vice Admiral Sir Tom Phillips as Vice Chief of the Naval Staff and in 1943 returned to sea as Second in Command of the Home Fleet with his flag in *Anson*. On 14 June 1944 he relieved Admiral Sir Bruce Fraser as Commander in Chief, Home Fleet. His major preoccupation during his tenure of

Admiral Sir Henry R Moore.   *Admiral Sir Tom S V Phillips.*

office was the immobilisation of the German battleship *Tirpitz* which, despite repeated attacks still posed a threat to the convoys to and from north Russia for which he was also responsible. His next appointment was Head of the British Naval Mission in Washington DC from December 1945 until September 1948 and he was also British Representative on the Military Committee of the Security Council of the United Nations Assembly. On his return to the UK he became Commander in Chief, the Nore and First and Principal ADC to HM the King. He retired in 1951 and was High Sheriff of Kent from 1959-60.

Admiral Sir Marshal L Clarke KBE CB DSC

Born on 9 May 1887, he joined the training ship *HMS Britannia* in 1902 and on 15 September 1903 the battleship *Emperor of India*. He qualified (N) in December 1908 and was appointed to the gunboat *Britomart* in China. On 26 November 1911 he joined the gunboat *Dwarf* on the west coast of Africa and after qualifying for First Class ships, on 9 April 1913, he was appointed Navigating Officer of the cruiser *Crescent* in the Training Squadron based on Queenstown. In December 1914 he transferred to the Armed Merchant Cruiser *Alsation* which replaced the *Crescent* as flagship of the 10th Cruiser Squadron on the northern patrol. He remained in this appointment until September 1918 having been awarded a DSC two years previously. He then joined the carrier *Argus*, a converted Italian merchant ship, and in June 1919 was a member of the first course at the RN Staff College at Greenwich. On 16 June of the following year he joined the staff of Vice Admiral Sir William Goodenough, Commander in Chief, South Africa and in 1922 was promoted to Commander. For the next seven years he held various staff and executive appointments at home and abroad. Promoted to Captain in June 1929; on 19 December he assumed command of the cruiser *Concord* and two years later was appointed Deputy Director of the Naval Staff College. In 1933 he took over command of the 6th Destroyer Flotilla in the Home Fleet and remained in this post for nearly three years. There followed two years as Commodore in Charge, Malaya and he subsequently commanded the carriers *Courageous* and *Furious* in the last named of which he served during the early part of the second world war. Promoted to Rear Admiral in June 1940, after a short spell as Second in Command of the 18th Cruiser Squadron in the Home Fleet, he was appointed Admiral Superintendent of Portsmouth Dockyard where he was faced with the many problems arising from the bombing attacks to which the yard was subjected in 1941-2 and later from the selection of Portsmouth as main springboard for the invasion of Normandy in June 1944 which entailed the fitting out of almost 1000 miscellaneous craft in addition to repairs to damaged ships. He had been advanced to Admiral in 1943 and retired in this rank in November 1945. He was created KBE in the New Years Honours List on 1 January 1946. He died on 8 April 1959.

Admiral Sir Tom S V Phillips KCB

Born in 1890 he entered the RN through the training ship *HMS Britannia* in 1903 and went to sea as a Midshipman in *Drake* on 15 May 1904. He remained in that ship until promoted to Sub-Lieutenant on 15 July 1907. A year later he was promoted to Lieutenant and in 1909 qualified (N) in *HMS Dryad*. After a short period as Assistant (N) in his old ship, *Drake* in the Atlantic Fleet, he was appointed to the 2nd Class cruiser *HMS Thetis* and on 10 November 1911 he joined the cruiser *Pegasus* in Australia. He returned to *HMS Dryad* for a 1st Class Ship course on 7 March 1913 and subsequently joined the destroyer depot ship *Woolwich* where he remained until 15 January 1915 when he joined the cruiser *Bacchante* off the Dardanelles. A year later, on 9 February 1916 he joined the cruiser *Lancaster* employed on trade protection duty in the Pacific. Returning to the UK after the war, in 1919 he underwent a course at the Naval Staff College on the conclusion of which he was attached to the Naval Advisory Committee studying naval disarmament at Geneva. In 1921 he was promoted to Commander and on 13 October 1922 he was seconded for temporary duty with the Limitations of Naval Armament Conference at Geneva. On 1 November 1924 he took over command of the sloop *Verbena* on the Africa station and eight months later, on 1 July 1925 he was appointed Staff Officer, Operations on the staff of Admiral Sir Roger Keys, Commander in Chief, Mediterranean.

Promoted to Captain in 1927, three years later he joined the Admiralty as Assistant Director of Plans. In 1932 he assumed command of the cruiser *Effingham* flagship of the Commander in Chief East Indies.

In 1935 he returned to the Admiralty as Director of Plans and remained in that post for three years after which he became Commodore, Destroyers, in the Home Fleet. He was ADC to HM the King from 1938 to 1939 and after promotion to Rear Admiral he was appointed Vice Chief of the Naval Staff. When it was decided to send a token force to the far east in an attempt to disuade the Japanese from attacking Singapore, he was offered the post of Commander in Chief, Far East with the acting rank of Admiral and hoisted his flag in the battleship *Prince of Wales.* He was not amongst the survivors when that ship, in company with *Repulse,* was sunk by torpedo aircraft in the South China Sea on 12 December 1941.

Admiral John Henry Godfrey, CB

Born on 10 July 1888, he entered the RN through the training ship *HMS Britannia* in 1903 and passed out as a Midshipman on 30 May 1904. He served in the battleships *Majestic* and *Exmouth* and was promoted to Lieutenant on 30 October 1908. The following year he qualified (N) in *HMS Dryad* and was subsequently appointed to the gunboat *Bramble* in West Africa. After completing a First Class Ship course, on 23 January 1913 he was appointed to the light cruiser *Blanche* attached to the Third Battle Squadron. Soon after the outbreak of war, on 24 October 1914, he joined the cruiser *Euryalus,* flagship of Admiral Sir Richard Peirse, commanding the 7th Cruiser Squadron which in 1915 formed part of the force covering the landing on W beach on the Gallipoli peninsula in April of that year. On 8 August 1917 he was appointed Assistant to the Chief of Staff to the Flag Officer, Malta. His next appointment was to the staff of the Commander-in-Chief, Atlantic Fleet, and on 30 June 1920 he was promoted to Commander. On 28 September 1921 he was appointed to Plans Division in the Admiralty and two years later he joined the staff of the RN Staff College, Greenwich. On 31 August 1925 he was appointed executive officer of the cruiser *Diomede* on the New Zealand station. Promoted to Captain on 30 June 1928, the following year he became Deputy Director of the Staff College. He returned to sea in command of the cruiser *Suffolk* on the China Station on 20 June 1931 and after two years in this appointment he returned to the Admiralty as Deputy Director of the Plans Division. His last sea-going command was the battle-cruiser *Repulse* which he joined on 2 January 1936. He was promoted to Rear Admiral on 22 February 1939 and, on the recommendation of Admiral Sir Dudley Pound, he succeeded to the post of Director of Naval Intelligence. That this was a wise selection was amply demonstrated during the next three years. He created an operational intelligence centre which was to play a vital part in the battle of the Atlantic and, after war broke out, he recruited a brilliant company of lawyers, writers, scholars and journalists to assist him in his important task. Although the early days of the war were marked by some obvious failures in the organisation, such as the surprise German invasion of Norway and the insecurity of the RN's cypher system, he continued to perfect his team, often in the face of scepticism on the part of the High Command, so that when, at the end of 1942, the time came for him to hand over to his successor, the division had reached a high pitch of efficiency.

On taking the post, he had been promised a sea command on relinquishing it, but this was not to be and he was sent out to India to command the Royal Indian Navy at a time when that country was in a state of turmoil clamouring for independence. Further when the war ended there were some demonstrations in that service over demobilisation which he suppressed with a firm hand, a policy which did not meet with approval in Whitehall. Despite his excellent war record, he was the only flag officer of his rank to receive no recognition of his distinguished services. He died on 29 August 1971 leaving a personal diary of the greatest value to historians.

Sir Geoffrey Miles, KCB, KCSI

Born on 2 May 1890, he joined the training ship *HMS Britannia* in 1905 and went to sea as a Midshipman in the battleship *Victorious* in 1906. He was promoted to Lieutenant on 15 June 1911 and was a member of the second class of Qualifiers to join *HMS Dryad* that year. On 5 January 1912 he joined *Neptune,* flagship of

Admiral John H Godfrey.

Admiral Sir Geoffrey Miles

the Commander-in-Chief, Home Fleet as Assistant (N) and six months later was appointed to the despatch vessel *Alacrity* which he took out to China. 'It was a lovely job,' he writes, 'poking about the Inland Sea of Japan and the excitement of navigating the Yangtse.' After returning to the UK he was appointed (N) of the half-leader *Botha* in the First Destroyer Flotilla in the Grand Fleet and in September 1916 he joined the light cruiser *Fearless,* leader of the First Flotilla and later leader of the 12th Submarine (K class) Flotilla. In November 1916, his ship was sent to Murmansk on the Kola Inlet. 'Just before you reach the anchorage,' he writes, 'there is an area of magnetic disturbance marked on the chart which used to swing the compass about 60°. One night we had just got under way to sail from the anchorage and when I steadied the Quartermaster with the ship's head pointing about north east, much to my surprise, he reported, "steady on south south west." The liquid in the steering compass had frozen; somebody had switched off the binnacle light, the warmth of which was just sufficient to keep it from freezing.' After completing a First Class Ship course in 1919, he qualified at the Naval Staff College and was subsequently appointed War Staff Officer on the Staff of the Rear Admiral (Destroyers) in the Home Fleet. After completing two years in this appointment, he became Squadron (N) to the Rear Admiral (D), Mediterranean who flew his flag in the cruiser *Coventry*. Those were the days of the great fleets and of manoeuvres on the grand scale. 'Looking back,' he writes, 'I think the incident which gave me greatest pleasure at the time — and which will be very unlikely to occur to any Navigating Officer in the future — was when I was Squadron (N) in the *Coventry*. The Combined Home and Mediterranean Fleets during the Spring of 1924 were to anchor in Pollensa Bay, Majorca. The Commander-in-Chief ordered the Rear Admiral (D) to follow the battleships and cruisers into the anchorage. We had six flotillas — something over 50 ships — and sailed in formation through the lines of heavy ships at anchor and brought the flotillas to anchor as one unit in their allotted berths beyond the big ships in a spectacular evolution.'

Promoted to Commander on 31 December 1924, in May of the following year he was appointed Staff Officer, Operations to the Vice Admiral Commanding the 3rd Battle Squadron and Second in Command of the Mediterranean Fleet who flew his flag in *Iron Duke* and later in *Barham*. In November 1927 he was appointed Squadron (N) and Staff Officer, Operations, to the Rear Admiral Commanding the Battle-cruiser Squadron who flew his flag in *Hood*.

On 25 November 1929 he joined the plans division of the Admiralty and, after promotion to Captain on 30 June 1931, he was appointed to command the First Minesweeping Flotilla at Portland. After serving as Deputy Director of the Naval Staff College at Greenwich, in July 1935 he was appointed Captain (D) of the Third Destroyer Flotilla in the Mediterranean Fleet and subsequently became Director of the Tactical School. In July 1939, he was appointed to command the battleship, *Nelson,* flagship of the Commander-in-Chief Home Fleet. Promoted to Rear Admiral in 1941, he was sent to Moscow as Head of the Military Mission there until 1943. In 1944 he was appointed Flag Officer Commanding the Western Mediterranean and in 1946 he went out to India as Commander in Chief of the Indian Navy, being the last British Officer to hold the post before the partition and independence of India. His portrait by Simon Elwes hangs in the main hall at Southwick House. 'I never regretted choosing (N) as my specialisation,' he says, 'and I thoroughly enjoyed all my appointments.'

Admiral Sir William Tennant KCB CBE MVO

Born on 2 January 1890 at Upton on Severn, he joined the training ship *HMS Britannia* in May 1905 as a member of the last term to be trained in that ship. After a cruise in *Highflyer* in September 1906, he joined the battleship *Prince of Wales* as a Midshipman, transferring a year later to the battleship *Venerable.* After completing his courses for the rank of Lieutenant to which he was promoted on 30 June 1912, he joined the *Tribal* class destroyer *Nubian.* In 1913 he qualified (N) in *HMS Dryad* and subsequently served in the destroyers *Lizard* and *Ferret* before being appointed Navigating Officer of the cruiser *Chatham* in which he later took part in operations off the Dardanelles. On 27 February 1916, he joined the cruiser *Nottingham* in the Grand Fleet and took part in the Battle of Jutland. In August 1916 his ship was torpedoed and sunk by U52 in the North Sea, but fortunately he was amongst the survivors and on 1 December 1916 he was appointed Navigating Officer of the cruiser *Concord* in the Harwich Force. In April 1918 he returned to *HMS Dryad* for a First Class Ship course and in May of the following year he joined the Royal Yacht *Alexandra* in which he remained until 1921 when he was appointed second (N†) of the battle-cruiser *Renown* for the tour of HRH The Prince of Wales to Australia and New Zealand on the conclusion of which he joined the Staff of the Navigation School. When, in 1923, the battle-cruiser *Repulse* was chosen to convey the Prince of Wales on an official visit to South Africa and South America, he was appointed to her as Navigating Officer and received an MVO for his services. In December 1925 he was promoted to Commander and after serving for 18 months in the operations division of the Admiralty, in 1927 he was selected to undergo the Naval Staff Course. His next appointment was to *Sussex* as executive officer and on 15 December 1930 he joined the staff of the RN Staff College. Promoted to Captain on 31 December 1932, after attending a course at the Imperial Defence College, he took command of the cruiser, *Arethusa,* flagship of the 3rd Cruiser Squadron in the Mediterranean Fleet. In July 1937 he joined the Staff of the Imperial Defence College as an instructor and on the outbreak of war in 1939, he became Personal Assistant to the First Sea Lord, Admiral of the Fleet Sir Dudley Pound. During the evacuation of the British Expeditionary Force from Dunkirk, he was sent to that port to take charge of the evacuation arrangements. He and General (later Field Marshal Lord) Alexander were the last two to leave after inspecting the beaches and the waterfront to make sure that there were no more troops to be taken off. For his outstanding work during that operation he was awarded a CB. In 1941 he assumed command of the battle-cruiser *Repulse* and, when on 10 December 1941 his ship was sunk in the China Sea by Japanese torpedo aircraft, once again he was among the survivors. On 6 February 1942, shortly after his return home, he was promoted to Rear Admiral and was appointed in command of the Cruiser Squadron attached to the Eastern Fleet. He returned to the UK in 1943 and joined the

Staff of Admiral Sir Bertram Ramsay to assist with the planning of the Normandy invasion. He was given the task of assembling and placing the two Mulberry harbours and for his services in this connection was awarded a CBE. His next post was that of Flag Officer Levant and Eastern Mediterranean in the acting rank of Vice Admiral in which he was confirmed in July 1945. In the post war Honours List published in December 1945 he received a KCB. In October 1946 he was appointed Commander-in-Chief, America and West Indies Station and was promoted to Admiral in October 1948. He retired the following year and subsequently became Chairman of King George's Fund for Sailors. In 1950 he was appointed Lord Lieutenant for the County of Worcester and in 1958 was made an Honorary Freeman of the City of Worcester. He died on 26 July 1963.

Admiral Sir Robin Bridge, KBE, CB

Born on 15 February 1894 he joined the RN College, Osborne in 1907 and went to sea as a Midshipman four years later. He was Sub-Lieutenant of the destroyer *Foresight* in the Dover patrol and on 21 January 1916 he joined the battleship *Marlborough* in the Grand Fleet and was present at the battle of Jutland when his ship was struck by a torpedo but managed to reach port. Having qualified provisionally at sea, on 7 July 1918 he was appointed (N) of the light cruiser *Royalist* in the Grand Fleet. On 13 October 1921 he joined the submarine depot ship *Platypus* in Australia and on return to the UK two years later he was appointed to the staff of *HMS Dryad*. On 5 March 1925 he returned to sea as Navigating Officer of the cruiser *Lowestoft* on the Africa station and on 3 January 1927 he joined the carrier *Furious* in the Atlantic Fleet. Promoted to Commander on 20 December 1929, he was appointed Squadron (N) to the Commander in Chief, America and West Indies, in *Desptach*. On 27 June 1932 he joined the Naval Staff College as a member of the directing staff and two years later he was appointed executive officer of the cruiser *Lowestoft* on the China station. Promoted to Captain on 30 June 1936, the following year he returned to *HMS Dryad* in command. On relief by Captain H A Rowley, on 16 June 1939, he was appointed in command of the carrier *Eagle* on the China station. After the outbreak of war, his ship was moved first to the East Indies and later to the Mediterranean Fleet where, until the arrival of the carrier *Illustrious* at the end of August 1940, she provided the only naval air support available to Admiral Sir Andrew Cunningham. In March 1941 he became Director of the Naval Air Division in the Admiralty and two years later was appointed Chief of Staff to the Flag Officer, Carrier Training. In 1944 with the rank of Commodore 1st Class he assumed the command of the Northern Naval Air Stations. Promoted to Rear Admiral in July 1945, he was appointed Flag Officer Air, on the East Indies Station, an appointment which, the following year, was combined with that of Flag Officer Air in the British Pacific Fleet. In June 1947 he became Senior Naval Representative of the Chiefs of Staff in Australia. He returned home in 1948 and was promoted to Vice Admiral, subsequently commanding the Reserve Fleet. He retired in 1951 being advanced to Admiral on the retired list in 1953. He died on 19 February 1971.

Admiral Sir Maurice Mansergh KCB CBE

Born on 14 October 1896 he joined the RN College Osborne in 1909 and went to sea on 13 May 1914 as a Midshipman in the battleship *Zealandia*. Promoted to Sub Lieutenant on 30 September 1916 he served in the destroyer *Alarm* and after promotion to Lieutenant on 30 March 1918, he joined the destroyer, *Rigorous*. He was a member of the first 1921 Qualifying class and his first appointment after qualifying was to the gunboat *Dwarf* in west Africa. On 1 July 1921 he joined the target-towing sloop *Chrysanthemum* and subsequently served in the destroyer depot ship *Woolwich*. On 5 May 1925 he returned to *HMS Dryad* as a member of the instructional staff and on 1 October 1927 he joined the battle-cruiser *Tiger* then being employed as a sea-going gunnery firing ship. On 5 December 1929 he was appointed to the carrier *Glorious*. Promoted to Commander on 31 December 1930; on 28 July 1931 he joined the staff of the Director of Navigation at the Admiralty. Two years later he attended a course at the Naval Staff College and on 23 December 1933 he joined the staff of the Commander in Chief, Mediterranean Sir William Fisher, as Staff Officer Operations. This was followed on 23 July 1936 by an appointment as executive officer of the battleship, *Rodney*. Promoted to Captain on 30 June 1937, the following year he attended a course at the Imperial Defence College and in January 1939 he joined the plans division of the Admiralty as Assistant Director. In April 1939 when the trade division was re-established, he became its Director and was faced with the task of recreating the convoy organisation against the possibility of war with Germany. In November 1941 he was appointed in command of the cruiser *Gambia* in the Eastern Fleet and in June 1943 he returned to the UK to take up the post of Deputy Chief of Staff to Admiral Sir Bertram Ramsay, Allied Naval Commander Expeditionary Force, to assist with the planning of the invasion of Normandy. When in September 1944 Admiral Ramsay moved to France, he became Chief of Staff. In March 1945 he was appointed Commodore in command of the 15th Cruiser Squadron in the Mediterranean and took part in the closing stages of the campaign in support of the army in Italy. When hostilities ceased, he was appointed Commodore in Charge, Levant and Eastern Mediterranean and in April 1946 he returned to the UK to take up his appointment as Naval Secretary to the First Lord. Promoted to Rear Admiral in July of that year, two years later he hoisted his flag in the light carrier *Theseus* in command of the Home Fleet Carrier Squadron and in the autumn of 1948 in company with four destroyers he made a goodwill visit to South Africa. In September 1949 he was appointed to the post of Fifth Sea Lord and Deputy Chief of the Naval Staff (Air) in the rank of Vice Admiral. From October 1951 to November 1953 he was Commander in Chief, Plymouth and in 1954 he retired. He died on 30 September 1966.

Admiral Sir John Frewen.

Admiral Sir Ian Easton

Admiral Sir John Frewen GCB

Born on 28 March 1911, the son of Captain E L Frewen RN, he joined the RN College Dartmouth in 1924 and on 1 January 1929 joined his first ship *Revenge,* as a Midshipman. After promotion to Sub-Lieutenant, he joined the cruiser *Caradoc,* on 17 August 1932 and four months later was promoted to Lieutenant. He qualified (N) in *HMS Dryad* in August 1934 and on 20 November of that year he joined the cruiser, *Lowestoft.* On 1 December 1937 he was appointed to the cruiser, *Ajax* on the North America and West Indies station and was in her when she took part in the battle of the River Plate on 13 December 1939. A year later, on 31 December 1940 he was appointed Squadron (N) in *London,* flagship of Rear Admiral L K Hamilton which was to play such an important part in the ill-fated Arctic convoy PQ 17 on 4 July 1942. It was while holding this appointment that he earned the gratitude of all members of the branch when he persuaded his Admiral and through him the Commander in Chief, Admiral Sir John Tovey, that it was a waste of a highly trained officer's time correcting charts when he could more usefully be employed on ship's duties. This led to the introduction of the Navigator's Yeoman, a rating trained to undertake this necessary but time-consuming task.

On 26 January 1943 he was appointed to the carrier, *Formidable* and on 30 June 1945 he was promoted to Commander. After two years as executive officer of the AS training establishment *Osprey,* on 23 March 1948 he was appointed in a similar capacity to *Duke of York,* flagship of the Commander in Chief Home Fleet. On 16 May 1949, he joined the plans division of Admiralty and on 30 June of the following year he was promoted to Captain. His first command was that of the frigate *Mounts Bay* which he assumed on 21 November of that year; then on 26 June 1952 he took up his appointment in command of the A/S training establishment, *Osprey*. Two years later he joined the staff of the Supreme Allied Commander, Atlantic as Assistant Chief of Staff, Intelligence. On 15 February 1958 he was appointed in command of the carrier *Eagle* and was advanced to Rear Admiral on 7 July 1959. The following month, he was appointed Chief of Staff to the Commander in Chief, Home Fleet, Admiral Sir William Davis GCB. In 1961 he went to the Far East as Second in Command of the fleet in those waters and the following year was promoted to Vice Admiral. Returning to the UK in 1963 he became Vice Chief of the Naval Staff a post which he held until 1965 when he returned to sea as Commander in Chief Home Fleet with the acting rank of Admiral in which he was confirmed on 9 February, the following year. In 1967 on hauling down his flag afloat, he rehoisted it ashore as Commander-in-Chief Portsmouth and when in 1969 the shore command organisation was changed, he became the first holder of the post of Commander-in-Chief Naval Home Command. He was First and Principal ADC to HM The Queen from 1968 to 1970 when he retired. Although offered many important posts connected with national and maritime affairs, he chose to devote his energies to the conversion and running of his family home, Brickwall House, as a school for children afflicted with dyslexia which, like everything he put his hand to, prospered. His untimely death on 30 August 1975 at the age of 64 deprived the country of a gifted and great-hearted officer who has been described by one who knew him well as, 'a great leader — a man of magnetic and inspiring personality and immense drive — no-one, whatever his nationality, had any doubts when they were under his command or sphere of influence. He was a dedicated professional who never ceased to encourage others to live and think professionally; a staff officer of the most piercing foresight and intellect who took infinite pains with every detail; but behind it all a humanist who was equally dedicated to the needs of men as well as the task.' A brother Admiral has also written of him, 'he brought to bear one of the clearest and most incisive brains, allied to complete fearlessness and integrity, on all naval and indeed defence problems which the country faced since the war.'

Admiral Sir Ian Easton, KCB, DSC

Born on 27 November 1917, he joined the RN College Dartmouth in 1931 and went to sea as a Midshipman in 1935 in the cruiser *York,* flagship of the Commander in Chief, America and West Indies. As an acting Sub-Lieutenant in 1939, he qualified as a pilot in the Fleet Air Arm and during World War II served in the carriers *Glorious, Ark Royal* and *Formidable.* He qualified as a Fighter Direction Officer at *HMS Dryad* in 1943 and on 26 October of that year was appointed Direction Officer in the carrier *Indefatigable.* On 16 July 1947, he returned to *HMS Dryad* to undergo an advanced course and the following year he joined the Admiralty Signal Research Establishment. On 31 October 1950 he was appointed to the carrier *Eagle* and on 30 June 1952, he was promoted to Commander. The following year he attended the RN Staff College and on 15 July 1955, he joined the staff of the British Joint Services Mission in Washington DC where he remained until 1957. His next appointment was as Staff (D) Officer to the Flag Officer Aircraft Carriers and he subsequently attended a course at the Joint Services Staff College. On 30 June 1960 he was promoted to Captain and joined the Admiralty Staff as Assistant Director Tactical and Weapons Policy Division. In 1962 he began two years exchange service with the Royal Australian Navy when he took command of *HMAS Watson*. After his return to UK and a year as naval member of the Templer Committee, in 1966 he was appointed Director of the Naval Tactical Weapons Policy Division. In 1968 he assumed command of the converted carrier *Triumph* in the Far East and on 7 July 1969 was promoted to Rear Admiral. From 1969 to 1971 he was Assistant Chief of Naval Staff (Policy) and subsequently Flag Officer of the Admiralty Interview Board. In 1973 he returned to Washington as Head of the British Defence Staff and Defence Attache. Promoted to Admiral on 6 January 1976, he is currently Commandant of the Royal College of Defence Studies.

Admiral Sir Anthony Griffin, GCB

Born at Peshawar on 24 November 1920, he joined the RN College, Dartmouth in May 1934 and went to sea as a Midshipman in the cruiser *Gloucester* in 1939. On 25 March 1941 when on passage to join *Hereward* in *SS Britannia* she was torpedoed and sank. He was rescued three days later and returned to the UK after being landed at Montevideo and on 25 June 1941 he joined the destroyer *Fury* attached to Force H. Promoted to Lieutenant on 1 October 1941, two years later on 10 May 1943 he joined the *Hunt* class destroyer *Talybont* operating in the channel and western approaches. For this service he was mentioned in despatches. In June 1944 he qualified (N) in *HMS Dryad* and in October joined the carrier *Implacable* as Assistant (N). On 3 January 1945 he was appointed Navigating Officer of the auxiliary carrier *Empress* on the East Indies station and in May 1945 received a second mention in despatches. On 11 March 1945 he returned to *HMS Dryad* for an advanced (N) course and two months later joined the cruiser *Sussex* as Navigating Officer and subsequently the battleship *Anson*. On 9 October 1947 he returned to *HMS Dryad* for an advanced ND course and remained as Staff Officer (ND). On 15 August 1949 he took up his appointment to the carrier *Glory* as second (D) officer and on 18 October 1950 he was appointed Staff (ND) Officer to the Flag Officer (Air) Mediterranean and the Cruiser Command. Promoted to Commander on 31 December 1951, after attending a course at the Naval Staff College, on 1 September 1952 he joined the Admiralty Signal and Radar Establishment, *Mercury* as Commander (ND). On 30 December 1954 he was appointed executive officer of the carrier *Eagle* and two years later he was promoted to Captain. On

11 June 1957 he joined the Admiralty as Deputy Director Navigation and Direction and returned to sea in August 1959 as Captain of the Inshore Flotilla. On 7 November 1960 he was appointed Deputy Director of the plans division in the Admiralty and in 1963 he attended a course at the Imperial Defence College on completion of which he was appointed in command of the carrier *Ark Royal.* Promoted to Rear Admiral on 7 January 1966, he returned to the Admiralty for a brief period as Naval Secretary which was followed by two years as Assistant Chief of the Naval Staff (Warfare). On 19 August 1968 he was appointed Flag Officer 2nd in Command Far Eastern Fleet and three months later he was advanced to Vice Admiral. On 30 September 1969 he became Flag Officer Plymouth and Commander Central Sub Area Eastern Atlantic and on 20 March 1970 his duties were extended to include Admiral Superintendent, Devonport. On 25 January 1971 he joined the Admiralty Board as Controller of the Navy and Third Sea Lord a post which he held until 15 December 1975 when he retired to become Chairman of the Organising Committee for British Shipbuilders and Chairman designate of the British Shipbuilding Corporation.

Admiral Sir Anthony Griffin.

Appendix III

LIST OF (N) & (ND) OFFICERS WHO

HAVE ATTAINED FLAG RANK 1903 TO 1976

ROYAL NAVY

Admirals of the Fleet	Sir Henry Oliver GCB KCMG MVO DL *1895* Sir John D Cunningham GCB MVO *1906*
Admirals	Lord Mountevans of Chelsea KCB DSO LLD *1901* Sir Wilbraham T R Ford KCB KBE *1905* Sir Frederick Edward-Collins KCB KCVO *1905* Sir Henry R Moore GCB CVO DSO DL *1908* Sir Marshal L Clarke KBE CB DSC *1908* Sir Tom S V Phillips KCB *1909* John H Godfrey CB *1909* Sir Geoffrey J A Miles KCB KCSI *1911* Sir William G Tennant KCB CBE MVO *1913* Sir A Robin M Bridge KBE CB *1917* Sir Maurice J Mansergh KCB CBE *1921* Sir John Frewen GCB *1934* Sir Ian Easton KCB DSC *1943* Sir Anthony Griffin GCB *1944*
Vice Admirals	J W Carrington DSO OBE *1900* E L Booty CB MVO A C Scott CBE Sir Richard H O Lane-Poole KBE CB *1904* Sir James A G Troup KBE CB *1904* H O Reinold CB *1904* The Hon A C Strutt CBE *1904* Sir Richard A S Hill KBE CB *1905* A H Norman CMG *1906*` A F B Carpenter VC *1907* R H C Hallifax CB CBE *1908* J G P Vivian CB *1909* B C Watson CB DSO *1910* E J Spooner DSO *1910* H J Egerton CB DL JP *1920* B B Schofield CB CBE *1920*

Sir Charles F W Norris KBE CB DSO *1924*
Sir Eric Clifford KCB, CBE *1924*
Sir John F Stevens KBE CB *1924*
Sir Maxwell Richmond KBE CB DSO *1925*
J S C Salter CB DSO OBE *1926*
Sir Ballin I Robertshaw KBE CB *1927*
Sir Hector D C MacLean KBE CB DSC *1933*
Sir Ian L T Hogg KCB DSC *1936*
Sir John O C Hayes KCB OBE *1936*
Sir David G Clutterbuck KBE CB *1938*
Sir John E L Martin KCB DSC FNI *1942*
Sir James G Jungius KBE *1946*
P E C Berger MVO DSC *1949*

Rear Admirals

D B Le Mottee
K D McPherson *1904*
J S G Fraser CBE DSO *1904*
A J Robertson MVO *1905*
G H G Benson DSO *1906*
Sir Kenneth E Creighton KBE, MVO *1907*
J D Campbell MVO, OBE *1907*
E R Corson MVO DSC *1908*
Sir Oswald Dawson KBE CB *1908*
R J R Scott CB AM DL *1909*
J Powell DSO *1909*
J W Clayton CBE *1910*
P K Kekewich CB *1910*
W S Chalmers CBE DSC *1911*
K H L Mackenzie CBE *1911*
W G Benn *1911*
M W S Boucher DSO *1911*
R K Dickson CB, DSO *1921*
W G Brittain CB CBE *1928*
J L Blackham CB DL *1935*
B C Durant CB DSO DSC DL *1935*
F B P Brayne-Nicholls CB DSC *1939*
C D Madden CB CBE MVO DSC *1940*
Sir Patrick J Morgan KCVO CB DSC *1940*
M N Lucey CB DSC *1944*
A R B Sturdee CB DSC *1944*
B C G Place VC CB DSC *1946*
A G Watson CB *1946*
Sir Ronald Forrest KCVO *1947*
H P Janion *1948*
P W Buchanan *1950*
A J Cooke *1953*

ROYAL AUSTRALIAN NAVY

Vice Admirals   Sir Henry M Burrell KBE CB *1930*
Sir David Stevenson KBE *1944*

Rear Admirals   C J Pope *1908*
H A Showers CBE *1923*
D H Harries CB CBE *1927*
G G O Gatacre CBE DSO DSC *1933*
J S Mesley CBE MVO DSC *1935*
B S Murray *1945*
N E McDonald *1946*
G J Willis AO *1948*

ROYAL CANADIAN NAVY AND CANADIAN DEFENCE FORCE

Vice Admirals   H T W Grant CBE DSO CD *1924*
H G de Wolf CBE DSO DSC CD *1928*
D S Boyle CMM CD *1947*

Rear Admirals   L W Murray CB CBE *1920*
R J Pickford CD *1945*
D L Hannington DSC CD *1946*
A L Collier DSC CD *1949*

INDIAN NAVY

Vice Admirals   N Krishnan PB PVSM DSC *1943*
K L Kulkarni *1945*

Rear Admiral   S H Sarma PVSM *1948*

Appendix IV

INSTRUCTIONS FOR

THE DIRECTOR OF NAVIGATION (1945)

1 The Director of Navigation will be responsible to the Board for the efficient performance of the duties of his Division. He will work under the supervision of the VCNS.

2 He is responsible for advising on:

a Navigation and Pilotage

i The Navigation and Pilotage of HM Ships and Fleets, and general questions relating thereto.

ii He is to maintain the closest touch with the Hydrographer and consult him on matters such as suitability of charts and channels, existence or placing of marks, set and drift of currents, latest publications, etc, which appertain to the safe navigation of ships.

iii Strategical, Tactical and Navigational plotting and all matters relating thereto.

iv Berthing of His Majesty's Ships and Fleets, and general berthing questions.

v Turning trials and manoeuvring generally.

vi Moorings, in so far as they concern berthing, but not with regard to priority or supply.

vii Dredging of ports and anchorages, from the Navigational point of view, after consultation with the Hydrographer.

viii Control of wartime navigational lighting appertaining to the navigation of ships, and of other lighting visible from the sea which may be mistaken for the above.

ix The use of all Navigational aids by HM Ships

x Collisions and groundings where the accuracy of the chart is not in question.

xi Collision regulations.

xii Damage sustained or caused by His Majesty's Ships.

xiii Damage caused to fishing gear, nets etc by His Majesty's Ships.

xiv Damage to, or loss of, anchors and cables, and other Navigational stores.

b. Radar

i The co-ordination of the requirements for surface warning and air warning radar.

ii The operational use of Shore Based Surface Watching Radar.

c. Shore Plotting

The organisation of Naval Shore Plotting methods.

d. Training and Personnel

i The Navigation School, syllabuses, instruction, and qualification in navigation of all officers and men of the Royal Navy, Royal Naval Reserve, the Royal Naval Volunteer Reserve.

ii Plotting. Schools for the training of officers, Radar Plot ratings, including syllabuses, instruction, and qualification in RP duties of all men of the Royal Navy, Royal Naval Reserve and Royal Naval Volunteer Reserve. Schools for the training of WRNS officers and ratings shore plotters. Air plotting syllabus for ratings in consultation with DAWT.

iii Action Information Training Centres, including syllabuses, and instruction carried out therein.

iv The instruction and training of Radar Plot ratings in His Majesty's Ships, and in shore plots.

v The co-ordinated training of AIO crews ashore and in His Majesty's Ships.

vi The co-ordinated training of Naval Shore plotting crews.

vii The entry of officers and men to meet the requirements of the Service for which the Navigation Branch is responsible.

e. *Material*
i The arrangements of Bridges and Charthouses.
ii The general layout of all navigational equipment and spaces.
iii The general layout of and co-ordination of all arrangements for Naval Shore Plotting Rooms.
iv The arrangement of Bridge Plotting Rooms and Operations Rooms. In the case of aircraft carriers, DACR is responsible for the arrangement and will consult with D of N regarding the layout of AIO equipment.
v The co-ordination of all arrangements for Action Information Organisation.
vi Requirements for Navigational and Plotting equipment, including trials thereof, with the exception of charts, navigational timepieces and compasses, and with the exception of Air Plotting equipment and of navigational and plotting equipment in aircraft.

NOTE: Any questions on the above matter which affect HM Surveying Ships will be dealt with by the Hydrographer.

3 He is responsible to the Board for:
a. Formulation of Staff Requirements for Bridges of His Majesty's Ships.
b. Formulation of Staff Requirements for Action Information Organisation (in conjunction with other technical staff divisions concerned).
c. Formulation of Staff Requirements for Naval Plotting Ashore at Home and Abroad.
d. Formulation of Staff Requirements for Warning and Navigational Radar, for Surface Watching Radar Ashore, and for Tactical and Operational Radar Teachers for Warning sets (in conjunction with DRE).
e. The allocation of priority of supply to His Majesty's Ships of navigational plotting and warning radar equipment, where such is necessary.
f. The inspection of navigational equipment except compasses fitted in His Majesty's Ships, and that part of AIO equipment which is provided to supply information to the Command.
g. The scrutiny of all reports of actions, exercises, practices and trials, collecting the data concerning navigation, warning radar and AIO therefrom, and calling the attention of Divisions and Departments to such points as particularly concern them.
h. Keeping the Naval Staff and Fleet informed of progress and general development of navigation, AIO, and shore plotting matters for which he is responsible.
i. The preparation and periodical revision of the following books:
1 The Seamanship Manual
2 The Navigation Manual
3 Handbook of Action Information Organisation
4 Remarks on handling Ships
5 Search and patrol by Surface Craft
6 Ports and Anchorages
7 Any additional books on subjects which come within the responsibility of the Branch

NOTE: Any question on the above matter which affects HM Surveying Ships will be dealt with by the Hydrographer.

4 Within the Admiralty, responsibility for the general direction of Technical training devolving upon The Captain *HMS Dryad* and the Captain *HMS Collingwood* (the latter only in as much as it affects RP training), will be vested in the Director of Navigation.
5 When proposals dealing with material are under consideration which affect the interests or welfare of Naval Personnel, he should consult the Director of Personal Services before the question is submitted to the Board.
6 He is regarded as the authority (below the Board) on all questions of practical seamanship.
7 He may sign correspondence with Dockyard and other Admiralty establishments at home and abroad, and with individual officers of His Majesty's Navy or Civil Service on matters dealing exclusively with the duties of his Division, but all correspondence communicating

Board decision, or concerning important questions of principle, or affecting other Departments, is to be in the name of the Board and is to be signed by the Secretary, and letters to the Dockyards (other than those signed by the Secretary), authorising work to be done are to be signed by the Director of Dockyards.

Appendix V

Directors of Navigation

Captain P Nelson-Ward MVO *11 December 1912 to 7 August 1916*
    Rear Admiral (Retd) *9 June 1916*
Captain J A Webster CBE MVO *8 August 1916 to 31 July 1919*
Captain J E T Harper MVO *1 August 1919 to 14 November 1921*
Captain F P Loder-Symonds CMG *15 November 1921 to 29 November 1923*
Captain The Hon A C Strutt *30 November 1923 to 29 November 1925*
Captain A H Norman CMG *30 November 1925 to 29 November 1927*
Captain O H Dawson *30 November 1927 to 13 January 1930*
Captain K E L Creighton MVO *14 January 1930 to 10 January 1932*
Captain J D Campbell MVO OBE *11 January 1932 to 1 October 1933*
    Rear Admiral (Retd) *5 January 1933*
Captain J W Clayton *2 October 1933 to 1 October 1935*
Captain W G Benn *2 October 1935 to 27 June 1938*
Captain C E Morgan DSO *28 June 1938 to 14 October 1940*
Captain R G Bowes-Lyon MVO *15 October 1940 to 8 June 1942*
Rear Admiral W G Benn (Retd) *9 June 1942 to 19 December 1945*
    (Serving in rank of Captain)
Captain R W Ravenhill CBE DSC *20 December 1945 to 30 June 1946*

Directors of Navigation and Direction

Captain R W Ravenhill CBE DSC *1 July 1946 to 9 December 1947*
Captain F B Lloyd OBE *10 December 1947 to 30 December 1949*
Captain W G Brittain CBE *31 December 1949 to 30 December 1951*
Captain E H Thomas DSC* *31 December 1951 to 13 January 1954*
Captain T D Ross *14 January 1954 to 8 February 1956*
Captain J E Jowitt DSC *9 February 1956 to 18 December 1956*
Captain D McEwen DSC *19 December 1956 to 16 October 1958*
Captain C D Madden MVO DSC *17 October 1958 to 5 January 1961*
Captain J W H Bennett DSC *6 January 1961 to 6 March 1962*
                   7 March 1962 to 31 March 1964

Directors of Navigation and Tactical Control

Captain J W H Bennett DSC *1 April 1964 to 4 June 1964*
Captain D N Forbes DSC *5 June 1964 to 27 December 1965*
Captain J S LeBlanc Smith *28 December 1965 to 6 June 1968*

Captain J D Hope *7 June 1968 to 23 June 1968*

Navigational Advisers to the Admiralty Board

Captain D T Smith *7 June 1968 to 9 July 1969*
Captain S A C Cassels *9 July 1969 to 17 December 1971*
Captain D R Reffell *17 December 1971 to 19 August 1974*
Captain M L'E Tudor-Craig *19 August 1974*

Appendix VI

CAPTAINS OF HMS DRYAD

H F Oliver MVO 18 June 1903
L E Power MVO 12 February 1907
H W Grant 1 January 1910
E L Booty MVO 15 January 1912
School Closed 1 September 1914-2 January 1919
A C S H D'Aeth CB 3 January 1919
O E Leggett CB 30 November 1920
H O Reinold CVO 30 November 1922
J W Carrington DSO 2 December 1924
J D Campbell MVO OBE 16 December 1926
J A G Troup 17 December 1928
W T R Ford 20 June 1930
O H Dawson 20 June 1932
E J Spooner DSO 27 July 1934
W H Gell DSO 17 August 1936
A R M Bridge 3 May 1937
H A Rowley 16 June 1939

J C Armstrong DSC (Retired) 5 December 1939
B B Schofield CBE 19 January 1944
C F W Norris DSO 8 February 1945
E G A Clifford 1 January 1947
C A G Nichols DSO MVO 29 December 1948
A A Thorold CBE DSO 4 December 1950
M J Evans CBE DSC 1 January 1953
R G Tosswill CBE 11 January 1955
R B Honnywill 10 May 1956
D S Tibbits DSC 19 June 1957
F B P Brayne-Nicholls DSC 9 October 1959
P J Wyatt CBE DSC 3 October 1961
D B N Mellis DSC 2 August 1963
M S Ollivant MBE DSC 1 July 1965
R D Butt 15 September 1967
A G Watson 12 August 1969
D W Foster 27 June 1972

School of Maritime Operations HMS Dryad

G I Pritchard 15 October 1974

J F Cadell 27 May 1976

Appendix VII

The first ship in HM Navy to bear the name of *Dryad* was a 16 gun frigate of 929 tons launched on the Thames in 1795. She was 142 feet long with a beam of 38 feet and a draught of 11 feet. Her complement was 270 and she saw much action during the Napoleonic Wars. Within a year of her completion on 2 May 1796, under the command of Commander John King Pulling, she captured the 14 gun French frigate *Proserpine* off Cape Clear and, after a fight lasting nearly two hours, the Frenchman struck to his smaller opponent.

The *Dryad* is next mentioned as forming part of Rear Admiral Sir Richard Strachan's fleet of 246 men o'war which sailed from the Downs on 28 July 1809 to take part in the unsuccessful Walcheren expedition. On this occasion she was commanded by Captain Richard Galway under whom she saw further action in 1812 and 1815. In the first she drove a 22 gun French brig ashore off Ile de Dieu and in the second, together with another British frigate, captured the 40 gun frigate *Clorinde*. After the end of the war, she was retained for a time as a receiving ship at Portsmouth but, in 1859, she was broken up and her timbers used in the construction of the screw sloop *Danae*.

Although work on the construction of a second *Dryad*, a single screw sloop, was begun in 1860, she was never completed. However the name was given to a single screw sloop of 1620 tons with a speed of 11.8 knots which was launched at Devenport in 1866. Commanded by Commander Thomas Butler Fellowes, she took part in the Abysinian war of 1868 when a naval brigade was landed to assist the troops under Lieut-General Sir Robert Napier in a compaign which resulted in the capture of Magdala. For his good services in command of the brigade, Fellowes was promoted to Captain and was relieved in command of the *Dryad* by Commander Philip Howard Colomb, later to become well known as an exponent of naval strategy. Nothing more is heard of the third *Dryad* until 1883 when under the command of Commander Charles Johnson she was given the difficult task of protecting British interests at Tamatave, in the island of Madagascar, during a dispute between the local authorities and the French when the French Admiral (later found to be insane) ordered the bombardment of the town. Thanks to the good work of *Dryad's* Royal Marines guarding the British Consulate, the resulting conflagration was controlled and much valuable property was saved. Commander Johnson's good service on that occasion was rewarded by his promotion to Captain. The following year, 1884, under a new Captain, Commander Edward Grey

Hulton, the ship took part in the Egyptian war and provided a company for the Naval Brigade which distinguished itself in action with the Mahdi's troops at the Battle of El Teb. The following year, 1885, the ship was sold and it was not until 1893 that the fourth and last ship to bear the name was launched at Chatham. She was a twin screw gunboat of 1670 tons with a speed of 18½ knots. She was 250 feet long with a beam of 30 feet and a draught of 10 feet and she mounted two 4.7 inch guns. (See plate   ) It was this ship which was ultimately chosen as a tender to the Navigation School when it was transferred ashore in 1906 and which gave its name to the establishment.

Index